POCKET GUIDE TO EVIDENCE

Second Edition

James C. Morton
B.Sc., LL.B., LL.M.
Certified as a Specialist in Civil Litigation
by the Law Society of Upper Canada

D1378748

Butterworths
A Member of the LexisNexis Group

Pocket Guide to Evidence, Second Edition
© Butterworths Canada Ltd. 2002
September 2002

The *Butterworth Group of Companies*

Canada:
75 Clegg Road, MARKHAM, Ontario L6G 1A1
and
1721-808 Nelson St., Box 12148, VANCOUVER, B.C. V6Z 2H2
Australia:
Butterworths Pty Ltd., SYDNEY
Ireland:
Butterworth (Ireland) Ltd., DUBLIN
Malaysia:
Malayan Law Journal Sdn Bhd, KUALA LUMPUR
New Zealand:
Butterworths of New Zealand Ltd., WELLINGTON
Singapore:
Butterworths Asia, SINGAPORE
South Africa:
Butterworth Publishers (Pty.) Ltd., DURBAN
United Kingdom:
Butterworth & Co. (Publishers) Ltd., LONDON
United States:
LEXIS Publishing, CHARLOTTESVILLE, Virginia

National Library of Canada Cataloguing in Publication

Morton, James C. (James Cooper), 1960-
    Pocket guide to evidence / James C. Morton. — 2nd ed.

Includes index.
ISBN 0-433-44017-1

1. Evidence (Law) – Canada. I. Title.

KE8440.M67 2002   347.71'06   C2002-904083-3
KF9660.M67 2002

Printed and bound in Canada.

Reprint #1, 2004.

PREFACE

Writing a book on evidence is a daunting task, even when the book is as modest as this volume. In drafting the second edition, I realized how much has changed in such a short period of time. The law of evidence is rapidly evolving. Regardless, my task has been immeasurably eased by the aid, assistance and encouragement of a large number of people.

This book emerges from courses in evidence I have had the pleasure of teaching at Osgoode Hall Law School and Thomas Cooley Law School since the 1990s. Such merit as this book has can be attributed to the faculty and the students I have dealt with; their insights have been central to the development of this book.

The editorial staff at Butterworths has guided me through the often difficult and frustrating task of producing a manuscript. They have taken a sheaf of typing and made an attractive text. In this regard, I want to thank Karen Davidson and Michelle Ecker for their help. They have been magnificent. Aiding them in this task, of course, has been my able assistant, Rosalie Antman, who turned what was close to illegible scribbles into a clearly drafted and grammatically sensible text.

Obviously, any faults, mistakes, errors or omissions in this text are solely the responsibility of the author; the credit for this book should go to those I have acknowledged; the blame, such as it is, rests with me.

I have tried to state the law as of September, 2002.

James C. Morton
Toronto, Ontario
September 2002

TABLE OF CONTENTS

TABLE OF CASES

SUMMARY ANALYSIS OF EVIDENCE PROBLEMS[1]

STEP ONE — IS IT RELEVANT AND PROBATIVE?

Does the evidence deal with a matter in dispute and does it tend to establish something about that matter? If the evidence is relevant and probative, it is admissible unless excluded by some other specific rule.

STEP TWO — DOES AN EXCEPTION TO THE GENERAL ADMISSION RULE APPLY?

Even if an exception applies, the evidence may still be admissible (*e.g.* not all confessions are excluded) but the relevant details of the exception must be considered.

The main exceptions to the general admissibility rule arise if the evidence is:

A. HEARSAY

A statement is hearsay and, *prima facie*, inadmissible, if it is (a) an out-of-court statement, (b) adduced in Court or (c) to prove the truth of the facts therein.

Exceptions to the Hearsay Rule

Evidence, even though hearsay, may be admissible if it falls within certain well-defined exceptions or, more generally, if the evidence is necessary and otherwise unavailable and there is some circumstantial indicia of trustworthiness. The specific exceptions include:

(*1*) *Testimony in Former Proceedings*
Testimony in a prior judicial proceeding between the same parties on the same factual issues where cross-examination was available is admissible if the witness is now unavailable.

(*2*) *Admissions*
Anything a party says can be used *against* that party.

(*3*) *Declaration Against Interest*

---

[1] This is a summary only; it should be considered as nothing more than an *aide memoire*.

A statement against a declarant's immediate pecuniary or penal interest is admissible, though hearsay.

(*4*)   *Business Records*
Common Law: A business record made at or near the time of the event described by someone with personal information of the event whose duty required them to note such an event as part of the ordinary course is admissible, though hearsay.
Statute: As Common Law except written notice must be given and personal knowledge is unnecessary.

(*5*)   *Past Recollection Recorded*
A written memorandum of an event now forgotten made at or near the time of the event may be admissible, though hearsay.

(*6*)   *Res gestae*
A hearsay statement relating to a startling event made while the declarant was under the stress of excitement caused by that event is admissible.

(*7*)   *Statements of Physical, Mental or Emotional State*
A hearsay statement of a declarant's *then* existing state of mind, emotion, sensation or physical condition is admissible.

(*8*)   *Dying Declarations*
A statement by a deceased about the circumstances of their death in a criminal prosecution for which the death is a necessary element is admissible if the declarant made the statement under a fixed and hopeless expectation of impending death.

(*9*)   *Official Statements*
Similar to business records — a written report or record of a public official is admissible to prove its truth if the official had first-hand knowledge of the reported facts and had a duty to make the report or record.

B. OPINION EVIDENCE

Opinions are not admissible evidence unless they are (a) a compendious way for the laity to testify to a common everyday experience or (b) opinions of someone skilled in a recognized science or art and necessary (or at least helpful) for the trier of fact to understand something otherwise beyond the trier's knowledge or understanding.

C. CHARACTER EVIDENCE

The State may not call evidence solely for the purpose of showing an individual is of bad character and therefore likely guilty of an offence. However, evidence may be called to prove guilt (or disprove a claim of good character) which incidentally shows bad character. The forbidden reasoning process is BAD CHARACTER, therefore GUILT; where GUILT leads to a conclusion of BAD CHARACTER, no problem arises.

An accused may call evidence of the accused's general reputation for character in the community to show the accused is not likely guilty. Where character is so raised, the State may rebut the claim by cross-examining or calling contrary evidence.

Evidence of bad character of non-parties may be called if otherwise admissible.

D. A CONFESSION

A confession, that is, (a) any statement made by (b) an accused to (c) a person in authority, is *prima facie* inadmissible unless the prosecutor shows it was free and voluntary.

E. OBTAINED CONTRARY TO *CHARTER* OR QUASI-CONSTITUTIONAL DOCUMENT

Evidence obtained as a result (direct or indirect) of a breach of a *Charter* right is inadmissible if its admission could bring the administration of justice into disrepute. Such rights are to be read broadly in light of Canada's constitutional heritage and *may* be broad enough to include rights under, for example, the *Bill of Rights*. The burden of showing the breach, the nexus between the evidence and the breach, and the disrepute lies on the party seeking to exclude the evidence.

F. OBTAINED IN BREACH OF A CONFIDENTIAL RELATIONSHIP

Relationship privilege (as opposed to settlement privilege) extends to criminal and civil proceedings. It applies by class or on a case by case basis. If a relationship is covered by a class, subject to exceptions special to each class, any communications within the class are privileged and not admissible. Classes include (a) solicitor-client (b) spousal (c) state policy making and (d) informant identity. Case by case privilege is established by Wigmore criteria which require that the communication (a) arose in confidence (b) confidence was essential to the communication (c) the relationship sought to be protected is valued by society and (d) the harm caused by disclosure is greater than the damage to the trial process.

G. OF CIVIL SETTLEMENT DISCUSSIONS

Civil settlement discussions are privileged and information disclosed therein cannot be used in evidence at the trial of the dispute the settlement discussions were intended to resolve.

STEP THREE — PREJUDICE VS. PROBATIVE VALUE?

Even if the evidence is otherwise admissible, the party opposing such admission can still argue that the probative value of the evidence is slight (usually an argument that the evidence is only marginally probative as opposed to relevant) and the prejudice of such evidence is out of all proportion to its value. The question is "would a jury, on seeing such evidence, decide to convict (acquit, *etc.*), regardless of the matters actually proven"?

Chapter 1

FUNDAMENTAL PRINCIPLES

INTRODUCTION

Evidence is one of the standard topics virtually all lawyers study in law school and, as a subject, it forms part of the structure of common knowledge held by all practising common law lawyers.[1]

Notice how I described evidence as forming part of the structure of lawyers' common knowledge. As with substantive topics such as contract or tort, evidence is something all common law lawyers know (or think they know) and they think of cases through the paradigm of evidence; it is part of the legal subconscious.

That said, the law of evidence purports to be a system, governed by well-known principles, that determines in an unambiguous way what a court will con-

---

[1] That having been said, some judges are of the view that standards of evidence have sadly fallen. Justice Reid, in an informal address to the Canadian Bar Association on February 7, 1986 noted:

One of the first things that judges learn about evidence is not to say to counsel who break elementary rules, "Surely you must have learned that in law school". That would have been a killing remark if a judge had made it to me when I was at the Bar because everyone had gone to Osgoode Hall and had had to take a course on evidence. No one notified the judges when the era of compulsory evidence ended.

It gradually dawned on me that something had happened when I said such things to counsel and got back nothing but blank stares. Talk at the lunch table indicated that other judges were having the same experience, of almost total ignorance of the law of evidence on the part of some counsel. Finally, one of our brethren who had been a law school teacher explained that evidence was not an elective course in law schools. I stopped saying, "Surely you must have learned that in law school". I realized we had to learn to deal with the Ripley factor: Believe it or not, some counsel don't know anything about evidence.

I suppose most people who come into the Supreme Court had some inkling when they were in law school that they might some day go into a court and therefore took a course in evidence. It is manifest, however, that some did not nor did they trouble to make a study of it on their own. The result is that they calmly make the most egregious mistakes. "There should be a law", as my mother used to say, that no one be allowed to appear as counsel in any court unless they can present a certificate saying that they have not only taken a course in evidence, but passed it. In the absence of such a law, anyone who appears as counsel in our courts without proper instruction in the law of evidence should be given a medal for chutzpah or have their professional insurance premiums raised.

sider in deciding a case. For example, is the plaintiff's age something a court will consider in a breach of contract case? In fact, the law of evidence does not, and cannot, be so precise and certain. The positivist view of law, that legal principles properly applied render unique, unequivocal answers, is not accurate. Evidence is what a court uses to justify a decision to consider, or exclude, some fact from analysis, but a justification is not an explanation. Almost anything can be admitted or excluded consistently with evidence law, and the decision to admit or exclude comes before the law is applied.

The failure of the positivist description of evidence does not mean the admission or consideration of some fact is wholly arbitrary — a competent practicing lawyer can predict quite well if something will be given a court's explicit consideration. Rather, the failure of positivism means the admission or exclusion of facts is based on unspoken shared assumptions and norms. These assumptions and norms are predictable — judges will give an elderly person more leeway as a civil defendant and will let them adduce items not adduceable for someone in their forties — but are not actually based on rules of hearsay and the like. A judge's decision is described, but not prescribed, by the law of evidence.

All that said, lawyers and judges discuss admission or exclusion of facts for consideration as if the law of evidence was dispositive. To argue cases and communicate with lawyers and judges, the law of evidence must be discussed as dispositive. Accordingly, from here on I will discuss the practical law of evidence as if it were dispositive.

ROLE OF EVIDENCE

Most disputes do not go to trial. Perhaps five in a hundred cases go to trial; the ratio being higher for criminal cases and lower for civil matters. But evidence only deals with admission of facts for consideration at trial. Accordingly, evidence will determine only what a judge will consider in deciding a case at trial.

The main purpose of evidence law is to limit the information put to a judge so he or she can make a practical decision in a limited time. Most trials are short — perhaps a week — and if a judge could consider anything the parties wanted to put forth (say, the plaintiff is not a nice person in a mortgage enforcement case), the trial would never end. Evidence acts as a gatekeeper limiting what a judge can see and hear thus making the practical business of conducting trials possible.

In its role as a gatekeeper, evidence acts to exclude unnecessary and irrelevant material. The goal is accurate, but practical, fact finding. Material and relevant facts are often excluded from consideration because they are only marginally helpful or because they were obtained in a fashion the court wants to discourage. Thus, Baron Rolfe notes:[2]

> The laws of evidence … as to what ought and what ought not to be received, must be considered as founded on a sort of comparative consideration of the time to be

---

[2]   *A.G. v. Hitchcock* (1847), 154 E.R. 38.

occupied in examinations of this nature, and the time which it is practicable to bestow upon them. If we lived for a thousand years instead of about sixty or seventy, and if every case were of sufficient importance, it might be possible, and perhaps proper, to throw a light on matters in which every possible question might be suggested ....

The rules of evidence are a set of standards that regulate the way facts may be proven at trial. Because triers of fact must base their decisions solely on the evidence presented in court, the rules are designed to limit the evidence to that which aids the trier of fact in determining the issue in dispute in a practical and pragmatic manner.

PROBABILITY, RELEVANCY AND MATERIALITY

Evidence fulfills its gatekeeper role by limiting what a judge considers to what is rationally relevant to the issues before the court and cutting even that back to exclude otherwise relevant material that is misleading or obtained in some way repugnant to the judge[3] (say, evidence obtained by physical abuse). Specifically,[4] *nothing which is not rationally relevant to issues in dispute is admissible. Subject to many qualifications, anything that is rationally relevant to issues in dispute is admissible.*
The "issues in dispute" are the questions the court must decide. For example, in a civil case, the issues are constrained by the pleadings. So, if A sues B for failing to pay for a sofa B bought from A, and B's only defence is B paid in cash, evidence showing, say, B took $500 from a bank machine is admissible — it is rationally relevant to whether B paid in cash. Evidence showing the sofa was poorly built is not admissible. Why? Because the quality of the sofa has nothing to do with the one issue before the court: did B actually pay A?
Similarly, in a criminal assault case where the only defence raised is one of identification, the violent tendencies of the victim cannot be proven since they have no impact on the issue of identification, which is all the Court has to decide.
Accordingly, in every case, considerable care must be given to determining what matters to the court, what does the court have to decide? If evidence does not relate to an "issue in dispute", then that evidence is inadmissible.
Two terms used in the context of "issues in dispute" are "relevancy" and "materiality". Relevancy speaks to the tendency of a fact to establish a proposition — say, in our sofa example, did B pay in cash? Materiality speaks to whether the proposition is an issue before the court. So, proof the sofa was poorly built is relevant to prove it is a bad sofa, but since the quality of the sofa is not an issue

---

[3] *R. v. Collins*, [1987] 1 S.C.R. 265.
[4] Lamer J., dissenting in *Morris v. R.*, [1983] 2 S.C.R. 190 at 201, noted the principle "(1) that nothing is to be received which is not logically probative of some matter requiring to be proved; and (2) that everything which is thus probative should come in, unless a clear ground of policy or law exclude it". This principle is usually called the Thayer principle named for the late Dean Thayer, a leading academic.

for the court, it is immaterial. For some fact to be considered by a court, it must be both (1) relevant (the fact tends to prove a proposition) and (2) material (the proposition it proves makes a difference to the court).

What is the test for relevancy? How strong a tendency to prove a proposition is needed? The standard is quite low. To be relevant, all a fact has to do is to render the relevant proposition more probable than it would be without the fact.[5] As the Supreme Court has noted:[6]

> ... the basic rule [is] that all *relevant* evidence is admissible. Relevance depends directly on the facts in issue in any particular case. ... To be logically relevant, an item of evidence does not have to firmly establish, on any standard, the truth or falsity of a fact in issue. The evidence must simply tend to 'increase or diminish the probability of the existence of a fact in issue'.... As a consequence, there is no minimum probative value required for evidence to be relevant.

Some older case law distinguishes between legal relevance, said to require something more than logical relevance, and logical relevance[7] — this distinction is no longer important and can be safely ignored. Janet Leiper, discussing the issue of relevance, set out a practical test:[8]

> A simple way to test the relevance of a piece of evidence ... is to subject it to the toddler test: Ask "why" it proves the fact, then ask why again and then ask it again. Repeat until you are impatient. If the logic breaks down after the second or third "Why?" then you may have spotted the problem with relevance. If the logic holds to the point of impatience then you are ready to argue relevance and defend your position in any courtroom.

Let us go back to the sofa example. In trying to show B actually did pay cash, would evidence that B had withdrawn money from a bank machine make it more probable that B paid cash? Obviously yes — such evidence is relevant and material. Is evidence that B is, say, a lawyer relevant? Well, is it more likely that B, as a lawyer, would honour a contract? Perhaps, perhaps not — here we get to a borderline question that could be argued. Is evidence that B has, say, red hair relevant? Almost certainly not — hair color does not make payment either more or less likely. In each of these examples, materiality was never an issue. Each piece of evidence was considered in light of an issue before the Court. The *Gurtler*[9] case provides an illustration of the interaction between relevance and materiality. The accused was charged with killing his spouse and the defence raised by his counsel was that she had committed suicide. In the context of the suicide defence, evidence raised by the prosecution about the deceased's plans, shortly before death,

[5]   *Ibid.*; the determination of probative value is based on the degree to which the evidence goes to prove the fact for which it is tendered and not the importance of that fact: *R. v. Pascoe* (1997), 113 C.C.C. (3d) 126 (O.C.A.).
[6]   *R. v. Arp* (1999), 166 D.L.R. (4th) 296 at 313.
[7]   *R. v. Cloutier*, [1979] 2 S.C.R. 709.
[8]   Leiper, J. "Fair Trial Issues" (2002) 6 *For the Defence* 25-26.
[9]   *R. v. Gurtler*, [1996] S.J. No. 665.

to take horseback riding lessons were relevant to prove the deceased was not suicidal. Suicidal intentions were material because suicide was a defence. If, by contrast, the defence was that the spouse was murdered by a stranger, the plans to take riding lessons would be neither relevant nor material.

It may then be seen that the law of evidence defines both what may be proved and how it may be proven. As M. Howard notes:[10]

> The province of the law of evidence is therefore twofold, *viz* to lay down rules as to what matter is or is not admissible for the purpose of establishing facts in dispute, and as to the manner in which such matter may be placed before the Court.

The substantive/procedural faces of evidence law make it peculiarly complex in application. Nevertheless, the general framework of evidence law is grounded on its inherent duality.

PROBATIVE VALUE AND COUNTERVAILING SOCIAL VALUES

The law of evidence is premised on a hearing before a jury and not a judge alone. Such a presumption is quite inaccurate: jury trials are rare in criminal matters and largely unheard of in civil cases. Juries are, perhaps unfairly, assumed to be quite susceptible to giving undue weight to evidence that is relevant and material, but only in a marginal way. The clearest example is a prior criminal conviction — in most cases, unless an accused testifies, no evidence of prior criminal convictions is admissible by the prosecutor against an accused. This exclusion of evidence that is of some probative value (someone who has been convicted of common assault is, probably, somewhat more likely to commit manslaughter than someone without a prior conviction) is intended to protect an accused from being convicted, not on the evidence, but rather the unreasoning prejudice of the jury[11] against convicted criminals.

As a general rule, if the evidence in question is likely to colour a jury's thinking — say, gruesome color photographs of a murder victim, or evidence the accused is a member of a despised religious minority — the court will exclude the evidence if the prejudicial effect of the evidence outweighs the evidence's probative value. Prejudicial effect means the likelihood a jury will decide a case on the basis of faulty or unfair reasoning because of an emotional, rather than intellectual, reaction to the evidence.

Similarly, evidence that is otherwise relevant and material is sometimes excluded to protect other social values. Evidence discovered in an illegal search is often excluded in this way — the idea is that the damage to society of allowing such searches to be used in court is greater than the gain in convicting one accused. The Canadian Constitution expressly recognizes that, on occasion, evidence may be excluded because the negative impact of its admission on society as

---

[10] *Phipson on Evidence* (15th ed.) (London: 2000) at 1.
[11] *Draper v. Jacklyn*, [1970] S.C.R. 92.

a whole outweighs any benefit to accurate fact finding. Thus, s. 24(2) of the *Charter*[12] provides, in part, that where:

> ... evidence was obtained in a manner that infringed or denied any rights or freedoms guaranteed by this Charter, the evidence shall be excluded if it is established that, having regard to all the circumstances, the admission of it in the proceedings would bring the administration of justice into disrepute.

Regardless of trial accuracy, where the conditions demand, Courts may exclude evidence to protect or promote significant societal goals.

PROBATIVE VALUE, PROCESS AND UNFAIR PREJUDICE

As mentioned, although relevant, evidence may be excluded if its probative value is substantially outweighed by the danger of unfair prejudice. Evidence may also be excluded if it tends to confuse the issues or mislead the jury, or if considerations of undue delay, waste of time, or needless presentation of cumulative evidence suggest evidence may be properly excluded. Probative value is the "tendency" of the evidence to prove a proposition. Since evidence need only affect the probability of a proposition, most evidence has some probative value. The probative value of evidence, as determined by a judge, is that value which the evidence would have if it is believed. Generally, if evidence has some probative value that evidence is admissible. That said, unfair prejudice, confusion, and waste of time represent countervailing considerations which may be a basis for excluding evidence, even if it is probative. Evidence is unfairly prejudicial if it encourages a decision based on improper reasoning, such as emotion. Where evidence is merely repetitive, or is confusing, a court has the discretion to exclude the evidence; however, such exclusions must be made with caution. Sometimes complex cases require difficult and complex evidence. Regardless, in both civil[13] and criminal matters the Court has the authority to exclude evidence the probative value of which is not commensurate with its prejudicial effect.[14] The American *Federal Rules of Evidence* describes this well:

> Although relevant, evidence may be excluded if its probative value is substantially outweighed by the danger of unfair prejudice, confusion of the issues, or misleading the jury, or by considerations of undue delay, waste of time, or needless presentation of cumulative evidence.[15]

---

[12] *Canadian Charter of Rights and Freedoms*, Part 1 of the *Constitution Act, 1982*, being Schedule B to the *Canada Act, 1982* (U.K.), 1982, c. 11.

[13] *Draper, supra*, note 11.

[14] *R. v. Harrer*, [1995] 3 S.C.R. 562; This power also extends to excluding evidence brought forward by an accused in a criminal trial: *R. v. B. (S.C.)* (1997), 119 C.C.C. (3d) 530 (Ont. C.A.).

[15] FED. R. EVID. 403.

IS THERE A DIFFERENT STANDARD TO EXCLUDE EVIDENCE IF ADDUCED BY AN ACCUSED?

When a person is accused of a crime, the risk of a wrongful deprivation of liberty or wrongful conviction leads the court to be very cautious before excluding evidence that *may* raise a doubt as to an accused's guilt. This does not mean that the rules of evidence are to be ignored — rather, technical rules of evidence may be somewhat relaxed to allow an accused to raise a doubt of guilt. Thus, the New Brunswick Court of Appeal notes:[16]

> Mr. Michaud's undoubted right not to be deprived of his liberty except in accordance with the principles of fundamental justice is not to be equated with an entitlement to the benefit of rules of evidence that will maximize his chances of acquittal. The pursuit of the truth with a view to properly determining the issues is what drives the rules of evidence.

The court's discretion to allow an accused to call evidence that may be technically inadmissible is not intended to allow an accused to evade justice, but rather to allow justice to be done. Justice Martin notes:[17]

> It seems to me that a court has a residual discretion to relax in favour of the accused a strict rule of evidence where it is necessary to prevent a miscarriage of justice and where the danger against which an exclusionary rule aims to safeguard does not exist.

To a similar effect, the Supreme Court notes:[18]

> Canadian courts, like courts in most common law jurisdictions, have been extremely cautious in restricting the power of the accused to call evidence in his or her defence, a reluctance founded in the fundamental tenet of our judicial system that an innocent person must not be convicted.

Put broadly, where the exclusion of evidence could risk an injustice, or raise a concern for wrongful conviction, the court has a narrow discretion to allow the evidence to be adduced.

---

[16] *R. v. Michaud* (2000), 144 C.C.C. (3d) 62 at 71; see also *Dersch v. Canada*, [1990] 2 S.C.R. 1505, 1515.

[17] *R. v. Williams* (1985), 18 C.C.C. (3d) 356 at 378 (Ont. C.A.).

[18] *R. v. Seaboyer*, [1991] 2 S.C.R. 577 at 611.

Chapter 2

THE JUSTICE SYSTEM

THE ADVERSARY SYSTEM

The Common Law system is premised on an adversarial trial regardless of the nature of the case. Evidence presumes that disputes will be resolved by an adversarial trial and the rules of evidence are based on the presumption.
There are three basic participants in an adversarial trial:

(1) Plaintiff/Prosecutor: A party seeking to have a judgment made against the Defendant/Accused;

(2) Defendant/Accused: A party seeking to have no judgment made against them; and

(3) Judge: The person or persons who decide if a judgment is made.

Most cases are heard by a judge sitting alone; this is true throughout North America, although some American states are disinclined to give major cases to judges alone. Similarly, in Canada some matters cannot be decided by a judge alone.[1] The judge decides what facts to accept and what law is properly applicable. Sometimes, however, a judge sits with a jury — in such cases the jury is the "trier of fact" and decides what facts to accept and what factual conclusions flow from the accepted facts. The judge, sitting with a jury, is restricted to rulings on law. The importance of this restriction for immediate purposes is that the admission of evidence is a legal matter — a judge decides if evidence is going to be heard by the jury. The jury then can accept the evidence in whole, in part, or not at all. The jury decides the facts, but the judge decides what those facts then mean in terms of legal relevance. Matters of law are determined by the judge and matters of fact by the jury:

> and quaestinem facti non respondent judices, and quaestionem juris non respondent juaratores.[2]

---

[1] Thus, s. 471 of the *Criminal Code* (Appendix A), R.S.C. 1985, c. C-46 requires, in general, that indictable offences be tried by a judge and jury.

[2] *Mechanical & General Inventions Co. Ltd. and Lehwess v. Austin and the Austin Motor Co.* [1935] A.C. 346.

Indeed, in civil matters, juries are customarily asked to decide specific factual questions rather than to rule on the liability, or otherwise, of the parties.[3] In terms of credibility, and other factual issues, there are no fixed rules and the findings of fact are to be left to the trier of fact.[4]

COUNSEL AND PARTIES

The adversarial system is so much a part of our history and culture that it usually does need much explanation. It is, however, worth emphasizing that (except for criminal prosecutors as described below) the parties' only goal, subject to a few ethical limitations, is to win. Each party does their best to bring forward helpful facts and counter other facts brought out by other parties. Parties, and their counsel, at trial are expected to be partisan and fiercely combative. The impartial party is the judge. The judge, in our system, does no investigating, conducts no independent review of the facts, and rules solely on what is put before the Court. If, say, the weather on July 1, 2000 is relevant to a case the judge may not call Environment Canada for historical data — the judge can only listen to what the parties put before the court. The adversarial system, rightly or wrongly, holds that the struggle of the parties will lead to the truth emerging and requires the lawyer's partiality as much as the judge's impartiality. Thus, Lord Brougham, in Queen Caroline's case,[5] acting as counsel, said:

> ... an advocate, by the sacred duty which he owes his client, knows in the discharge of that office but one person in the world — [the] client and no other .... Nay, separating even the duties of a patriot from those of an advocate, and casting them if need be to the wind, he must go on reckless of the consequences, if his fate it should unhappily be to involve his country in confusion for his client's protection.

Lord Brougham's statement is classic, but is limited to honest partisanship. A lawyer cannot break the law for a client — even if a client would win a case by the destruction of a videotape, the lawyer is not thereby allowed to destroy evidence.[6] Similarly, a lawyer may not intentionally mislead a court.

There is well known case law dealing with the duty of defence counsel. In *Tuckiar v. The King*,[7] an accused confessed to defence counsel who passed the confession on to the court. The facts in *Tuckiar* are unusual, but many counsel are confused about their duty when someone tells them facts that would hurt their client. The duty of counsel (with the exception of Crown counsel described below) is clear — counsel cannot mislead the court but counsel has absolutely no

---

[3]   For example, a jury may be asked questions such as "did the plaintiff slip in the defendant's store" and not a general question of "is the defendant liable to pay the plaintiff and, if so, how much is to be paid". In criminal matters juries are usually left with the general question of guilty or not guilty.

[4]   *White v. R.*, [1947] S.C.R. 268.

[5]   (1820), 129 E.R. 976.

[6]   *R. v. Murray* (2000), 48 O.R. (3d) 544 at 567 (S.C.J.): "There is no obligation on a citizen to help the police, but taking positive steps to conceal evidence is unlawful".

[7]   *Tuckiar v. The King* (1934), 52 C.L.R. 335.

duty to volunteer information except as required by disclosure requirements. Thus, in a civil case a party has a duty to produce all relevant documents and as counsel you must ensure this is done — that said, you have no duty to highlight the weaknesses of your client's case. The other counsel's job is to destroy your client's case — you do not have a duty to do their job for them.

The role of counsel is well described in *Tombling v. Universal Bulb*[8] where the Court notes:

> The duty of counsel to his client in a civil case ... or in defending an accused person ... is to make every honest endeavour to succeed. He must not, of course, knowingly mislead the Court, either on the facts or on the law, but, short of that, he may put such matters in evidence or omit such others as in his discretion he thinks will be most to the advantage of his client.

Allowing a party to testify falsely and relying on that testimony amounts to misleading the court. Thus, in *Meek v. Fleming*[9] defence counsel relied on, or at the least took no steps to correct, important testimony of the defendant that was, to defence counsel's knowledge, false. If counsel know of a falsehood, they cannot allow the court to accept it. Of course, actual knowledge is very rare — counsel are seldom involved in the facts giving rise to litigation and seldom have knowledge of the facts. This issue of actual knowledge usually arises only when a party tells a lawyer they plan to lie. It is quite proper to accept a client's description of the facts and urge those facts even if counsel doubts the veracity of the facts — counsel is not to judge the case but only to help present it to the court. Of course, as a matter of advocacy it is sensible to test implausible stories since they are unlikely to convince a judge, but this is a practical, and not ethical, matter.

The major exception to the openly partisan position of counsel is that of a criminal prosecutor. A prosecutor has a duty, not to win, but to ensure justice is done. In practice, many prosecutors see justice as being done best if they win but the theory has an important implication — a prosecutor must disclose their case to an accused so the accused can make a full answer and defence. The prosecutor does not have discretion to omit facts, even if the prosecution does not intend to rely on them. Put otherwise, the results of police investigations are not the property of the prosecutor to secure a conviction but rather belong to the public to ensure justice is done.[10]

---

[8] [1951] 2 T.L.R. 289.

[9] [1961] 2 Q.B. 366 (C.A.).

[10] *R. v. Stinchcombe*, [1991] 3 S.C.R. 326. See also S. Hutchison, "Production of Criminal Documents" in *CBAO Institute 2000* (Toronto, 2000).

THE DUTY TO DISCLOSE

As noted above, unlike defence counsel in criminal cases who have no legal obligation to disclose the facts they rely on to defend the accused,[11] the prosecutor is under an obligation to disclose everything in the prosecutor's possession or control[12] unless it is (a) clearly irrelevant (b) privileged or (c) falls within the ambit of the personal information provisions[13] of the *Criminal Code*. The disclosure of materials by the Crown is essential to the right of an accused to make full answer to charges brought and is a principle of fundamental justice.[14] As the Chief Justice notes in *Mills*:[15]

> ... the right of an accused to make full answer and defence is a pillar of criminal justice on which we rely heavily to prevent the conviction of the innocent. It is a principle of fundamental justice protected by [the Constitution]. Flowing from the right to make full answer and defence is the Crown's constitutional and ethical duty to disclose all information in its possession reasonably capable of affecting the accused's ability to raise a reasonable doubt concerning his innocence.

The duty to disclose is triggered whenever there is a reasonable possibility of the information to be disclosed being useful to the accused.[16] Disclosure should be made before the accused is required to elect a mode of trial or enter a plea, and disclosure must be sufficient to allow the accused to make an informed decision to the plea or election.[17] The obligation to disclose is a continuing obligation, with the prosecution having an obligation to ensure ongoing disclosure is made as new materials come to light.[18]

JUDGES

A judge has two functions at trial. The first, during the testimony, is to deal with evidentiary issues and ensure a smooth trial. The second is the decision making process after the evidence is adduced.

Dealing first with the conduct of a trial, the judge's role, broadly speaking, is to sit, listen and only intervene if called on to rule. For example, otherwise inadmissible evidence will be admitted unless counsel object — generally speaking, a

---

[11]   As a practical matter, disclosure should be made of alibi or mental disorder defences. Failure so to do can lead to an adverse inference: see *R. v. Cleghorn*, [1995] 3 S.C.R. 175 (alibi) and *R. v. Stevenson* (1990), 58 C.C.C. (3d) 464 (Ont. C.A.) (mental disorder).

[12]   *Stinchcombe, supra*, note 10; *R. v. Egger*, [1993] 2 S.C.R. 451; *R. v. Trang*, [2002] 2 W.W.R. 317 (Alta. Q.B.); *R. v. Harvie* (2001), 9 M.V.R. (4th) 98; *R. v. O. (W.A.)* (2001), 207 Sask. R. 208 (C.A.).

[13]   Section 278.1 of the *Criminal Code*; see also *R. v. O'Connor*, [1995] 4 S.C.R. 411 for personal records in the hands of third parties and not the prosecution.

[14]   *Stinchcombe, supra*, note 10.

[15]   *R. v. Mills*, [1999] 3 S.C.R. 668, para. 5, *per* Lamer C.J.C. dissenting in part.

[16]   *R. v. Dixon*, [1998] 1 S.C.R. 244.

[17]   *R. v. Girimonte* (1997), 121 C.C.C. (3d) 33 (Ont. C.A.).

[18]   *Ibid.*

judge will not intervene and say, "wait that's inadmissible".[19] The judge is not to determine, say, what witnesses will be called, what order they will be called or, subject to tidy-up questions to clarify obscurities, what questions the witnesses are to be asked. All this is subject to an overall judicial discretion to intervene to ensure a fair trial. Thus, if a judge sees an apparently unfair trial, say where a party is not represented by counsel, the judge has a duty to step in and make the trial process fair — for example, raising the question of the admission of evidence.[20]

As the Court noted in *Jones v. National Coal Co.*:[21]

> In the system of trial which we have evolved in this country, the judge sits to hear and determine the issues raised by the parties, not to conduct an investigation or examination on behalf of society at large.

> ...it is for the advocates, each in his turn, to examine the witnesses, and not for the judge to take it on himself lest by so doing he appears to favor one side or the other .... And it is for the advocate to state his case as fairly and strongly as he can, without undue interruption, lest the sequence of his argument be lost.... The judge's part in all this is to hearken to the evidence, only himself asking questions of witnesses when it is necessary to clear up any point that has been overlooked or left obscure; to see that the advocates behave themselves seemly and keep to the rules laid down by law; to exclude irrelevancies and discourage repetition; to make sure by wise intervention that he follows the points that the advocates are making and can assess their worth; and at the end to make up his mind where the truth lies. If he goes beyond this, he drops the mantle of a judge and assumes the role of an advocate. ...

What about the judge's second role — deciding the case? In judge alone trials, the judge considers the evidence and gives a decision with reasons for that decision. In such cases the judge is both the trier of law and the trier of fact. The judge's reasons normally include findings of law and fact and ought to be full enough for the parties to understand why the judge ruled the way the judge ruled.[22] In jury cases the judge's role is restricted to instructing the jury on the law, or, alternatively, tò apply the law to facts found by the jury. As a procedural point, after both sides have made their case, the judge speaks to the jury and tells them what law is applicable to the case before the jury convenes to decide the relevant facts. In deciding what law to explain to the jury the judge makes certain factual assumptions — a judge does not outline the law of theft in a medical malpractice case. This last point complicates matters. A judge must help the jury to clarify issues and indeed a judge must review the evidence in some detail pointing

---

[19] The rule differs somewhat between criminal and civil matters. In civil cases a failure to object is normally taken as agreement to admission: *McLeod v. Pearson*, [1931] 3 W.W.R. 4 (Alta. T.D.). In criminal cases a failure to object is normally taken as intentional and the evidence admitted (*R. v. Lomage* (1991), 44 O.A.C. 131 (C.A.)), however, a criminal accused should not be deprived of the right to a full and fair trial because of an error of counsel: (*R. v. Stewart*, [1969] 2 C.C.C. 244 (B.C.C.A.)).

[20] *R. v. Schwartzenhauer* (1935), 64 C.C.C. 1 (S.C.C.).

[21] [1957] 2 All E.R. 155 at 159 (C.A.).

[22] *Wagman v. Blue Mountain Resorts Ltd.* (1984), 47 C.P.C. 53 (Ont. H.C.).

out weaknesses in testimony but the judge must not say either side's case is better than another.[23]

A judge must assist the jury to decide facts but at all times make it clear it is the jury who is to decide what the facts are. This is well set out in *McRae v. Eldridge*[24] where the Court notes:

> It is the function and the duty of a trial Judge to see that the jury have a clear understanding of the issues to be determined by them. He should, in the course of his charge, refer to such portions of the evidence as in his opinion will enable the jury to proceed to consider the whole evidence and make their findings in accordance therewith.

DIVISION OF DUTIES BETWEEN JUDGE AND JURY

In a jury trial, the judge must determine the admissibility of evidence. In determining the admissibility of evidence the judge generally decides questions of law and, in some cases, preliminary questions of fact.

Thus, the judge is required to determine preliminary questions of fact relating to the admission of evidence in question, such as in exclusionary rules like hearsay, privilege, or the incompetency of a witness. By contrast, generally, the jury determines issues of fact dealing with the weight and meaning of evidence. For example, where two witnesses give different versions of what happened, the jury decides who to believe. The judge's role is limited to deciding if, in the last example, the witnesses can testify and not as to who is to be believed.

If there is some evidence in support of a proposition, even evidence the judge thinks is weak and unconvincing, the judge must turn the case to the jury because the judge is not a trier of fact.[25] By contrast, if there is no evidence supporting a proposition, the judge is to withhold the case from the jury and decide against that proposition.[26] The distinction is an important one; as the Court noted in *Metropolitan Railway Co. v. Jackson*:[27]

> The Judge has a certain duty to discharge, and the jurors have another and a different duty. The Judge has to say whether any facts have been established by evidence from which negligence *may be* reasonably inferred; the jurors have to say whether, from those facts, when submitted to them, negligence *ought to be* inferred. It is, in my opinion, of the greatest importance in the administration of justice that these separate functions should be maintained, and should be maintained distinct.

A judge's role in fact-finding is limited to ensuring the jury is limited to rational determination; so long as a rational jury could make a fact-finding determination —

---

23   *R. v. Sims*, [1992] 2 S.C.R. 858.
24   [1958] O.R. 128 at 130 (C.A.).
25   *Ontario v. O.P.S.E.U.* (1990), 37 O.A.C. 218 (Div. Ct.).
26   *R. v. Rowbotham*, [1994] 2 S.C.R. 463.
27   (1877), 3 App. Cas. 193 at 197 (H.L.).

so long as there are reasonable grounds to find something is true — the judge must leave the question to the jury.

Chapter 3

APPEALS AND EVIDENTIARY REVIEW

STRUCTURE OF COURTS

The concept of an appeal court, that is, a court that exists to review decisions of lower courts is quite modern and emerged clearly only with the Judicative Acts of the 1870s. Previously, judicial review of trial decisions was rather haphazard, and was based on considerations of equity rather than law.[1] Regardless, the concept that trial decisions are subject to review is well-established in the common law world.

Generally, trial level courts are subject to have final decisions[2] reviewed on appeal. While the structure varies somewhat from province to province, trial decisions can be appealed as of right to a provincial appeal court. A further appeal, to the Supreme Court of Canada, exists but the Supreme Court must grant leave to bring the appeal and such leave is very seldom granted. The Supreme Court grants leave only on matters of national importance; evidence cases seldom raise such issues.

All that said, the issue of weight of evidence — taken to an extreme — can be an issue of law. The trier of fact must act in a rational manner. As mentioned, if there is no admissible evidence in support of a proposition then, as a matter of law, the proposition must be rejected.[3] So, if, at the end of a jury theft trial, there is no admissible evidence of ownership (an element of theft), then as a matter of law the charge must be dismissed. If there is some evidence, a jury's decision to convict, or acquit, based on that evidence, can stand. The trier of law admits the evidence. The trier of fact weighs the evidence, but only if there is evidence to weigh. The judge should only withdraw a case from the jury if there is no evidence on which a jury could reasonably find for the party bearing the onus of proof.

---

[1]   See for example, *Bright v. Eynon* (1757), 1 Burr. 390 (K.B.).
[2]   Interlocutory matters are often not subject to appeal.
[3]   *R. v. Rowbotham*, [1994] 2 S.C.R. 463.

THE NEED FOR ERROR

Appellate courts exist in order to, among other things, rectify errors made at first instance. Accordingly, absent some error by the court of first instance, there is no ground to appeal. Since most issues concerning the admission of evidence occur during trial, and are dealt with during trial (as opposed to in substantive reasons for judgment) the error necessary to found an evidentiary-based appeal must come in a trial ruling. However, unless an objection to evidence is raised, there will be no trial ruling and little upon which to ground an appeal. Unless a piece of evidence is objected to, it will usually be presumed that the parties are content that the evidence go to the trier of fact and no appeal based on its admission will be allowed.[4] This rule is sometimes waived by appellate courts if the admission of the evidence would lead to a substantial wrong or miscarriage of justice.[5] Thus, the Court notes:[6]

> ... a party in a civil case generally should not bring an appeal on the basis of some aspect of the trial proceeding to which it did not object. For example, if no objection is made to the admissibility of evidence in a civil trial, an objection on appeal will usually be unsuccessful.

An appellate court is far more likely to see such miscarriage of justice in criminal matters.[7] Thus, Justice Krever, in *Lomage*,[8] writes:

> The judge in a criminal case assumes a greater responsibility to see that justice prevails than that in the pure adversary system ....

THE APPELLATE COURT

As a general rule, following a trial, any party who disagrees with the result may appeal to a higher court for review. Normally there is at least one appeal as of right. That higher court is usually known as the Court of Appeal although the specific title varies from jurisdiction to jurisdiction. Appellate courts may have broad jurisdiction to deal with various matters; in this section we will consider only their role in considering appeals based on evidentiary concerns.

At the outset, it is important to segregate questions of law from questions of fact. Generally speaking, the Court of Appeal has absolute authority to review questions of law and rule differently than the trial judge. That does not mean the Court of Appeal will, on finding the trial judge erred in law, automatically overturn the lower court's decision. It may be that the Court of Appeal will say that a

---

4   *McLeod v. Pearson*, [1931] 3 W.W.R. 4 (Alta. T.D.).
5   *Mann v. Balaban*, [1970] S.C.R. 74.
6   *Marshall v. Watson Wyatt* (2002), 57 O.R. (3d) 813 at 820 (C.A.).
7   *R. v. D. (L.E.)*, [1989] 2 S.C.R. 111; *R. v. Lomage* (1991), 44 O.A.C. 131, especially *per* Krever J.A. at 140 (C.A.).
8   *R. v. Lomage* (1991), 44 O.A.C. 131 at 140 (C.A.).

ruling of law at trial was wrong but the ruling made no difference to the ultimate outcome of the case; in such situations the error made no difference and the appeal will be refused. So, in a wrongful dismissal case the Court of Appeal might say that a trial judge erred in ruling that one month severance for each year employed was a standard and still uphold the final decision if the Court of Appeal agrees with the final result. You can come to the right answer by the wrong reasoning. So, in a typical provision, s. 134(6) of the *Ontario Courts of Justice Act*[9] precludes an appeal court from ordering a new trial "unless some substantial wrong or miscarriage of justice has occurred". If an appeal is to be allowed the error of law made by the trial judge must be one that made, or could have made, a difference. All that said, the Court of Appeal's power to correct errors of law is significant — errors of fact, as set out below, usually go unremedied.

With respect to questions of fact Appellate Courts have a very limited authority. The reasoning here is that, unlike questions of law (which the Court of Appeal can decide as well as the trial court), on issues of fact the trial court saw the witnesses, looked at the exhibits and, generally, had a better chance to figure out what happened. The presence at trial does give a great advantage to the trial judge — one can see a witness giving testimony and conclude that witness is lying but, when reading the transcript only, think the testimony is truthful. Further, some witnesses are not very articulate and a trial transcript does not say very much — much of their meaning comes from body language. The Court of Appeal sees and hears no witnesses — all the Appellate Court gets is a trial transcript and so its ability to decide facts is limited.

As the Court notes in *Watt v. Thomas*:[10]

> ...but if the evidence as a whole can reasonably be regarded as justifying the conclusion arrived at at the trial, and especially if that conclusion has been arrived at on conflicting testimony by a tribunal which saw and heard the witnesses, the appellate court will bear in mind that it has not enjoyed this opportunity and that the view of the trial judge as to where credibility lies is entitled to great weight.

The Court of Appeal is not to retry cases on the facts but only to review determinations of facts to see if the factual finding was clearly unreasonable.[11] As Justice Laskin notes in *Marshall v. Watson Wyatt*,[12] in the context of a claim that a jury erred, "an appellate court is justified in intervening only if the jury's verdict was "plainly unreasonable"". In a similar passage, the Supreme Court notes[13] "where it is found that the evidence did not permit a jury acting judicially to reach

---

9   R.S.O. 1990, c. C.43.
10   [1947] 1 All E.R. 582 at 583-584 (H.L.).
11   *C.N.R. v. Muller*, [1934] 1 D.L.R. 768 (S.C.); *R. v. Corbett*, [1975] 2 S.C.R. 275. See s. 686 of the *Criminal Code* (Appendix A) for an appellate court's power on a criminal appeal.
12   (2002), 57 O.R. (3d) 813 at 819.
13   *McKinley v. B.C. Tel*, [2001] 2 S.C.R. 1612, para. 59; see also *McCannell v. McLean*, [1937] S.C.R. 341, 343:

> [T]he verdict of a jury will not be set aside as against the weight of evidence unless it is so plainly unreasonable and unjust as to satisfy the Court that no jury reviewing the evidence as a whole and acting judicially could have reached it.

the conclusion that it did, an appellate court is entitled to set it aside". An appellate court is not entitled to second-guess the trier of fact, whether judge or jury.[14]

Put otherwise, a trier of fact must act judicially. If a trier of fact comes to a conclusion that, based on admissible evidence, is reasonable and possible, an appeal court cannot intervene. If, however, a jury's decision (or the factual findings of a judge) cannot possibly be right, the Court of Appeal can and will intervene.

---

[14] *R. v. Armstrong*, 2002 Carswell N.S. 11 (N.S. C.A.).

Chapter 4

ONUS, BURDEN AND PRESUMPTION

BURDEN OF PROOF

The concepts encompassed by "burden of proof" can be confusing at first glance but are not too difficult if reduced to basics. Essentially, "burden of proof" is an ambiguous term covering two different ideas:

(1)   the burden of producing evidence; and
(2)   the burden of persuasion.

The burden of producing evidence, also called the burden of going forward, is the responsibility of providing *some* evidence that a fact exists. When a party fails to satisfy this burden, there is insufficient evidence for a reasonable trier of fact to find a fact is even in issue. For example, if a plaintiff is suing for goods delivered but not paid for, that plaintiff must adduce some evidence of delivery (the testimony of the delivery person, a signed receipt, or the like) or the plaintiff's case will automatically fail. The evidence does not have to be such as to prove delivery but it must be enough that a rational decision maker *could* find delivery occurred. If the burden of producing evidence is not met and the fact in issue is necessary as a legal matter, then a directed verdict is appropriate. Put otherwise, unless the burden of production is met, a judge will withdraw the issue from the jury and decide the issue as a matter of law.

The party with the burden of producing evidence is the party who must establish a fact — this party is sometimes the plaintiff and sometimes the defendant. Thus, in our example of goods delivered the plaintiff must produce evidence of delivery. On the other hand, if the defence is one of confession and avoidance, such as, in the delivery example, "yes, the product was delivered but it was defective", then the defendant has the burden of production on the issue of defective product. The burden of producing evidence is determined by the pleadings or charge — who must establish a fact?

Once a fact has been put into issue by some evidence a directed verdict is inappropriate. The parties try to persuade the trier of fact. The trier of fact considers all the evidence and decides one way or another. There is enough evidence, from the burden of production, that either decision could be proper — the question is, what is the decision?

The question of persuasion takes us to the second meaning of burden of proof, or to the level of persuasion required.

In a criminal case, the trier of fact must be convinced of the accused's guilt to "beyond a reasonable doubt". What does "beyond a reasonable doubt" mean? A phrase often used to describe "beyond a reasonable doubt" is "to a moral certainty".[1] The trier of fact must be morally certain the accused is guilty to convict. Of course, these are just words — the concept is that any lingering doubt must be resolved in favour of an accused.[2] This does not mean that the trier of fact must be convinced of every fact in dispute to be morally certain of guilt. It may be, say, that the trier of fact is unsure how the accused killed the deceased but is certain the killing was wrongful and was done by the accused. The trier of fact, in determining criminal guilt, does not segregate each fact but rather looks at the overall picture to see if guilt follows.[3]

In a civil case the level of proof is much lower — it is customarily considered to be a balance of probabilities. As Lord Denning stated in *Miller v. Minister of Pensions*:[4]

> [The burden of proof in civil cases] must carry a reasonable degree of probability, but not so high as is required in a criminal case. If the evidence is such that the tribunal can say: "We think it is more probable than not," the burden is discharged, but, if the probabilities are equal, it is not.

If the trier of fact thinks it is something more likely than not that something happened, then the trier has passed the necessary persuasive burden to make a finding of fact.

Some confusion arises in civil suits for criminal acts — there the burden of persuasion is still, in theory, a civil standard but the court gives a special scrutiny to the facts to be proven. Thus, to find civil fraud, a trier of fact need only find the trickery more likely than not, but extra care will be taken in the finding. Sometimes the court will say "clear and convincing evidence" is needed. The level of proof in civil cases for allegations of crimes or acts of moral turpitude is confusing. The Supreme Court of Canada, in *Continental Insurance Co. v. Dalton Cartage Co.*,[5] is clear that the relevant burden of proof is to a balance of probabilities; but, in the very same case, the Court approved a passage from *Bater v. Bater*[6] saying:

> The degree depends on the subject matter. A civil court, when considering a charge of fraud, will naturally give a higher degree of probability than that which it would require if considering whether negligence was established. It does not adapt so high a degree as a criminal court, even when it is considering a charge of a criminal

---

[1]   It should be noted that the Supreme Court suggests trial judges avoid using this phrase.
[2]   As Blackstone notes, "... it is better that ten guilty persons escape, than that one innocent suffer". *Commentaries* (1769), IV, 27, 352.
[3]   *R. v. Morin*, [1988] 2 S.C.R. 345.
[4]   [1947] 2 All E.R. 372 (K.B.).
[5]   [1982] 1 S.C.R. 164.
[6]   [1950] 2 All E.R. 458 at 459 (C.A.).

nature, but still it does require a degree of probability which is commensurate with the occasion.

Perhaps the best approach is to conclude that allegations of morally blame-worthy acts must be proven to a standard somewhat higher than the usual civil standard, but not to a standard of moral certainty. Accordingly, whenever an act of moral turpitude is asserted, the burden of proof persuasion is to an enhanced standard;[7] the evidence and proof offered must be analyzed with considerable care.[8] With any allegation of moral turpitude, a very clear proof is needed.
In the well-known decision in *Sodeman v. R.*,[9] the Court notes:

> ...questions of fact vary greatly in nature and in some cases greater care in scruti-nizing the evidence is proper than in others, and a greater clearness of proof may be properly looked for.

CIRCUMSTANTIAL EVIDENCE

Circumstantial evidence poses a special problem in criminal cases. Generally, the trier of fact is to consider all the evidence together, and not one piece of evidence at a time, in deciding whether an accused has been proven guilty beyond reasonable doubt.[10] But what if the State's entire case is circumstantial?[11] Must the evidence exclude every possible explanation other than guilt,[12] and, if this is the case, ought the judge to withdraw a circumstantial case from the jury unless all explanations other than guilt are excluded? The general rule is that a purely circumstantial case can succeed only if "the circumstances [are] consistent with the conclusion of guilt and inconsistent with any other rational conclusion".[13]
The case law is clear that the decision whether every possible explanation, other than guilt, is excluded in a circumstantial case is a matter for the jury.[14] That having been said there is no set formula that a trial judge must give a jury when considering circumstantial evidence.[15] As the Court notes in *Cooper*:[16]

---

[7] *Continental Insurance Co. v. Dalton Cartage Co.*, [1982] 1 S.C.R. 164; *Smith v. Smith*, [1952] 2 S.C.R. 312; R.M. Novick *Blond's Evidence* (1994) at 103.
[8] *R. v. Simpson* (1977), 35 C.C.C. (2d) 337 (Ont. C.A.).
[9] (1936) 2 All E.R. 1138 (P.C.).
[10] *Stewart v. R.*, [1977] 2 S.C.R. 748.
[11] Justice Watt defines circumstantial evidence thusly:
> Circumstantial evidence is any item of evidence, testimonial or real, other than the testi-mony of an Eyewitness to the material fact. It is any fact from the existence of which the trier of fact may infer the existence of a fact in issue.

D. Watt, *Manual of Criminal Evidence* (Toronto: Carswell, 1999) at 40.
[12] See *McGreevy v. D.P.P.* (1973), 57 Cr. App. R. 424.
[13] *R. v. Handy* (2002), S.C.C. 56, para. 96; *Hodge's Case* (1838), 168 E.R. 1136.
[14] *R. v. Comba*, [1938] S.C.R. 396.
[15] *R. v. Fleet* (1997), 36 O.R. (3d) 542 (C.A.).
[16] *R. v. Cooper*, [1978] 1 S.C.R. 860 at 881.

It [a judge's charge to the jury] is enough if it is made plain to the members of the jury that before basing a verdict of guilty on circumstantial evidence they must be satisfied beyond a reasonable doubt that the guilt of the accused is the only reasonable inference to be drawn from the proven facts.

WHO BEARS THE ONUS OF PROOF?

Broadly speaking, it is the plaintiff or the prosecutor who bears the burden of proving their case. That said, on specific issues, the defendant or accused may have the burden of producing evidence. The defendant or accused has the burden of producing evidence for affirmative defences: pleas of confession and avoidance. For example, if, in a homicide case, self-defence is pleaded, the defendant has the burden of producing enough evidence to show self-defence could apply. The persuasive burden remains with the prosecution — the accused does not have to do more than raise a doubt that self-defence applies, but that doubt, for affirmative defences, must be raised by the accused. In a civil case the same rule applies, but since persuasion is only to a balance of probabilities, raising a doubt is not enough and an affirmative defence needs to be established to a balance of probabilities. It should be noted that there is no onus to call evidence and inferences drawn from a failure to call evidence are likely improper.[17]

The burden of persuasion is the responsibility of persuading a trier of fact that some fact actually is true. This is the burden to beyond reasonable doubt in criminal and to a balance of probability in civil cases. Thus, going back to the delivery case, to satisfy the burden of producing evidence it may be enough to produce an invoice. The trier of fact may, or may not, find delivery based on the invoice alone. To satisfy the burden of persuasion the plaintiff must go further and actually convince the trier of fact, to a balance of probabilities, that delivery in fact occurred. Similarly, in a criminal case for assault, testimony that the accused and complainant, say, willingly went outside to fight raises the issue of consent, and meets the accused's evidentiary burden. The prosecutor's burden of persuasion then requires that consent be disproven to beyond a reasonable doubt.

PRESUMPTIONS

A presumption is a reasoning process whereby, to some degree, proof of one fact is taken to be evidence of another fact. For example, if you demonstrate an individual is an adult, it is presumed that individual is legally competent. That does not mean that you cannot argue the individual suffers from a legal disability, some mental instability, say, and is incompetent — but it does mean that if no other evidence is led a court will find that individual competent. The *Downey*

---

[17]   *Wiche v. Ontario* (2001), 9 C.C.L.T. (3d) 72.

case[18] gave another example. Section 195(2) (now s. 212(3)) of the *Criminal Code*[19] provided that evidence a person lives with, or is habitually in the company of, prostitutes is, absent evidence to the contrary, proof that person lives on the avails of prostitution — a crime. What this means is that a Crown can focus on proof that someone, say, lives with a prostitute rather than proving that person actually lives on the avails of prostitution. In effect, the presumption in s. 195 (2) of the *Criminal Code* makes living with a prostitute a crime subject to a defence, to be raised by the accused, that the accused was self-supporting. A civil law example is the presumption of regularity.[20] This presumption says that, absent evidence to the contrary, a court will assume everything was done in the ordinary course. Thus, an item mailed will be assumed to have been received a few days later. This allows proof of receipt of mail by proof of mailing.

TYPES OF PRESUMPTIONS

Presumptions come in various forms depending on how difficult it is to convince a court not to follow them. Professor Morgan has described the types of presumptions as follows:[21]

Presumption of facts — Such presumptions are not prescribed by law but rather arise from common sense. For example, someone has a driver's licence, it follows that they can drive. If the ability to drive is an issue in an action, proof that someone has a driver's licence *allows*, but does not require, the Court to find that person can drive.

Rebuttable Presumptions of Law — Such presumptions are prescribed by law but not conclusive if there is evidence to the contrary. The avails of prostitution example [from *Downey*] is an example of a rebuttable presumption of law. Such presumptions reverse the onus of producing evidence.

Irrebuttal Presumptions of Law — These presumptions are prescribed by law and conclusive as to some issue. An example could be impaired driving legislation providing that proof [of] blood alcohol of a certain level is proof that the driver is impaired regardless of any other evidence. With such a presumption, the crime of impaired driving is, in effect, mirrored by a related crime of driving with blood alcohol over a certain level. In Canada, rather than rely on a presumption, the same result is obtained by criminalizing both impaired driving *and* driving with blood alcohol in excess of a certain level. Irrebuttable presumptions do not allow for evidence to the contrary, and, indeed, an irrebuttable presumption may fly in the face of common sense. For example, the Eighteenth Century presumption that a contract

---

[18] *R. v. Downey* (1992), 2 S.C.R. 10.
[19] R.S.C. 1985, c. C-46.
[20] *Omnia praesumuntur rite et solenniter esse acta.*
[21] J. Morton, *Cases and Materials on Evidence*, 4th ed. (Butterworths: Toronto, 1960).

made at sea was actually made at the Royal Exchange in Cornhill was both irrebuttable and absurd.[22]

Such legal fictions are rare in modern times.

JUDICIAL NOTICE

Triers of fact, be they judges or juries, are assumed to have a fund of general knowledge about the world and specific facts in it. *Phipson on Evidence* says:[23]

> Judicial notice is the cognisance taken by the court itself of certain matters which are so notorious, or clearly established, that evidence of their existence is deemed unnecessary.

This fund of information changes and develops over time.

All educated Canadians today know what, say, a photocopier is and, generally speaking, that copies of documents made on a photocopier do not necessarily reproduce exactly the original — copies can be enlarged, parts of the original whited out, and the like. This was not true, say, in the early 1960s. If a case in 1962 dealt with photocopied copies of documents it might be necessary for someone to explain, by testimony, what a photocopier was and how it operated. By contrast, it might be that in 1897 a trier of fact could be assumed to have a knowledge, say, of the behaviour of horses that today would need proof by evidence.

The principle of judicial notice can be stated as follows:

The trier of fact will take judicial notice of such facts as are generally known in the community and which are not capable of dispute among reasonable people.

Judicial notice is the acceptance of a fact as true without the introduction of evidence of that fact. Once a fact is taken judicial notice of, in Canada, it is incontestable.[24] Thus, if judicial notice is taken that, say, Poland was occupied by German and Soviet troops in the early stages of the Second World War, no evidence to the contrary may be led and the trier of fact will not consider any other fact possible.

Obviously, the concept of judicial notice can lead to problems if it is too widely extended. Just because a view is widely held in a community and not disputed among reasonable members thereof does not mean it is correct. In 1944 Professor Morgan said[25] that "to warrant judicial notice the probability [of truth of the matter to be noticed] must be so great as to have the truth of the proposition notoriously indisputable". United States Federal Rule of Evidence 201 says:

---

[22] W. Blackstone, *Commentaries on the Laws of England* (Clarendon Press: Oxford, 1765) III, at 7, 107.
[23] *Phipson on Evidence*, 15th ed. (London: 2000) pp. 1-11.
[24] *R. v. Zundel* (1987), 58 O.R. (2d) 129 (C.A.).
[25] (1944), 57 Harv. L. Rev. 269, 271.

A judicially noticed fact must be one not subject to reasonable dispute in that it is either (1) generally known within the territorial jurisdiction of the trial court or (2) capable of accurate and ready determination by resort to sources whose accuracy cannot reasonably be questioned.

And yet, notoriously indisputable propositions may be wrong. At the turn of the century it was an accepted commonplace among educated North Americans that intelligent beings lived on Mars, built great canals and suffered a severe water shortage. It is hard to think of a lawsuit turning on the judicial notice of Martian society but, similar, less appealing commonplaces about gender and race were assumed until very recently by triers of fact as being facts beyond dispute. Nevertheless, when properly confined, judicial notice is a sensible way to limit the court's investigation to matters really in dispute. Perhaps the point is to recognize judges are human and matters that judges are certain to be true will influence them — it is probably better these certainties be stated rather than being passed over in silence.

Chapter 5

TESTIMONIAL EVIDENCE

USE OF TESTIMONIAL EVIDENCE

As a general rule, evidence in a trial is given either by the testimony of a witness telling the court what happened or by the court itself inspecting physical evidence. The distinction is important because a witness's testimony suffers from the defects of faulty perception, memory and bias. Real evidence, physical evidence, may be misinterpreted, misunderstood or given too much weight, but it will not suffer from being translated through another's experience. Thus, in the *Nikolovski*[1] case, a videotape was played of a robbery and that was found sufficient to found a conviction. Speaking of audio tapes, the Ontario Court of Appeal in *R. v. Rowbotham*[2] noted:

> It is true that the tapes themselves constitute the evidence which should be and must be considered by the jury.

Similarly, courts will often inspect products alleged to be defective to determine if the product really is defective. Thus, a court may inspect, for instance, representative examples of allegedly defective product packaging and decide for itself if the alleged defects are real. All that said, for a court to consider real evidence, some authentification of the evidence is necessary.[3] Authentification is generally accomplished by testimony of a witness so witness testimony is usually

---

[1] *R. v. Nikolovski* (1996), 141 D.L.R. (4th) 647 (S.C.C.).
[2] (1988), 41 C.C.C. (3d) 1 at 47 (Ont. C.A.).
[3] Describing videotapes of a crime, the evidentiary effect of these tapes and the need for authentification, the Court in *R. v. Murray* (2000), 48 O.R. (3d) 544 at 566-67 (S.C.J.) notes:
It would be difficult to over-estimate the evidentiary significance of these tapes. The making of them formed an integral part of the crimes. The victims were forced to participate not just in perverse sexual acts, but also actively in the videotaping of them. The resulting images amounted to the basest kind of forced child pornography. The tapes were the products and instrumentalities of crime and were far more potent "hard evidence" than the often-mentioned "smoking gun" and "bloody shirt". Once it possessed either of those items, the prosecution would still have to connect them to the accused and the accused would have room to raise issues such as self-defence. Here, jurors became eyewitnesses to Bernardo committing most of the crimes with which he was charged. Once the jury viewed the tapes, Bernardo was left with no defence to anything but the murder charges and little chance of a successful defence on those.

needed even in a case of real evidence. The witness must give testimony that the real evidence is, in fact, the item actually in dispute. Thus, in the product packaging case the witness must testify that truly representative examples of the actual packaging in issue is before the court. Absent the authenticating witness, the court has nothing.

Witnesses, unlike real evidence, must communicate to the court what they perceived. To do so they must be: (1) able to perceive an event (2) able to understand and remember the event in a coherent fashion and (3) able to relate that understanding and memory to the court.[4] Errors in the perception and recitation can come in at all stages — memory changes over time. Even if memory were not variable, language is always imprecise, and the recounting of an event does not necessarily lead to the court understanding precisely what the witness was trying to convey. Nevertheless, and in spite of all its limitations, testimony of witnesses is the most practical way to get facts before the court. Testimony amounts to a structured method of allowing the parties to tell their story. As such, it serves the purpose of adducing facts and, additionally, allows for the cathartic release of emotions engendered by "having one's say".[5]

COMPETENCE

Competence is the legal ability to give testimony in court.[6] The determination of who is or is not competent is a legal matter decided by a judge. In practice, except for children, competence rarely causes a problem. All adults are, until shown otherwise, presumed competent.[7] The exceptions for adults are (1) spouses of criminal accused, who are not competent to testify for the prosecution (except in specific cases of spousal or child abuse) and (2) criminal accused, who are not competent to testify for the prosecution.

At one time the ability, or lack of ability, to swear on oath was a significant issue.[8] In practice, no one is ever challenged on taking an oath — to use an affirmation it is sufficient to say "I prefer to affirm". If children are mature enough to understand the solemnity of giving testimony under oath or affirmation, they can give sworn evidence. As the Court noted in *R. v. Hayes:*[9]

> The important consideration, we think, when a judge has to decide whether a child should properly be sworn, is whether the child has a sufficient appreciation of the

---

[4] These issues are to be decided at time of trial and not when the perceived event occurred: *R. v. Marquard*, [1993] 4 S.C.R. 223.

[5] Indeed, as a practical matter, many parties, even after losing at trial, are pleased that they were able to tell their story and be heard. A problem with "paper trials" — hearings conducted solely by affidavit — is that the parties often feel left out of the court process.

[6] Competence also has other meanings in other contexts, such as testamentary capacity, but we are limiting our discussion to the testimonial context.

[7] See, for example, ss. 18 and 18.1 of the *Evidence Act*, R.S.O. 1990, c. E.23.

[8] See, for example, Robinson C.J.'s lengthy discussion of an oath taken by a non-Christian in *R. v. Pah-May-Gay* (1860), 20 U.C.Q.B. 195 (C.A.).

[9] [1977] 2 All E.R. 288 at 291 (C.A.).

solemnity of the occasion, and the added responsibility to tell the truth, which is involved in taking an oath, over and above the duty to tell the truth which is an ordinary duty of normal social conduct.

If a child, or indeed an adult, cannot understand the meaning of testifying under oath or affirmation, they may give evidence on promising to tell the truth. The situation of unsworn but accepted testimony is rare and is contrary to the general rule that evidence must be given under oath. Unsworn testimony is admissible only by statutory amendment to common law.[10] The conditions precedent for accepting such unsworn evidence, while less than that required for sworn evidence, are not trivial. The Ontario Court of Appeal in *Khan*[11] notes:

> ... in determining whether to receive the unsworn evidence of a child of tender years who does not understand the nature of an oath, a judge ... must form an opinion as to whether the child (a) is possessed of sufficient intelligence to justify the reception of the evidence, and (b) understand the duty of speaking the truth.

Once allowed, evidence of a witness testifying on promising to tell the truth is to be weighed in the same fashion as evidence given under oath or affirmation.[12] The ability to communicate is also required as part of competence. The witness must be able, at the time of trial, to adequately relate the events testified about to the trier of fact.[13] Sometimes a degenerative disease stops this — Alzheimer victims are common examples of people who may lose competence to testify.

Finally, competence presumes an ability to perceive the events testified about at the time of their occurrence.[14] Even if a person is able to relate testimony at the time of trial, they cannot testify if, at the time of the incident, they were unable, through disease, drugs or extreme youth, to perceive the incident. This last is a result of irrelevance — without the ability to perceive the incident a witness's testimony is irrelevant.

The inability of a criminal accused, or their spouse, to testify in favour of the Crown reflects a deep-seated societal opposition to compulsory testimony. Of course, an accused can always plead guilty and eliminate the need for any testimony. In the case of an accused's spouse, the bar on competence seems to be rooted in the importance placed on marital harmony. That said, where intra-family crimes occur the accused's spouse is quite competent. The *Canada Evidence Act*, s. 4, provides:

> 4.(1) Every person charged with an offence, and, except as otherwise provided in this section, the wife or husband, as the case may be, of the person so charged, is a

---

[10] See, for example, s. 18.1(3) of the Ontario *Evidence Act* and s. 16(3) of the *Canada Evidence Act*, R.S.C. 1985, c. C-5.

[11] *R. v. Khan* (1988), 42 C.C.C. (3d) 197 at 204 (Ont. C.A.); incidentally, the *voir dire* to determine a child witness's competence may be conducted in front of the jury: *R. v. Ferguson* (1996), 112 C.C.C. (3d) 342 (B.C.C.A.).

[12] *R. v. McGovern* (1993), 22 C.R. (4th) 359 (Man. C.A.).

[13] *Udy v. Stewart* (1886), 10 O.R. 591 (C.P.).

[14] *Hildreth v. Key* (1960), 341 S.W. (2d) 601.

competent witness for the defence, whether the person so charged is charged solely or jointly with any other person.

(2) The wife or husband of a person charged with an offence against subsection 50(1) of the *Young Offenders Act* or with an offence against any of sections 151, 152, 153, 155 or 159, subsection 160(2) or (3), or sections 170 to 173, 179, 212, 215, 218, 271 to 273, 280 to 283, 291 to 294 or 329 of the *Criminal Code*, or an attempt to commit any such offence, is a competent and compellable witness for the prosecution without the consent of the person charged.

...

(5) Nothing in this section affects a case where the wife or husband of a person charged with an offence may at common law be called as a witness without the consent of that person.

(6) The failure of the person charged, or of the wife or husband of that person, to testify shall not be made the subject of comment by the judge or by counsel for the prosecution.

The common law compellability of a spouse against an accused includes, broadly speaking, offences against the spouse, or children, affecting their person, health or liberty.[15]

LEVEL OF PROOF

Competence of a witness is distinct from belief in that witness's testimony. Put otherwise, a witness may be accepted as competent and then be totally disbelieved because, say, the trier of fact thinks they are incredible. Accordingly, the level of proof needed to find a witness competent is limited to balance of probabilities. As the Court noted, albeit provisionally, in *Ferguson*:[16]

... I think that it is sufficient for the court to be satisfied on a balance of probabilities that the child is capable of communicating the evidence, and understanding the nature of a promise, whether the proposed witness is tendered by the Crown or by the defence. To require the higher standard of proof might preclude the jury from hearing relevant and credible evidence, and would involve the establishment of a double standard, depending on who called the witness. Once that witness has testified, of course, the jury weighs his or her evidence on the criminal standard.

[15] *R. v. Singh*, [1970] 1 C.C.C. 299 (B.C.C.A.).
[16] *R. v. Ferguson* (1996), 112 C.C.C. (3d) 342 at 361 (B.C.C.A.).

COMPELLABILITY OF WITNESS

A compellable witness is a witness that can be forced to give testimony. Specifically, a witness is compellable if, upon receiving a subpoena, that witness will be arrested and brought to court if the witness fails to attend at court and testify.

Subject to constitutional considerations, all competent witnesses are compellable except heads of state, foreign ambassadors and their direct staff and judges (see below). Thus, if the Russian President is visiting Canada and sees a car crash, they can testify if they want to but they cannot be obliged so to testify.

COMPELLABILITY OF JUDGES

As a general rule judges cannot be required to testify regarding their reasons for a decision.[17] That having been said, judges are competent and compellable witnesses regarding matters occurring during trial, but collateral to the trial. Specifically, in order for an incident to be collateral to the trial, the incident must have no bearing whatsoever on the trial or its process — if the incident would in some way lead to questioning the judge about the nature of the trial, the incident is not collateral.[18]

Administrative or chambers matters occurring during the course of trial which are related to trial are not incidental and judges cannot be compelled to give testimony regarding those administrative or chambers matters.[19] Although highly unusual, an example of a collateral incident for which a judge is compellable arose in the *Thanet*[20] decision. In *Thanet*, a riot broke out following sentencing in a criminal matter and judges, being witnesses to the riot, were compellable. Similarly, if an assault occurred during trial or in chambers, the judge could be compelled to testify about the assault even if the assault arose, say, as a result of testimony heard at trial.

COMPELLABILITY AND THE CONSTITUTION

As a fundamental constitutional[21] principle, a person cannot be required to give testimony against themselves in a criminal proceeding. Thus, an accused is not even competent as a witness for the prosecution. But, what if an accused is called to testify for the prosecution against someone else who is charged with

---

[17] *MacKeigan v. Hickman*, [1989] 2 S.C.R. 796; there is no distinction between Superior Court judges and lower court judges for purposes of judicial compellability.

[18] *Clendenning v. Belleville (Municipality) Commissioners of Police* (1976), 15 O.R. (2d) 97 (Div. Ct.).

[19] *Edwards (Litigation Guardian of) v. Canada (Attorney General)* (1999), 182 D.L.R. (4th) 736 (Ont. S.C.J.).

[20] *R. v. Thanet* (1799), 27 St. Tr. 821.

[21] See s.7 of the *Canadian Charter of Rights and Freedoms*, Part I of the *Constitution Act*, 1982, being Schedule B to the *Canada Act 1982* (U.K.), 1982, c. 11.

committing crimes together with the witness? Can the witness be compelled to testify even when such testimony touches on crimes the witness may have committed?[22]

In *R. v. S. (R.J.)*,[23] the Supreme Court of Canada held that there is a presumption that an accused person is a compellable witness in a parallel criminal proceeding against someone alleged to have committed a crime with the accused unless it is established that the predominant purpose in compelling the testimony of the accused is incrimination of the accused.

The test to determine whether a witness is compellable in a particular proceeding has evolved into a two-stage analysis by virtue of the subsequent decisions of the Supreme Court of Canada in *British Columbia (Securities Commissions) v. Branch*,[24] and *Phillips v. Nova Scotia (Commissioner, Public Inquiries Act)*.[25] In *Cadagan* the Court describes the two-stage analysis as follows:[26]

> First, the court must consider the importance to the state of obtaining compelled testimony from the witness; if the court is of the opinion that the proceedings are undertaken or are functioning primarily in such a way as to obtain evidence for the prosecution of the witness, rather than for some legitimate public purpose, s. 7 requires that the witness be exempted from testifying.
>
> Secondly, in the event it is found that the proceedings in question were commenced to achieve goals of substantial public importance rather than to further a collateral criminal prosecution, the court must continue to the second stage of the analysis. This second stage requires that the court balance the right of the witness/accused against the interest of the state in receiving the compelled testimony, in a way which insures that all the requirements of the Charter are upheld. The result of the balancing will depend upon the circumstances of each case. The witness will not be compellable if he can show that his right to a fair trial will be jeopardized even if he is protected from any derivative use of his prior testimony against him at his trial.

The two-stage test is strictly applied and it is a rare case where a person will be found to be non-compellable as a result of constitutional considerations.[27]

INTERPRETERS

As is almost self-evident, evidence cannot be taken by the court unless it is presented in a form the court can understand. Accordingly, if a witness cannot testify in a language understood by the court, a translator may be used, as

---

[22] It should be remembered that such testimony cannot be used at the witness's own trial, except to cross-examine as to credibility: *R. v. Kuldip* (1990), 61 C.C.C. (3d) 385 (S.C.C.).
[23] (1995), 96 C.C.C. (3d) 1 (S.C.C.).
[24] [1995] 2 S.C.R. 3 (S.C.C.).
[25] [1995] 2 S.C.R. 97 (S.C.C.).
[26] *R. v. Cadagan* (1998), 165 D.L.R. (4th) 747 at 752 (S.C.J.).
[27] *R. v. Jobin* (1995), 97 C.C.C. (3d) 97 (S.C.C.).

necessary,[28] to allow the testimony to be heard.[29] The question of necessity is one of fact; does the witness "possess a sufficient knowledge of the language to really understand and answer the questions put".[30] Only when necessary will an interpreter be allowed.

The reason an interpreter is not allowed except as necessary is because translated evidence (a) loses much of its immediacy[31] and (b) an unscrupulous witness, pretending to have poor language skills, could use the translator to shield answers and fabricate evidence.[32] Moreover, translation invariably changes the meaning of questions and answers and, unless really needed, ought to be avoided.

In situations where a translator is needed, the translator must, at a minimum, be competent in the languages involved[33] and be impartial between the parties.[34] These last issues seldom pose a problem.

---

[28] *Filios v. Morland* (1963), N.S.W.R. 545.
[29] *The Tripca Mines* (1950), 3 All E.R. 798; rev'd (1960), 3 All E.R. 304.
[30] *Donkin Creeden Ltd. v. "Chicago Maru (The)"* (1916), 28 D.L.R. 804.
[31] *Filios, supra,* note 28.
[32] *R. v. Burke* (1858), 8 Cox C.C. 44.
[33] *R. v. Walker* (1910), 16 C.C.C. 77 (B.C.C.A.)
[34] *Unterreiner v. R.* (1980), 51 C.C.C. (2d) 373 (Ont. Co. Ct.).

Chapter 6

EXAMINING WITNESSES

WITNESS PREPARATION

The trier of fact generally learns the facts of each case from the testimony of witnesses asked questions by counsel in court. The order of examination is, first, direct examination, where a witness is examined by the party calling them, second, cross-examination, where that witness is examined by the party opposite and, finally, re-examination, where the party who first called the witness has a chance to clarify anything new or confusing arising in cross-examination.

Since the only way to prepare for trial is to find out what each witness will say, it is proper to speak to as many witnesses as possible to find out what they will say. The only significant exception is speaking directly to a party represented by a lawyer other than yourself; parties can be dealt with only through counsel.

From a general discussion of what witnesses say they will say to witness preparation is but a short step. And it is a perfectly proper step. Most people go to court very seldom and will be confused and awkward unless they are given some explanation of what to expect. Louis Nizer writes:[1]

> The law permits you — it does more than permit you, it makes it your duty — to examine your witness carefully in advance to refresh his recollection as to dates and details by exhibiting documents to him which establish these matters; to acquaint him with the sequence of questions so that the truth may be established in orderly fashion and without confusion which may throw doubt on it. It is the only way, in fact, in which you can present the truth. For truth never walks into a court room. It never flies in through the window. It must be dragged in by you ....

Many counsel arrange to have important trial witnesses examined, and then cross-examined, in a mock trial with a full courtroom set-up. Once a witness has been through this they are much less nervous and they can focus on giving their evidence in a straightforward and coherent fashion. The limitation, of course, is that, in witness preparation counsel may not "prepare away" inconvenient facts. As a practical matter, it is worth noting that attempts to alter a witness's testimony usually fail and generally in a catastrophic matter. Ethical issues aside, witnesses are best prepared if they are ready to tell the truth as they see it.

---

[1] "The Art of the Jury Trial" (1946), 32 Cornell L.Q. 59, 66.

In summary, counsel may prepare a witness for trial and rehearse the anticipated evidence, provided that the testimony of the witness is not altered or skewed in any way.

DIRECT EXAMINATION

Direct examination is the examination by a party of witnesses called to testify by that party. The key to understanding direct examination, as opposed to cross-examination, lies in the concept of leading and non-leading questions. Subject to the exceptions set out below, leading questions are not allowed in direct examination.

A leading question is a question that directly or indirectly suggests the answer or which directly or indirectly assumes the truth of a matter in issue.

For example, the following two questions would be leading in a mortgage case where default under the mortgage is in issue:

(1)   "I put it to you that you knew the mortgage was in default when you wrote to the real estate agent" — the question suggests the answer; and

(2)   "What did you write to the real estate agent after the mortgage default"? — the question assumes default, a matter in issue.

The first question suggests its own answer and is leading. The second, more subtle, question assumes the fact of the default and is also leading.[2]

The rule of when it is proper to lead can be briefly stated as:

Counsel may not lead their witnesses on material issues but should lead them on introductory or non-contentious matters.

The well-known comments of the Supreme Court of Alberta in *Maves v. Grand Trunk Pacific R. Co.*[3] are helpful:

> The chief rule of practice relative to the interrogation of witnesses is that which prohibits "*leading questions*", *i.e.*, questions which directly or indirectly suggest to the witness the answer he is to give. The rule is, that on *material points* a party must not lead his own witnesses, but may lead those of his adversary; in other words, that leading questions are allowed in cross-examination, but not in examination-in-chief.... On all matters, however, which are *merely introductory, and form no part of the substance of the enquiry*, it is both allowable *and proper* for a witness to lead his own witnesses, as otherwise much time would be wasted to no purpose.

---

[2]   Note, if the default was uncontested, the second question would not be leading.
[3]   (1913), 14 D.L.R. 70 at 73 (Alta. S.C.), quoting W. M. Best, *Principles of the Law of Evidence*, 11th ed.

The exceptions to the leading question rule are hostile witnesses and witnesses who, for some reason, cannot testify otherwise coherently except in response to leading questions.

The hostile witness is a witness who by demeanor or manner shows a refusal to testify willingly. The question of whether a witness is hostile is one of fact. The Court considers whether the witness shows a mind hostile to the party calling him or betrays a desire not to tell the truth in concluding a witness is or is not hostile.[4] If on questioning the witness simply refuses to answer responsively, counsel may turn to the judge and say, "Your Honour, the witness is clearly hostile, I wish the witness declared so". If the judge declares the witness hostile, counsel may lead the witness on all points.

The other exception to the prohibition on leading questions in chief is for witnesses who cannot sensibly testify otherwise. In cases like that the witness cannot testify except on being led.

The Court in *Maves*[5] notes:

> A case which not infrequently arises in practice is that of a witness who recounts a conversation and in doing so omits one or more statements, which counsel examining him is instructed formed part of it. The common and proper practice is to ask the witness to repeat the conversation from the beginning. It is often found that in his repetition he gives the lacking statement — possibly omitting one given the first time. This method may be tried more than once and as a matter of expediency — so as to have the advantage of getting the whole story on the witness' own unaided recollection — counsel might pass on to some other subject and later revert to the conversation, asking him to again state it. But when this method fails, the trial Judge undoubtedly ought to permit a question containing a reference to the subject matter of the statement which it is supposed has been omitted by the witness. If this method fails, then and not till then — that is when his memory appears to be entirely exhausted, the trial Judge should allow a question to be put to him containing the supposedly omitted matter.

Since, as a matter of advocacy, leading your own witnesses is unconvincing, leading should be avoided as much as possible even when, technically, it is permitted.

CROSS-EXAMINATION

After direct examination is finished, the party opposite is entitled to cross-examine, or ask questions of the witnesses called on direct examination. Leading questions are quite proper in cross-examination. The purpose of cross-examination is, in general, threefold:

---

[4] *Boland v. Globe & Mail*, [1961] O.R. 712 (C.A.); unless a witness is found hostile, leading questions are improper: *R. v. Rose* (2001), 153 C.C.C. (3d) 225 (Ont. C.A.).

[5] *Supra*, note 3 at 77.

(1)   To destroy or weaken the force of the witness's testimony in direct examination;
(2)   To elicit something favourable; and
(3)   To discredit the witness.

But the process of cross-examination is a perilous one. Legal literature is full of illustrations of cross-examination that has had the effect of damaging the cross-examining party. It is important that counsel not conduct a cross-examination that merely repeats the chief; such examination reinforces the evidence in chief. Similarly, as a noted counsel[6] once said, good cross-examination is not examining crossly, it is more akin to smothering with love.

Written in the criminal context, Earl Levy, Q.C., put the difficulty well, writing:[7]

> There is nothing sadder than seeing the cross-examiner use an aimless and scatter-gun attack on the prosecution witnesses hoping that something fruitful will occur for the defence. The almost inevitable result will be that the prosecution's case is made stronger by this Russian roulette approach as the cross-examiner fills in gaps in the Crown's case or, because he foolishly repeats the same questions as those asked in-chief, the witness repeats the same damaging answers. Worse, it may distract attention from the genuinely strong parts of the defence case.

In Canada there is no limit on the scope of cross-examination — any relevant question may be put to any witness. That said, generally speaking, unless cross-examination has a clear and unambiguous purpose it is better not to conduct cross-examination. No cross-examination is far more helpful than a bad cross-examination. The only exception to the principle that cross-examination ought to be avoided if it serves no immediate purpose is the rule in *Browne v. Dunn*.[8] The rule is well set out in the *R. v. Dyck*[9] decision:

> As a rule a party should put to each of his opponent's witnesses in turn so much of his own ease as concerns that particular witness, or in which he had a share, *e.g.*, if the witness has deposed to a conversation, the opposing counsel should indicate how much he accepts of such version, or suggest to the witness a different one. If he asks no questions he will in England, though not perhaps in Ireland, generally be taken to accept the witness' account.

In effect, unless counsel cross-examines a witness on a topic the counsel may be deemed to accept that witness's story. This sometimes leads to bizarre examinations beginning as follows:

---

6   Personal memory of Mr. Williston as related by E.L. Stone, Esq.
7   *Examination of Witnesses in Criminal Cases* (Toronto: Carswell, 1991) at 145.
8   (1893), 6 R. 67 (H.L.).
9   [1970] 2 C.C.C. 283 at 291 (B.C.C.A.), citing with approval, *Phipson on Evidence*, 10th ed., at para. 1542.

"Now, witness, I am going to ask you a series of questions that we all know how you will answer, but I am obliged to put these questions to you in fairness and so as to comply with the rule in *Browne v. Dunn.*"

The witness is put questions which are always leading and usually denied.[10] No matter how unnecessary this may seem, omit to do it and counsel may be barred from putting their case at all if it is based on a denial of testimony counsel have been deemed to accept. As the Ontario Court of Appeal noted:[11]

> ... a party wishing to impeach the credibility of a witness must ordinarily put the contradictory material to the witness in order to give the witness an opportunity to explain it.

Even if there was no rule from *Browne v. Dunn*, good advocacy would suggest the confrontation of a witness with a damaging statement or contradiction is far more effective than the mere adduction of evidence inconsistent with that of the witness whose evidence is to be discredited.

Cross-examination of an opposite party's witnesses is a matter of right — but what about co-defendants? Can one defendant cross-examine the witnesses of another defendant? The question is not without difficulty but the better view is that where the defendants are taking adverse positions, cross-examination is to be allowed. Adversity was described in *Menzies* thusly:[12]

> ...an actual issue in tangible form spread upon the record is not essential, so long as there is a manifest adverse interest in one defendant against another defendant. "Adverse interest" is a flexible term, meaning pecuniary interest, or any other substantial interest in the subject-matter of litigation.

Of course, even if cross-examination is not proper, examination-in-chief (by non-leading questions) must be allowed.[13] A right to examine witnesses (whether in chief or by cross) is a fundamental part of a fair trial.[14]

RE-EXAMINATION

After cross-examination, the party who conducted direct examination may ask questions to clarify answers given during cross-examination. These questions may not seek to repeat the testimony from direct or raise new issues — they may only clarify or expand on matters raised on cross-examination. The questions tend to be of the form:

---

[10] Occasionally witnesses will not respond as expected and will admit the facts put.
[11] *O'Brien v. Shantz* (1999), 167 D.L.R. (4th) 132 at 136 (Ont. C.A.).
[12] *Menzies v. McLeod* (1915), 34 O.L.R. 572, cited with approval in *Aviaco v. Boeing* (2000), 2 C.P.C. (5th) 48 at 50 (Ont. S.C.J.).
[13] *Whiten v. Pilot Insurance Co.* (1996), 132 D.L.R. (4th) 568 (Ont. Gen. Div.).
[14] *Marchand (Litigation Guardian of) v. Public General Hospital Society of Chatham* (2000), 51 O.R. (3d) 97 (Ont. C.A.).

"In cross-examination you mentioned you met Mr. S and Ms. W on January 22 last, was anyone else at that meeting?", or

"In cross-examination, you started to explain how hot dogs are manufactured and my friend cut your answer short — can you please finish your answer?"

An attempt to deal with matters in re-examination that ought to have been dealt with in chief will not be allowed — counsel are not permitted to split their case.[15]

---

[15] J. Sopinka, S. Lederman & A. Bryant, *The Law of Evidence in Canada* (Toronto: Butterworths, 1992) at 880.

Chapter 7

HEARSAY

INTRODUCTION

In order to understand why hearsay evidence is normally inadmissible, consider the children's game of broken telephone. In that game, a verbal statement is given to one child and is then verbally passed from child to child, one to another, numerous times. The fun of the game is to see how garbled the statement gets by the last transmission. Each time the statement is repeated a small error creeps in until its sense and meaning becomes totally changed. It is this "broken telephone" problem that the rule against hearsay evidence is meant to address.

Before going into more detail about why hearsay is usually excluded, a definition is helpful. Hearsay evidence is (1) any out-of-court assertion (2) repeated in court (3) to prove the truth of that assertion. The classic formulation of hearsay is in *Subramaniam v. Public Prosecutor*[1] where the Court holds:

> Evidence of a statement made to a witness by a person who is not himself called as a witness may or may not be hearsay. It is hearsay and inadmissible when the object of the evidence is to establish the truth of what is contained in the statement. It is not hearsay and is admissible when it is proposed to establish by the evidence, not the truth of the statement but the fact it was made.

Why is hearsay evidence problematic? First, cross-examination is effectively impossible. No amount of cross-examination will establish anything since the witness knows nothing of the substantive facts but only the statement made. Second, the functional witness is not testifying; all we know is the witness heard something someone else said. That other person is the one whose veracity is to be accepted or rejected. But that person is not, and never was, under oath or even aware their statement might be relied on. The person whose statement is being repeated could be joking, speculating, making a wish or flat out lying and the trier of fact cannot put their statement into context to examine what they meant. Finally, the witness in court may have misunderstood what they heard. Perhaps, as in "broken telephone", the witness made a slight mistake when they heard the out-of-court statement the first time and another mistake in the repeating of the statement. Perhaps the out-of-court statement was absolutely true, but the witness did

---

[1] (1956), 1 W.L.R. 965 at 970 (P.C.).

not properly repeat it. For all these reasons, hearsay evidence is, subject to many exceptions, generally rejected.

The policy behind the hearsay rule was well stated by Sir John Simon, K.C., in argument in *R v. Christie*,[2] as follows:

> By the law of England evidence is not admissible through the mouth of one witness to shew what a third person said for the purpose of proving the truth of what that third person said (a) because to admit such evidence would be to accept the statement of a person not on oath, and (b) because that person could not be cross-examined on his statement. But the evidence may be admitted upon some other principle. The maxim "Hearsay is no evidence" should be "Hearsay is no evidence of the truth of the thing heard".

Lord Normand said in *Teper v. R.*:[3]

> The rule against the admission of hearsay evidence is fundamental. It is not the best evidence and it is not delivered on oath. The truthfulness and accuracy of the person whose words are spoken to by another witness cannot be tested by cross-examination, and the light which his demeanor would throw on his testimony is lost.

HEARSAY DANGERS

Describing the dangers posed by hearsay evidence without first defining the meaning of hearsay is a difficult task. Unfortunately, defining hearsay without considering the dangers the exclusionary rule is designed to avoid is at least equally problematic. As a working definition of hearsay for the purposes of considering the dangers such evidence implies we can say, as before, hearsay is evidence of a statement made out of court that is called to prove the truth of that statement. An illustrative example might be a witness called to prove that an automobile was properly repaired.

If the mechanic who did the repairs is called and describes the work done by that mechanic, then the trier of fact can consider the mechanic's statement and decide if the repairs were proper. But, if the mechanic is not called, and someone else is called to repeat a statement made by the mechanic as to what was done, the hearsay rule is triggered. The mechanic is not before the court and the mechanic's statement is repeated to prove its truth.

The problems posed by the recitation of an out-of-court statement for its truth are fairly obvious. The trier of fact cannot assess the credibility of the person whose credit is really at issue (the person whose statement is being repeated) and, regardless, cross-examination is limited to ensuring the testifying witness properly repeated the out-of-court statement. In a comprehensive analysis, Phipson notes:[4]

---

2 [1914] A.C. 545 at 548 (H.L.).
3 [1952] 2 All E.R. 477 at 449 (P.C.)
4 J. Buzzard, R. Amlot, & S. Mitchell, eds., *Phipson on Evidence*, 11th ed., (London: Sweet & Maxwell, 1970) at 278.

... rejection [of hearsay evidence] has been based on its relative untrustworthiness for judicial purposes, owing to (1) the irresponsibility of the original declarant, whose statements were neither under oath, nor subject to cross-examination; (2) the depreciation of truth in the process of repetition; and (3) the opportunities for fraud its admission would open; to which are sometimes added (4) the tendency of such evidence to prolong legal inquiries, and (5) to encourage the substitution of weaker for stronger proofs.

Canadian courts have been quite cognizant of the hearsay dangers, albeit without being quite so fulsome in analysis. Thus, in *R. v. B.(K.G.)*[5] the Chief Justice described the dangers of hearsay evidence as:

... the absence of an oath or solemn affirmation when the statement was made, the inability of the trier of fact to assess the demeanour and therefore the credibility of the declarant when the statement was made (as well as the trier's inability to ensure that the witness actually said what is claimed), and the lack of contemporaneous cross-examination by the opponent.[6]

Similarly, in *Abbey*[7] Justice Dickson, as he then was, notes:

The principal justification for the exclusion of hearsay evidence is the abhorrence of the common law to proof which is unsworn and has not been subjected to the trial by fire of cross-examination. Testimony under oath, and cross-examination, have been considered to be the best assurances of the truth of the statements of facts presented.

In brief, hearsay poses the twin dangers of unsworn and untested evidence being treated as reliable and worthy of belief. Any definition of hearsay must be based on the concern for these dangers.

Before leaving the topic of the dangers posed by hearsay, a point worth noting is that the main problem with hearsay is not, as is often asserted,[8] that the trier of fact is particularly gullible but rather that the person repeating the out-of-court statement may not understand that statement. As Professor Morgan notes:[9]

---

5   [1993] 1 S.C.R. 740 at 764.
6   See also Lord Normand in *Teper v. R.*, [1952] 2 All E.R. 447 at 449:
    The rule against the admission of hearsay evidence is fundamental. It is not the best evidence and it is not delivered on oath. The truthfulness and accuracy of the person whose words are spoken to by another witness cannot be tested by cross examination, and the light which his demeanour would throw on this testimony is lost.
7   *R. v. Abbey*, [1982] 2 S.C.R. 24 at 41.
8   See, for example, Justice L'Heureux-Dubé's dissent in *R. v. Starr*, [2000] 2 S.C.R. 144, at para. 46; see also J. Sopinka, S. Lederman, and A. Bryant, *Law of Evidence in Canada*, 2nd ed. (Toronto: Butterworths, 1999) at 176 for a subtle analysis of jury weakness.
9   E.M. Morgan, *Some Problems of Proof* (New York: Columbia, 1956) at 112. Similarly, at p. 106, Professor Morgan notes that the view "that the rules which exclude relevant information from intelligent persons, and particularly the hearsay rule, owe their origin to a distrust of the jury's capacity to evaluate evidence ... has little, if any, support in history." See also E.M. Morgan, "Hearsay Dangers and the Application of the Hearsay Concept" (1948), 62 Harv. L. Rev. 177.

... the reasons for rejecting hearsay ... have to do with the credulity not of jurors but of witnesses .... Each of these reasons [to reject hearsay] is as applicable to one sort of tribunal as to another. Not one of them even suggests a peculiar incapacity of jurors to evaluate such evidence.

In a similar vein, Lord Chief Baron Gilbert, after noting that hearsay is generally inadmissible,[10] justifies its exclusion on the basis that "it is his [*i.e.* the witness's] knowledge that must direct the Court and jury in the judgment of the fact, and not his mere credulity, which is very uncertain and various in several persons".[11]

The best proof that hearsay rests on a distrust of witnesses, as opposed to a distrust of juries, is the way Canadian courts deal with impliedly assertive conduct. As we shall see, Canadian courts[12] do not see such conduct as raising a hearsay issue; this is because such conduct, unlike hearsay, does not rely on its truth value for the intermediate assertion of the sworn witness (who may be deceived) but rather on the conduct itself and the trier of fact seeing through that conduct to the implicit fact.

HEARSAY DEFINED BY PURPOSE

The classic description of hearsay is worth repeating, and comes from the decision of Privy Council in *Subramaniam v. Public Prosecutor*[13] where the Court held:

Evidence of a statement made to a witness by a person who is not himself called as a witness may or may not be hearsay. It is hearsay and inadmissible when the object of the evidence is to establish the truth of what is contained in the statement. It is not hearsay and is admissible when it is proposed or established by the evidence, not the truth of the statement, but the fact it was made.

Professor McCormick defined hearsay as follows:[14]

Hearsay evidence is testimony in court, or written evidence, of a statement made out of court, the statement being offered as an assertion to show the truth of matters asserted therein, and thus resting for its value upon the credibility of the out-of-court assertion.

---

[10] *Law of Evidence*, 6th ed. (London: Clarke and Sons, 1801). His Lordship rested the exclusion of hearsay largely on the absence of oath and the fact that "nothing can be more uncertain than the loose and wandering witnesses that are taken upon the uncertain reports of the talk and discourse of others": at 135. That said, His Lordship earlier restricted certain evidence since to allow its admission would "dispossese your adversary of the liberty to cross-examine": at 61.
[11] *Ibid.* at 135.
[12] Although English courts generally see implicit assertions as amounting to hearsay: see, for example, *R. v. Kearley* (1992), 95 Cr. App. R. 88 (H.L.). This may suggest English courts have a greater distrust of juries than Canadian courts.
[13] (1956), 1 W.L.R. 967 (P.C.).
[14] *McCormick on Evidence*, 2nd ed. (St. Paul: West Publishing Co., 1972) at 584.

Similarly, in *R. v. Starr*, Mr. Justice Iacobucci, cites *Cross on Evidence*, stating hearsay is:[15]

...an assertion made other than one made by a person while giving oral evidence in the proceedings is inadmissible *as evidence of any fact asserted*. [Emphasis in original]

The Supreme Court of Canada has been careful not to overdefine hearsay;[16] that said, in general, the court's definitions are uncontroversial and follow the traditional view of hearsay being (a) an out of court assertion, (b) repeated in court, or (c) to prove the truth of that assertion.[17] Such a black letter definition, standing alone, is unhelpful; rules are, or should be, reified reasons and the function of any rule is a necessary element of its definition.[18]

Justice Iacobucci, in *Starr*, combines the definition of the hearsay rule with its purpose. His Lordship notes:[19]

More recent definitions of hearsay have focussed upon the precise evidentiary concerns underlying the exclusionary rule, namely the absence of an opportunity for meaningful, contemporaneous cross-examination of the out-of-court declarant in court under oath or solemn affirmation, regarding the truth of the specific statement or expressive conduct that is sought to be admitted as proof of its contents.

His Lordship continues in combining the definition and purpose of the hearsay rule where he notes:[20]

These articulations of the hearsay rule make clear that hearsay evidence is defined not by the nature of the evidence *per se*, but by the use to which the evidence is sought to be put: namely, to prove that what is asserted is true. When the out-of-court statement is offered for its truth, the inability to cross-examine or "test" the source of the evidence in court under oath or affirmation as to the truth of the assertion undermines its reliability.

An appropriate definition of hearsay must combine the traditional elements of hearsay with a recognition of the functional issues the rule is designed to address. The hearsay dangers must inform that definition of the exclusionary rule. Thus,

---

[15] *R. v. Starr*, *supra*, note 8, quoting R. Cross, *Cross on Evidence*, 7th ed. (London: Butterworths, 1990) at 42.

[16] Thus, in *R. v. Smith*, [1992] 2 S.C.R. 915 at 918 the Chief Justice declines to undertake a comprehensive definition of hearsay preferring merely to "establish the parameters of the debate" by reference to *Subramaniam*. The difficulty of an authoritative definition of hearsay was referred to by Lord Reid in *Myers v. D.P.P.* [1965] A.C. 1001 at 1070 (H.L.) where he pointed out that "it is difficult to make any general statement about the law of hearsay which is entirely accurate".

[17] *R. v. Starr*, *supra*, note 8 at para. 167.

[18] The hearsay rule is intended to ensure fair and expeditious trials. Its continued vitality rests on its function and not "a superstitious awe... about having any truck with evidence that involves A's telling the court what B said": Cross, "What Should be Done about the Rule Against Hearsay?" [1965] Crim. L.R. 68, 82.

[19] *R. v. Starr*, *supra*, note 8 at para. 159.

[20] *Ibid.* at para. 162.

hearsay may be considered to be any intentional assertion made outside of a judicial hearing repeated in that hearing for the truth of the contents of the assertion. Intentional assertions carry with them the risk of acceptance without the support of cross-examination or the ability to consider the demeanour and effect of the person making the assertion; these assertions must be caught as hearsay if the rule is to deal with the dangers it is designed to address. Our definition captures the function of hearsay and bars, in general, out-of-court assertions repeated for their truth value.[21]

In terms of the definition of hearsay, it should be noted that the leading Supreme Court of Canada decision on hearsay, *R. v. Starr*, was a majority decision of Justice Iacobucci with strong dissents by Madame Justice L'Heureux-Dubé and Chief Justice McLachlin. All reasons for judgment have roughly similar definitions of hearsay. Neither of the dissenting decisions differs significantly from Justice Iacobucci's decision in the determination of what is or is not hearsay. Justice Iacobucci does emphasize the centrality of the hearsay rule in the trial process. His Lordship explicitly states that the admission of unreliable hearsay evidence "would compromise trial fairness",[22] strong language affirming the rule's continued viability. In a similar albeit less vigorous tone, Justice L'Heureux-Dubé refers to the hearsay rule as "the most characteristic rule of our system of judge-made rules of evidence".[23]

HEARSAY IMPLIED BY ASSERTIVE CONDUCT

The implementation of our hearsay definition can be seen in the issue of conduct that implies an assertion. Now, we will examine whether such conduct creates a hearsay problem.

Consider a letter written to a deceased whose legal competence at the time of their death is in doubt. The letter is written in language suggesting the deceased was sensible and of reasonable intelligence.[24] Is the letter a hearsay assertion of competence? Clearly, if the letter stated expressly "X [the deceased] is competent" it would be hearsay, but here the competence of the deceased is merely implied. If the concern in hearsay is the trier of fact, the implied assertion is just as problematic as express hearsay. An easily misled jury will be, if anything, even more easily misled by implied assertions than by express assertions. But, if the concern with hearsay is the witness only, the implied assertion poses no problem. The trier of fact is not viewing the ultimate fact through the mediation of a witness without actual knowledge; the trier gets the facts and decides what, if anything,

---

[21] It also captures the surprisingly common situation where the witness testifying is also the out-of-court declarant. If the witness is merely repeating what they previously said, or, more commonly, wrote with no current recollection all the dangers of hearsay remain: see H. Stewart, "Prior Identification and Hearsay: A Note on *R. v. Tat*" (1998), 3 Can. Crim. L.R. 61.

[22] *Starr*, para. 200.

[23] *Ibid.* at para. 45.

[24] This is the *Wright v. Tatham* (1838), 7 E. R. 559 (H.L.) case, where the House of Lords held implied assertions could be hearsay.

to imply from them. Since the declarant is not aware they are making a declaration there is a substantial indication of truthfulness.[25] Speaking in *Smith*[26] Chief Justice Lamer notes:

> If a statement sought to be adduced by way of hearsay evidence is made under circumstances which substantially negate the possibility that the declarant was untruthful or mistaken, the hearsay evidence may be said to be 'reliable'....

The implied assertions of out-of-court declarants do not raise the issue of a duplicitous or deceived witness, and, so, hearsay and its attendant dangers are not present.

Canadian courts, consistent with our definition of hearsay, do not treat implied assertions or assertive conduct as hearsay.[27] For example, in *R. v. McKinnon* a body was located by police in a remote area. The police were accompanied by the accused's spouse. The accused objected to the evidence of the spouse accompanying the police, saying this implied the location was given to the police by the spouse who received the information from the accused. Rejecting this argument Justice Finlayson notes:[28]

> In the first place, her presence was a fact, and was part of the police officers' testimony as to the search and discovery, which search and discovery surely was a relevant fact in the light of the Crown's theory of the "plan" to kill and hide the body. In the second place, her presence in the manner described cannot be characterized as hearsay by conduct. It has always been my understanding that such hearsay usually amounted to a description of actions or behaviour which are themselves means of expression, such as shrugs, headshakes or other gestures that are a substitute for or supplement to oral communication. Evidence of such conduct is tendered as evidence of an assertion by the person who performed the action. As such, it is inadmissible hearsay. On the facts of this appeal I see nothing in the evidence about the wife's accompanying the police officers to the gravesite which amounts to an assertion or a statement that she received information about its location from her husband, from her husband alone, and from no other source. The evidence is not tendered as evidence of an assertion by the wife. It is not hearsay.

Implied assertions are not hearsay; the concern with deceived witnesses is not present.[29] The distinction between explicit assertions, which give rise to hearsay issues, and mere conduct, which does not, shows that implied assertions are not subject to hearsay concerns. Consider a case where a party behaves in an unusual fashion — that behaviour can be powerful circumstantial evidence. The behaviour

---

[25] Of course, error remains possible, but this is true of any declaration whether made in court under oath or not.

[26] [1992] 2 S.C.R. 915 at 933.

[27] See *R. v. Ly*, [1997] 3 S.C.R. 698; *R. v. Edwards* (1994), 34 C.R. (4th) 113, aff'd [1996] 1 S.C.R. 128; *R. v. McKinnon* (1989), 70 C.R. (3d) 10 (Ont. C.A.); *R. v. Wysochan* (1930), 54 C.C.C. 172 (Sask. C.A.).

[28] *R. v. McKinnon, supra*, note 27 at 16-17.

[29] See A. Rein, "The Scope of Hearsay" (1994), 100 L.Q.R. 431 for an analysis of the English position on hearsay from implied assertions.

may be forced, or intentionally deceptive, but it is not hearsay as it is non-assertive.[30]

HISTORY OF THE RULE

As noted above, the hearsay rule is of great age. For several hundred years, the concerns raised by hearsay have been dealt with, more lor less, consistently by common law courts; the rejection of hearsay evidence was based on the absence of an oath and, later, the inability to cross-examine. In common law, witnesses are to testify to what they saw and heard directly;[31] thus, in 1441 a witness's evidence on an issue about which the witness was "so informed" was rejected on the basis that the witness was not testifying.[32] Similarly, the report of *Braddon and Speke* (1684)[33] provides:

> Jeffries, L.C.J.: Does she know anything of her own knowledge?
> Braddon: She can tell what she heard, my lord.

> L.C.J.: 'Tis no evidence .... Where is the woman that told her? Why is she not brought?

> Counsel for Braddon: They say, she is so big with child she can't come.

> L.C.J.: Why, if that woman were here herself, if she did say it, and would not swear it, we would not hear her; how then can her saying be an evidence before us? I wonder to hear any man that wears a gown, to make a doubt of it.

The Chief Justice raised, quite expressly, the lack of sworn testimony as a basis for rejecting hearsay. By 1700, the hearsay rule was well-established[34] as was the basis for excluding hearsay on the further ground that cross-examination

---

[30] *R. v. D. (G.N.)* (1993), 81 C.C.C. (3d) 65 (Ont. C.A.); leave to appeal to S.C.C. refused (1993), 82 C.C.C. (3d) vi (note) (S.C.C.).

[31] Witnesses are to say what they have seen and heard: "*quod vidi et audivi; de visu suo et auditu*". Accordingly, in *Bushel's Case* (1670), 84 E.R. 1123, 1124 (K.B.) the report of Chief Justice Vaughan reads:

> He put this difference between the oath of a witness and that of a juror. The witness swears more generally on his senses, the juror by collection and inference, by the act and force of his understanding.

It is of some interest that Chief Justice Vaughan, while apparently barring hearsay from a witness still accepted that a *jury* may rely on "*other evidence than is deposed in open Court*": p. 1125. The exclusion of hearsay, at least in the seventeenth century, was not yet completely the same as our modern rule.

[32] Y.B. 20. Hen. VI, 20, 16.

[33] *Ibid.* at 1188.

[34] R.J. Delisle, "Hearsay Evidence" in *1984 Special Lectures* (Toronto: Richard De Boo Publishers, 1984) at 59.

was unavailable.[35] In 1813, Chief Justice Marshall was stating settled law when he commented:[36]

> Its intrinsic weakness, its incompetency to satisfy the mind of the existence of the fact and the frauds which might be practised under its cover, combine to support the rule that hearsay evidence is totally inadmissible.

In this regard, the definition and exclusion of hearsay evidence, has changed little over time. For example, arguing in *R. v. Christie*,[37] Sir John Simon, at the start of the First World War, noted:

> By the law of England evidence is not admissible through the mouth of one witness to shew what a third person said for the purpose of proving the truth of what that third person said (*a*) because to admit such evidence would be to accept the statement of a person not on oath, and (*b*) because that person could not be cross-examined on his statement.

The consistency of the hearsay rule over half a millennium is a powerful testament to the rule's centrality to, and viability in, common law trials; it is difficult to think of any other common law principle older than the exclusion of hearsay.

EXCEPTIONS TO THE HEARSAY RULE

Starting with the decision in *R. v. Khan*[38] and continuing through to *Starr*, the Supreme Court has adopted what it calls a principled approach to hearsay evidence and exceptions to the general exclusionary rule. Under the principled approach, evidence may be admitted, though hearsay, if it is necessary and reliable.[39] The principled approach recognizes that the dangers hearsay evidence can attract are not always present and, in specific cases, hearsay evidence is just as good a basis for judicial decision-making as sworn and cross-examined testimony.

Broadly speaking, and prior to the *Khan* case, the analysis of hearsay in Canadian courts was relatively mechanical. A determination would be made as to whether or not evidence was hearsay and, if it was, a further consideration would be made as to whether the evidence was admissible, though hearsay, pursuant to a specific previously existing exception to the general exclusionary rule. These exceptions are numerous and do not always fall within the obvious ambit of the principles of necessity and reliability.

---

[35] *Supra*, note 4 at 649 referring to *Hawkins, Pleas of the Crown*.
[36] *Mima Queen v. Hepburn*, 11 U.S. 290, 296 (1813).
[37] [1914] A.C. 545 at 548.
[38] [1990] 2 S.C.R. 531; see also *R. v. Smith, supra*, note 16; *R. v. U. (F.J.)*, [1995] 3 S.C.R. 764; *R. v. Rockey*, [1996] 3 S.C.R. 829; certainly, the Supreme Court had earlier revised the hearsay rule but only in rather limited ways: see *Ares v. Venner*, [1970] S.C.R. 608 (business records), *R. v. O'Brien*, [1978] 1 S.C.R. 591 (statements against interest).
[39] See, generally, D. Watts, *Manual of Criminal Evidence* (Toronto: Carswell, 2000), para. 28.01 ff. The principles come from Wigmore, Vol. II, p. 1793, 1794.

For example, in the *Pelletier*[40] decision, the defendant sought to adduce a statement made to police by a witness who had disappeared. The Court initially considered whether or not the statement was hearsay and then considered at some length whether or not the statement, having been found hearsay, fell within the scope of a pre-existing exemption to the hearsay rule.[41] The analysis, in this older case law, turned entirely on the mechanical determination of whether or not evidence fell within the scope of the exclusionary rule and, if it did, whether some exemption to that exclusionary rule applied. Whether the evidence was, regardless of the existence of the specific exemption, necessary or reliable, did not enter into the analysis at all; the question was not one of principle but rather the fulfilment of each condition prior to the application of the specific exemption. As Justice Buller suggested in *Eriswell*:[42]

> The true line for the courts to adhere to is, that, wherever evidence not on oath has been repeatedly received, and sanctioned by judicial determination, it shall be allowed; but beyond that, the rule, that no evidence shall be admitted, but what is upon oath, shall be observed.

The old approach followed precedent alone — the function of cross-examination or value of the hearsay itself was not considered.

The decision in *Khan*[43] began a change in this approach. Specifically, following *Khan*, evidence which would otherwise be inadmissible as hearsay, could be admitted even if it did not fall within any previously existing hearsay exception provided the evidence was necessary and reliable. Writing in *Khan*, Justice McLachlin, as she then was, noted:

> The first question should be whether reception of the hearsay statement is necessary. Necessity for these purposes must be interpreted as "reasonably necessary". The next question should be whether the evidence is reliable.[44]

Similarly, in *Finta*[45] Justice Cory noted:

> ... in recent years courts have adopted a more flexible approach to the hearsay rule, routed in the principles and policies underlying the hearsay rule, rather than in the narrow strictures of the traditional exceptions. The requirements for the admission of hearsay evidence are that it be necessary and reliable.

The hearsay exclusionary rule has always been subject to exceptions. Thus, in 1836 Baron Parke held:[46]

---

[40]   *R. v. Pelletier* (1978), 38 C.C.C. (2d) 515 (Ont. C.A.).
[41]   *Ibid.* at 524. In this case declaration against penal interest.
[42]   *R. v. Eriswell* (1790), 3 T.R. 707 at 721.
[43]   *Supra*, note 38.
[44]   *Ibid.* at 540.
[45]   *R. v. Finta* (1994), 28 C.R. (4th) 265, para. 85.
[46]   *Stobart v. Dryden* (1836), 150 E.R. 581 at 623.

The general rule is, that hearsay evidence is not admissible as proof of a fact which has been stated by a third person. This rule has been long established as a fundamental principle of the law of evidence; but certain exceptions have also been recognized, some from very early times, upon the ground of necessity or convenience.

The concept that the exceptions to the hearsay exclusionary rule are based on unifying principles has been a theme of Canadian jurisprudence for some time. Thus, in 1922 Justice Stuart, writing in a concurring minority judgment for the Alberta Court of Appeal, noted:[47]

> ... the records were ... admissible in evidence as proof of the facts stated therein. There is first the necessity principle. ... Then there is the circumstantial guarantee of trustworthiness....

Justice Stuart's twin bases (necessity and trustworthiness) for a proper exception to the hearsay exclusionary rule were picked up by the Supreme Court of Canada in *Ares v. Venner*.[48] Although *Ares* was largely taken as a mere clarification of the business records exception to the hearsay rule, the case explicitly held that the rule is subject to judicial modification to ensure the hearsay rule assists the ascertaining of facts.[49]

Despite the invitation of the Supreme Court of Canada in *Ares* to view hearsay in a principled, as opposed to formal, fashion, little change in the mechanical application of the exclusionary rule occurred until *Khan*.[50] Justice McLachlin, in *Khan*, discussing the principled and formal approach to the hearsay rule commented:[51]

> The hearsay rule has traditionally been regarded as an absolute rule, subject to various categories of exceptions, such as admissions, dying declarations, declarations

---

[47] *Omand v. Alberta Milling Co.*, [1922] 2 W.W.R. 412 at 413; although it was *obiter*, the various decisions in *Sugden v. Lord St. Leonards* (1876), 1 P.D. 154 illustrate the principled and more mechanistic approach to hearsay and its exclusions. The Master of the Rolls, at 242, was prepared to expand the admission of hearsay on principle:

> The Court should be anxious, not narrowly to restrict the rules of evidence, which were made for the purpose of furthering truth and justice, but, guided by those great principles which have guided other tribunals in other countries in admitting this kind of evidence generally, to admit it at all events in the special case which we have under consideration.

Holding a contrary view, Lord Mellish wrote, at 251:

> ... you cannot admit it [the contested evidence] unless you can bring it within some of the exceptions to the general rule, that hearsay evidence is not admissible to prove a fact which is stated in the declaration. It does not come within any of the rules which have been hitherto established, and I doubt whether it is an advisable thing to establish exceptions in a case which has never happened before, and may never happen again, for you then establish an exception which more or less throws a doubt on the law.

The choice of uncertain principle or certain mechanics is not limited to the new millenium.

[48] [1970] S.C.R. 608.

[49] Justice Hall endorses the minority decision in *R. v. Myers*, [1965] A.C. 1001 and agrees with Lord Pearce, in *Myers*, in saying that a refusal to reform hearsay judicially amounts to "a surrender to formalism".

[50] *R. v. Khan*, [1990] 2 S.C.R. 531.

[51] *Ibid.* at 540.

against interest and spontaneous declarations. While this approach has provided a degree of certainty to the law on hearsay, it has frequently proved unduly inflexible in dealing with new situations and new needs in the law. This has resulted in courts in recent years on occasion adopting a more flexible approach, rooted in the principle and the policy underlying the hearsay rule rather than the strictures of traditional exceptions.

So as to make clear that *Khan* signalled a new approach to hearsay, the Supreme Court in *Smith*[52] explicitly says the principles underlying the rule and its exceptions are necessity and reliability.[53] Having said this, the Court continues[54] "... *Khan*, therefore, should be understood as the triumph of a principled analysis over a set of ossified judicially created categories". The case law following *Smith*, up to and including *Starr*, expands on this principled approach.[55]

INTERACTION OF EXCEPTIONS TO HEARSAY RULE AND PRINCIPLED APPROACH

A difficulty that has arisen from the determination that hearsay exceptions should be dealt with in the principled approach arises from the impact of the exceptions to the exclusionary rule. Are the exceptions to the exclusionary rule to be followed, as traditionally done, and then the principled approach applied only if no previously existing exception applies?[56] If this is the approach to be taken, the

---

[52] *R. v. Smith* [1992] 2 S.C.R. 915.
[53] The Court writes at 931:
> It has long been recognized that the principles which underlie the hearsay rule are the same as those that underlie the exceptions to it. Indeed, *Wigmore on Evidence*, (2nd ed., 1923), vol. III, described the rule and its exceptions at § 1420 in the following terms:
> > The purpose and reason of the Hearsay rule is the key to the exceptions to it. The theory of the Hearsay rule ... is that the many possible sources of inaccuracy and untrustworthiness which may lie underneath the bare untested assertion of a witness can best be brought to light and exposed, if they exist, by the test of cross-examination. But this test or security may in a given instance be superfluous; it may be sufficiently clear, in that instance, that the statement offered is free from the risk of inaccuracy and untrustworthiness, so that the test of cross-examination would be a work of supererogation. Moreover, the test may be impossible of employment — for example, by reason of the death of the declarant — so that, if his testimony is to be used at all, there is a necessity for taking it in the untested shape. These two considerations — a Circumstantial Guarantee of Trustworthiness, and a Necessity, for the Evidence — may be examined more closely ....
[54] *Ibid.* at 932.
[55] Not without its critics. D. Thompson in *"The Supreme Court Goes Hunting and Nearly Catches a Hearsay Woozle"* (1995), 37 C.R. (4th) 282 at 294 comments:
> *Necessity and Reliability.* For better or worse, the Supreme Court has adopted Wigmore's too-tidy explanation for the hearsay exceptions, namely the twin criteria of necessity and reliability. These two factors have become the means of expanding the admissibility of hearsay.
[56] As the British Columbia Court of Appeal held in *R. v. Collins* (1997), 118 C.C.C. (3d) 514; see also, to the same effect, *R. v. Duff* (1994), 32 C.R. (4th) 153 (Man. C.A.); see also Justice L'Heureux-Dubé's dissent in *Starr*, *supra*, note 8, at para. 44.

principled approach expands the scope of admissible evidence but does not restrict the admission of hearsay evidence to that which is necessary and reliable — it is possible that evidence which is not necessary or reliable might fall within an exception to the hearsay rule but still be admissible.[57] That having been said, eliminating the traditional exceptions and holding that hearsay is generally inadmissible save when some overall test of necessity and reliability has been met could lead to greatly expanded inquiry at trial, lengthening of trials and considerable unpredictability in the trial process. As Madame Justice L'Heureux-Dubé points out in her dissent in *Starr*[58] changes in which the existing hearsay exceptions are subject to review under the twin guides of necessity and reliability can lead to "major and far reaching" effects on the trial process and will lead to "uncertainty in the law". Her Ladyship continues[59] and notes that such "analysis mandated in every case of hearsay evidence on this approach would inevitably and unnecessarily complicate and lengthen trials".

That having been said, writing for the majority, Justice Iacobucci holds that evidence which is admissible under a hearsay exemption may not be admissible if it does not meet the twin test of necessity and reliability. Justice Iacobucci notes:[60]

... it is clear that the existing exceptions are a long-standing and important aspect of our law of evidence. I am cognizant of their important role, and the need for caution in reforming them. Given their continuing importance, I would expect that in the clear majority of cases, the presence or absence of a traditional exception will be determinative of admissibility.

...

All this being said, it is also clear that the logic of the principled approach demands that it must prevail in situations where it is in conflict with an existing exception. For example, had there been any doubt in this appeal whether the present intentions exception required that the statement not be made under circumstances of suspicion, the principled approach would require holding that it does now. Hearsay evidence may only be admitted if it is necessary and reliable, and the traditional exceptions should be interpreted in a manner consistent with this requirement.

In some rare cases, it may also be possible under the particular circumstances of a case for evidence clearly falling within an otherwise valid exception nonetheless not to meet the principled approach requirements of necessity and reliability. In such a case, the evidence would have to be excluded. However, I wish to emphasize that these cases will no doubt be unusual, and that the party challenging the admissibility of evidence falling within a traditional exception will bear the burden of showing that the evidence should nevertheless be inadmissible. The trial judge will determine the procedure (whether by *voir dire* or otherwise) to determine admissibility under the principled approach's requirements of reasonable necessity and reliability.

---

[57] Thus, in *Gormley v. Canada Permanent Trust*, [1969] 2 O.R. 414 (H.C.) a hearsay statement was found admissible pursuant to the exception allowing declarations against a pecuniary interest even though the statement exposed the declarant to nothing more than a possibility of a $4.00 liability. Such a trifling amount would hardly seem sufficient to ensure trustworthiness or reliability.

[58] *R. v. Starr* at para. 48.

[59] *Ibid.* at para. 49.

[60] *Ibid.* at paras. 211, 213, 214.

The concerns raised by Madame Justice L'Heureux-Dubé, that Justice Iaco-bucci's approach may lengthen trials and increase uncertainty in the trial process, may well have some merit. Under Justice Iacobucci's analysis, any hearsay evi-dence, otherwise admissible under an exception to the hearsay rule, can be chal-lenged as being neither necessary nor reliable. The exceptions, although being general guidelines for admissibility, would cease therefore to govern and, par-ticularly where evidence was important to the determination of a case, a thorough trial within a trial would have to be conducted on the issues of necessity and reli-ability regardless of the existence of an exception. Granted, the onus of who must prove evidence is necessary and reliable changes depending on whether an ex-ception exists or not, however, the effect of lengthening trials and raising legal uncertainty may well be considerable.

With respect, the dissenting decision of Chief Justice McLachlin in *Starr*, while perhaps somewhat mechanistic, would seem more practical than Justice Iacobucci's majority approach. Justice McLachlin, in very brief reasons, deals with the admissibility of hearsay evidence as follows:[61]

> In my view, the following principles govern the admissibility of hearsay evidence:
>
> (1) Hearsay evidence is admissible if it falls under an exception to the hearsay rule;
> (2) The exceptions can be interpreted and reviewed as required to conform to the values of necessity and reliability that justify exceptions to the hearsay rule;
> (3) Where the evidence is admissible under an exception to the hearsay rule, the Judge may still refuse to admit the evidence if its prejudicial effect outweighs its prohibitive value;
> (4) Where evidence is not admissible under an exception to the hearsay rule, the Judge may admit it provided that necessity and reliability are established.

Again, with great respect, Chief Justice McLachlin's approach permits the court flexibility to exclude evidence that would otherwise be admissible as long as its prejudicial effect outweighs its probative value (thus protecting the concept of a fair trial) and gives the court scope to modify and vary the exceptions to the hearsay rule in accordance with developments in society. Chief Justice McLachlin's approach does this without introducing great uncertainty into the trial process.

The case law since *Starr* has, in general, followed the reasoning in that case without lengthy analysis of it. Typical of the decisions referencing *Starr* is a deci-sion of the British Columbia Provincial Court, *Adiwal*,[62] where the Court held:[63]

> It is clear from the judgment of Iacobucci, J. for the majority that the ambit of the principled approach in relation to the potential admissibility of hearsay has been substantially expanded to the extent that traditional exceptions will now also be subject to analysis in terms of their necessity and reliability, and subject to inclusion

---

[61] *Ibid.* at para. 2.
[62] *R. v. Adiwal*, [2000] B.C.J. No. 2693.
[63] *Ibid.*

or exclusion to improve trial fairness. The continuing trend is towards expansion of the principled approach.

A number of other decisions,[64] including *Parrot*[65] in the Supreme Court of Canada, have adopted and followed *Starr* in varying factual circumstances.

OUT-OF-COURT ASSERTIONS THAT ARE NOT HEARSAY

Consider again the definition of hearsay as any (1) out-of-court assertion, (2) repeated in court, (3) to prove the truth of that assertion. All three elements must be present before a question of hearsay arises. Elements (1) and (2) are fairly straightforward (although they have a few twists as seen below). It is element (3) that causes difficulty. Unless the statement is being repeated to prove the truth of its contents, there is no hearsay issue.

Thus, if a statement is repeated in court for a reason other than its truth, the statement is not hearsay. What might be other reasons for adducing an out-of-court statement? An example might be an oral contract, which is established by the fact that a statement is made. If X says, "I will buy your car for $200" and Y says "I accept", a contract (subject to the *Statute of Frauds*) is established. It does not matter if X was lying when X said "I will buy your car for $200"; the truth of the statement is irrelevant, its importance arising from its making and not its truth. The statement establishes the contract — truth is not relevant.[66] Similarly, to show A was careful in, say, docking a boat, it is proper to show A was told by someone with apparent authority that any wrecks were clearly marked. If A testifies "the harbour master said the wrecks were marked", A is not trying to prove the wrecks were marked but rather that A was acting reasonably at the time in thinking the wrecks were marked.[67]

The leading case here, yet again, is *Subramaniam*.[68] Here, an accused was charged with possessing illegal ammunition and wanted to testify, in his defence, that he had been forced to by guerillas who told him they were Communists and would kill him if he did not co-operate. The question before the court was, is the repetition of what the guerillas said hearsay? No, and this is because the truth of the statements "We are Communists and will kill you if you don't co-operate" is irrelevant. They could be Royalists who would give him kudos for refusing to help. The truth is irrelevant; what counts is that the statement was made and Mr.

---

[64] *R. v. Hynes*, [2000] N.B.J. 434 (N.B.C.A.); *R. v. Lauzon*, [2000] O.J. No. 3940 (O.C.A.); *R. v. Deschenes*, [2000] O.J. No. 4658 (O.S.C.J.); *R. v. Beaucage*, [2000] O.J. No. 4255 (O.S.C.J.); *R.D.A. v. B.C.T.D.C.* 2000 Carswell B.C.C.A. 674 — it can be argued, as set out below, that this case does not adopt *Starr*.

[65] *R. v. Parrot*, 2001 Carswell S.C.C. 3; the Supreme Court of Canada referred to *Starr* in *R. v. Sutton* (2000), 38 C.R. (5th) 39 at 41 but only to point out that the implications of *Starr* for the admission of co-conspirator hearsay evidence would not be considered.

[66] *Creaghe v. Iowa Home Mutual*, 323 F2d 981 (1963).

[67] *The Douglas* (1882), 7 P.D. 151.

[68] *Supra*, note 1.

Subramaniam believed it and was, accordingly, justified in doing what he did. The Court notes:[69]

> The fact that the statement was made, quite apart from its truth, is frequently relevant in considering the mental state and conduct thereafter of the witness or of some other person in whose presence the statement was made.

PRESENT KNOWLEDGE AND REFRESHING MEMORY

If a witness does not recall the events they are called upon to give evidence concerning, there is nothing wrong with allowing them to review notes to refresh their memory. The notes refresh the witness's memory and, accordingly, they are giving testimony of their own recollection. If the memory is not refreshed, and all the witness can do is read the notes to the court, there is a hearsay problem — the notes are an out-of-court assertion being repeated to prove the truth of that assertion. The testimony is then hearsay and excluded unless it falls within one of the exceptions to the hearsay rule. Merely because the hearsay statement is being repeated by its initial author does nothing to alter the fact the statement is hearsay. As noted in *Jewett v. U.S.*:[70]

> It is one thing to awaken a slumbering recollection of an event but quite another to use or memorandum of a recollection, fresh when it was correctly recorded, but presently beyond the power of the witness so to restore that it will exist apart from the record.

---

[69] *Ibid.* at 963.
[70] 15 F. 2d 955, 956 (1926).

Chapter 8

EXEMPTIONS TO THE HEARSAY RULE

INTRODUCTION

As noted in Chapter 7, there has been a recent revolution in the analysis of when evidence, though hearsay, may be admissible. Prior to *Starr*,[1] there were three stages in the analysis of hearsay. First, was there a hearsay issue? If so, did a traditional exception to the hearsay rule apply? If not, could the evidence be admitted anyway, on the basis the evidence was both necessary and reliable?[2] *Starr* changed all this. Now the analysis is as follows: (1) is there a hearsay issue? (2) does a traditional exception apply? (3) if a traditional exception applies, can the party opposing admission show that the evidence is, nevertheless, not necessary and reliable? (3a) if a traditional exception does not apply, can the party seeking admission show that the evidence is both necessary and reliable? Obviously, a key element in the new analysis of the nature and scope of the traditional exceptions. While challenged, the traditional exceptions remain central to the admission of hearsay evidence.

The traditional exceptions to the hearsay rule are numerous and not always consistent. They cannot be reduced to a single rule; each exception is isolated from the others. That said, the exceptions usually apply where there is good reason to believe the hearsay evidence is particularly likely to be accurate or correct. Broadly put, most of the exceptions can be explained based on two elements of the Wigmore criteria:

1. **the evidence is relevant, material and important but cannot be adduced except by hearsay; and**
2. **there is some circumstantial indicia of trustworthiness that suggests the hearsay is believable.**

In *Stobart v. Dryden*,[3] Parke B. said:

> The general rule is, that hearsay evidence is not admissible as proof of a fact which has been stated by a third person. This rule has been long established as a funda-

---

[1] *R. v. Starr*, [2000] S.C.R. 144.
[2] See, for example, *R. v. Duff* (1994), 32 C.R. (4th) 153.
[3] (1836), 1 M. & W. 615, 150 E.R. 581 at 623.

mental principle of the law of evidence; but certain exceptions have also been recognized, some from very early times, upon the ground of necessity or convenience.

More recently, the Supreme Court of Canada has turned to a functional approach for hearsay exceptions and it *may* be that ultimately the exceptions will be assimilated to the Wigmore criteria.[4]

THE EXEMPTIONS

A. TESTIMONY IN PREVIOUS HEARINGS

This exception to the hearsay rule is very simple and set out clearly by the Supreme Court of Canada in *Erdman*[5] where Justice King notes citing Taylor on Evidence, s. 464:

> Where a witness has given his testimony under oath in a judicial proceeding, in which the adverse litigant had the power to cross-examine, the testimony so given will, if the witness himself cannot be called, be admitted in any subsequent suit between the same parties, or those claiming under them, provided it relate to the same subject or substantially involve the same material questions.

The key to this exception to the hearsay is that the evidence deals with the same issue in the previous and current litigation, cross-examination was available at the first hearing, and the witness examined is unavailable through death, illness, mental instability or just cannot be found even though reasonable attempts to locate the witness have been made. A similar statutory provision exists under the *Criminal Code*.[6]

B. ADMISSIONS

As a general rule, *anything* a party says can be used in evidence by the opposite party. This is an extremely important and broad exception to the hearsay rule. No issue of unavailability, circumstantial guarantees of trustworthiness or anything similar is required for this exception to the hearsay rule to apply — if one party said it, wrote it or in any way indicated it, a party opposite can use it. This exception to the hearsay rule is well set out in the *Jacks*[7] decision where the Court writes:

> Admissions are ordinarily admissible as original or substantive evidence of the truth of the statements made or of the existence of facts which they tend to establish;

---

[4] *R. v. Khan*, [1990] 2 S.C.R. 531; *R. v. Starr*, [2000] S.C.R. 144.
[5] *Walkerton v. Erdman* (1894), 23 S.C.R. 352.
[6] R.S.C. 1985, c. C-46, s. 715 (Appendix A); see also s. 715.1 (Appendix A).
[7] *Jacks v. Woodruff*, 132 N.E.2d 603, 607.

while they may be used to impeach or contradict the testimony of the party who made them, their admissibility does not depend on, nor should their effect be confined to, their tendency to do so.

The admissions exception to the hearsay rule is limited in several respects. First, an admission is evidence only with respect to the party making the admission. Thus, if there are two defendants and one makes an admission, the plaintiff may use the statement in the plaintiff's case against the defendant making the admission and not the other. The case against the co-defendant must be made out some other way.

Second, silence may be used as an admission,[8] but only where silence necessarily implies an admission. A person may be taken to have adopted an admission where, based on conduct or silence when confronted with accusations, the person is seen as adopting the truth of the accusations. This is illustrated by the *MacKenzie*[9] case where the Court found that silence in the face of an allegation a car was stolen amounted to some type of admission of the theft. The Court notes:

> One would expect a normal, honest vendor, when told that he had sold stolen goods, to deny the allegation vehemently... Under these circumstances, (the defendant vendor) must be taken to have impliedly admitted the truth of the allegations.

But this reasoning cannot be taken too far. Thus, in the *Eden*[10] case an allegation put to a youth while in the back of a police car and not responded to was not taken to be adopted by silence. The Court of Appeal pointed out that the youth "was entirely within his rights in remaining silent and no imputation unfavourable to him should be placed upon the exercise of that right". An admission from silence will only be implied if silence inescapably implies that admission.[11] As a practical matter, admissions from silence will rarely be found.

Third, admissions, particularly by businesses, may also be made by agents or employees. If a law firm is sued for, say, breaching a contract to buy photocopy paper, a statement made by that firm's bookkeeper about the contract is going to be an admission against the law firm. The bookkeeper's job encompasses things like making contracts for photocopy paper. The very same statement, however, made by the receptionist probably would not be an admission — the receptionist's job does not (or should not) go so far as to making contracts for a law firm. Broadly put, a statement by an employee or agent within the scope of their employment or agency can be admitted as an admission.

C. STATEMENT AGAINST INTEREST

The statement against interest exception to the hearsay rule is often confused with the admission exception. Recall, under the admission exception, anything a party

---

[8] To wit, silence denotes consent.
[9] *MacKenzie v. Commer* (1973), 44 D.L.R. (3d) 473 at 475 (N.S.S.C.).
[10] *R. v. Eden*, [1970] 2 O.R. 161 (C.A.).
[11] See also *R. v. Christie*, [1914] A.C. 545 at 559; *R. v. Pammer* (1979), 1 Man. R. (2d) 18 (C.A.).

says can be used against that party regardless of the hearsay rule. The admission exception applies *only* to parties. The statement against interest exception to the hearsay rule differs from the admission exception in that it applies to anyone and can be used to adduce, for proof of its truth, any out-of-court statement if that statement was "against interest" and the declarant is unavailable.

Narrowly put, a statement against interest is a statement that, at the time it was made, was so contrary to the declarant's interest that a reasonable person would not have made the statement if it were not true. The statement can be against either financial or penal interest but it must be to the declarant's immediate prejudice. Further, the statement must be wholly against the declarant's interest — a confession to shoplifting that gives the declarant an alibi for murder will not amount to a statement against interest.

The statement against interest exception to the hearsay rule can be stated thusly:

An oral or written declaration, by an unavailable person, of a fact that person knows to be against their immediate pecuniary or penal interest is admissible, though hearsay, of the facts contained in the declaration.

An example of the exception may help to clarify the nature of the statement against interest exception. If someone, while drinking at a tavern, says that they stole thousands of dollars from their employer, but only gives their first name and no details, then the exception cannot apply. If that same person goes to a police station and makes a full statement to the same general effect to the police the exception does apply. The *O'Brien*[12] case turned on this very issue. In *O'Brien* a now deceased witness, Jensen, went to a lawyer, confessed a crime but said he would not expose himself to prosecution. The Supreme Court of Canada rejected the out-of-court statement made by Jensen, saying it was hearsay not falling within the statements against interest exception. Justice Dickson writes:

> ... the entire circumstances in which the statement was made negative the conclusion Jensen apprehended exposing himself to prosecution ... The guarantee of trustworthiness of a statement made out of Court flows from the fact that the statement is to the "deceased's immediate prejudice." To be admissible there must be a realization by the declarant that the statement may well be used against him. That is the very thing Jensen wished to avoid. He had no intention of furnishing evidence against himself.

If the statement cannot be used to the declarant's prejudice, the statement cannot amount to a declaration against interest.

---

[12] *R. v. O'Brien* (1977), 76 D.L.R. (3d) 513 at 520 (S.C.C.).

D. BUSINESS RECORDS

As a practical matter, organizations generate a great deal of paper much of which is, effectively, anonymous. For example, shipping invoices contain important information that is relied on every day by business but which are often prepared by several unnamed authors. Such invoices, however, if allowed to prove their contents, are hearsay evidence. As a practical matter, an exception to the hearsay rule exists to allow business records to be proven for their truth. The business records exception is justified because (a) such evidence is generally reliable and (b) it usually cannot be adduced otherwise. Consider, for example, an automobile manufacturer's records of engine block numbers. Such records are relied on daily to determine entitlements to warranty protection; the evidence is reliable. Further, no one could possibly have an independent memory of such engine block numbers and the only way to prove such a number (assuming it is an issue) is through a business record.[13]

At common law a business record is admissible to prove the truth of its contents if:

1. it was made at or near the time of the matter recorded;
2. it was made by someone with personal knowledge of the matter recorded and whose position obliged them to record the information; and
3. it was made in the ordinary course of business.[14]

Business records are admissible as an exception to the hearsay rule if the common law principles apply. *Palter Cap Co. Ltd. v. Great West Life Assurance Co.*[15] is a fairly typical business record case. A doctor made a physical exam and took some notes and then died. Obviously the doctor could not testify; the Court had to determine if the notes were admissible. In finding the notes admissible, the Court noted they were made (1) at the time of the exam, or thereabouts, (2) by the doctor personally, and (3) in the ordinary course of a medical practice. The Court referred, with approval to a statement in Halsbury's, 2nd ed., Vol. 13, p. 588, para. 658:

... the statement must (1) relate to some act or transaction performed by the person making it in the ordinary course of his business and duty; (2) be made in the ordinary course of his business under a duty to make it; and (3) be made at or near the time at which the act or transaction to which it relates was performed.

The Supreme Court in *Ares v. Venner*[16] comments:

---

[13] See *Myers v. D.P.P.*, [1965] A.C. 1001 (H.L.); and the discussion of that case in J. Sopinka, S. Lederman & A. Bryant, *Law of Evidence in Canada*, 2nd ed. (Toronto: Butterworths, 1999) p. 213ff.
[14] See, for example, *Cargill Grain v. Davie Shipbuilding Co. Ltd.*, [1977] 1 S.C.R. 659.
[15] [1936] O.R. 341.
[16] [1970] S.C.R. 608 at 626.

... hospital records, including nurses' notes made contemporaneously by someone having a personal knowledge of the matters then being recorded and under a duty to make the entry or record should be received in evidence as *prima facie* proof of the facts stated therein.

Business records may also be admitted into evidence by statute. The statutory requirements to adduce business records are less onerous than the common law prerequisites and it is more common for business records to be admitted pursuant to statute than common law. The key differences between common law and the statutory exception are that personal knowledge of the facts recorded is irrelevant under statute, except as to weight, but written notice of the intention to call business records must be given before the evidence is to be called. A typical provision appears in the Ontario *Evidence Act*,[17] s. 35, which provides:

s. 35(2) Any writing or record made of any act, transaction, occurrence or event is admissible as evidence of such act, transaction, occurrence or event if made in the usual and ordinary course of any business and if it was in the usual and ordinary course of such business to make such writing or record at the time of such act, transaction, occurrence or event or within a reasonable time thereafter.

(3) Subsection (2) does not apply unless the party tendering the writing or record has given at least seven days notice...

To similar effect is s. 30 of the *Canada Evidence Act*,[18] which allows the admission of "a record made in the usual and ordinary course of business" provided at least seven days notice of the intention to adduce business records is given.

Merely delivering notice of the intention to call business records and then filing with the court those (allegedly) business records is not sufficient to allow the use of those documents to prove the truth of their contents. The other conditions precedent to the use of the documents (the circumstances of creation and their use as actual business records) must be proven independently.[19] Mere production of a document is not sufficient to prove the document or its contents.[20]

In calling business records, counsel should consider both the common law and statutory exceptions to the hearsay rule. Generally speaking, the only time the common law exception is needed is if notice was not served — this is rare, but when it does happen the common law exception is of great assistance.

Although not often required, the common law business record exception to the hearsay rule is available as necessary.

---

[17]   R.S.O. 1990, c. E. 23.
[18]   R.S.C. 1985, c. C-5.
[19]   *O'Brien v. Shantz* (1999), 167 D.L.R. (4th) 132 (Ont. C.A.).
[20]   *Murphy v. Predator* (2002) Carswell Alta. 547 (Alta. Q.B.).

E. PAST RECOLLECTION RECORDED

Often, a witness at trial has no recollection of a relevant and material fact, but did make written notes about the fact earlier. The classic example is a witness who saw a car speeding away, wrote down the licence plate number, but at trial has no memory of the licence plate number. Since such evidence is often necessary and has the reliability of being recorded at a time when memory was fresh, an exception to the hearsay rule is made for past recollection recorded.[21] The American *Federal Rules of Evidence* set this exception out well:[22]

> Recorded recollection. A memorandum or record concerning a matter about which a witness once had knowledge but now has insufficient recollection to enable the witness to testify fully and accurately, shown to have been made or adopted by the witness when the matter was fresh in the witness' memory and to reflect that knowledge correctly. If admitted, the memorandum or record may be read into evidence but may not itself be received as an exhibit unless offered by an adverse party.

The Alberta Court of Appeal in *Meddoui*[23] stated the rule as follows:

1. The past recollection must have been recorded in some reliable way.
2. At the time, it must have been sufficiently fresh and vivid to be probably accurate.
3. The witness must be able now to assert that the record accurately represented his knowledge and recollection at the time. The usual phrase requires the witness to affirm that he 'knew it to be true at the time'.
4. The original record itself must be used, if it is procurable.

It should be noted that if the person whose past recollection is said to be recorded does not acknowledge making the recording of the recollection, then the exception does not apply.[24]

F. RES GESTAE

This is a rather confusing exception to the hearsay rule. It has been used, and is still used, by some counsel to try to admit hearsay without giving serious consideration to the issue of hearsay. Thayer reminds us that the exception was first used by "Garrow and Lord Kenyon — two famously ignorant men".[25] That said, the *res gestae* exception to the hearsay rule is quite clearly established and

---

[21] See, for example, *R. v. Rouse*, [1977] 4 WWW 734, aff'd [1979] 1 S.C.R. 588.

[22] FED. R. EVID. Rule 803(5).

[23] *R. v. Meddoui* (1990), 2 C.R. (4th) 316 at 323 (Alta. C.A.), citing *Wigmore on Evidence*, Chadbourn Rev., vol. 3 (Boston: Little Brown, 1970), para. 744, et. seq.

[24] *R. v. Courchene* (1999), 135 Man. R. (2d) 267 (Q.B.).

[25] J.B. Thayer, "Res Gestae" (1881), 15 Amer. L. Rev. 1, 10. If anyone other than Thayer said such a thing, it might bespeak contempt, but even abuse by Thayer conveys a measure of respect. In any event, one doubts Garrow or Lord Kenyon are disturbed by the reference.

fairly easily defined. The *res gestae* exception to the hearsay rule can be stated thusly:

A hearsay statement relating to a startling evidence or condition that was made while the declarant was under the stress of excitement caused by the event or condition is admissible though hearsay.

The reasoning here is that the event was so startling that the declarant does not have reflective capacity and will only speak the truth as the declarant sees it. The statement must be made while the declarant still feels the shock of the event; if the shock had worn off and reflective thought occurred, the statement will not be admitted. The Court in *Gilbert*[26] accepted the following definition of the *res gestae* exception:

> Whatever act, or series of acts, constitute, or in point of time, immediately accompany and terminate in, the principal act charged as an offence against the accused, from its inception to its consummation or final completion, or its prevention or abandonment, — whether on the part of the agent or wrong-doer in order to its performance, or on that of the patient or party wronged, in order to its prevention — and whatever may be said by either of the parties, during the continuance of the transaction, with reference to it, including herein what may be said by the suffering party, though in the absence of the accused, during the continuance of the action of the latter ... form part of the principal transaction, and may be given in evidence as part of the *res gestae*, or particulars of it.

The view of *res gestae* in *Gilbert* comes out of the case law. The *Wilkinson*[27] decision is fairly typical. A deceased made a statement suggesting that she was in the midst of a fight with her husband — she was then shot by an unseen shooter. The prosecutor wanted to adduce the deceased's statement to prove she was fighting with her husband. Clearly, the statement was hearsay, being an out-of-court statement adduced to prove the truth of its contents. Was the statement admissible as part of the *res gestae*? The statement was made contemporaneous with the fight and flowed from it and, as a result, was admissible as being part of the *res gestae*. Justice Hall notes:

> She [the deceased] had no opportunity for fabrication and her statements were not mere narrative of events but were part of the transaction itself, and are admissible on this ground.

Similarly, Lord Wilberforce notes in *Ratten v. R.*:[28]

> As regards statements made after the event it must be for the judge, by preliminary ruling, to satisfy himself that the statement was so clearly made in circumstances of spontaneity or involvement in the event that the possibility of concoction can be dis-

---

[26] *R. v. Gilbert* (1907), 12 C.C.C. 127 at 138 (S.C.C.).
[27] *R. v. Wilkinson*, [1934] 3 D.L.R. 50 at 56 (N.S.S.C.).
[28] [1971] 3 All E.R. 801 at 807 (P.C.).

regarded. Conversely, if he considers that the statement was made by way of narrative of a detached prior event so that the speaker was so disengaged from it as to be able to construct or adopt his account, he should exclude it … But if the drama, leading up to the climax, has commenced and assumed such intensity and pressure that the utterance can safely be regarded as a true reflection of what was unrolling or actually happening, it ought to be received.

G. EXISTING STATEMENT OF PHYSICAL, MENTAL OR EMOTIONAL STATE

As a general rule, an otherwise hearsay statement of the declarant's then existing state of mind, emotion, sensation or physical condition is admissible. The statement must be of an existing state or condition and a recollection thereof is not sufficient to be admitted. United States Federal Rule of Evidence 803(3) sets out the exception as follows:

> Then existing mental, emotional, or physical condition. A statement of the declarant's then existing state of mind, emotion, sensation, or physical condition (such as intent, plan, motive, design, mental feeling, pain, and bodily health), but not including a statement of memory or belief to prove the fact remembered or believed unless it relates to the execution, revocation, identification, or terms of declarant's will.

The *Hillmon*[29] case is the leading decision on this exception to the hearsay rule. It was material to determine if a deceased did or did not go to a place in Kansas called Crooked Creek. The deceased had written letters saying he intended to go to Colorado. This was an intention held at the time the letters were written and it was sought to adduce these letters to prove that intention. The Court ruled:

> Wherever the bodily or mental feelings of an individual are material to be proved, the usual expressions of such feelings are original and competent evidence. Those expressions are the natural reflexes of what it might be impossible to show by other testimony. If there be such other testimony, this may be necessary to set the facts thus developed in their true light, and to give them their proper effect. As independent explanatory or corroborative evidence, it is often indispensable to the due administration of justice. Such declarations are regarded as verbal acts, and are as competent as any other testimony, when relevant to the issue. Their truth or falsity is an inquiry for the jury.

An important limitation on this exception to the hearsay rule is that statements of existing intention are proof of the intention only of the declarant and cannot be used to prove the act or intention of any other person.[30]

---

[29] *Mutual Life v. Hillmon* 145 U.S. 285 (1892); see also *R. v. Moore* (1984), 5 O.A.C. 51.
[30] *R. v. Smith*, [1992] S.C.R. 915.

H. DYING DECLARATIONS

The dying declaration exception to the hearsay exclusion is rarely seen. Briefly stated, the dying declaration exception is as follows:

Where a hearsay statement is made by a dying declarant, who knows death is imminent, and that statement is sought to be adduced in a criminal proceeding for which the death of the declarant is a necessary element and the statement relates to the circumstances of death, the statement is admissible.

It is important to notice how limited the dying declaration exception is — it applies only where five elements all apply:

1. Declarant is deceased;
2. Declarant knew of impending death;
3. The statement related to death;
4. Criminal case; and
5. Element of criminal charge is death of declarant.

This exception is generally found in homicide cases. There are very few offences other than homicide for which the death of someone is an essential element. Thus, in the *Jurtyn*[31] decision the Court describes the exception as follows:

> It was a general rule that dying declarations are only admissible where the death of the deceased declarant was the subject of the charge, and they concerned the circumstances of the death ... it [the declaration] must be proferred as testimony in a public prosecution [it must be] not merely for an act which had resulted in fact in death, but for an act involving legally the resulting death as a necessary element ....

The rather tragic *Schwartzenhauer*[32] case illustrates how narrow the dying declaration exception is. Here, an accused was charged with an offence, "namely, to use unlawfully on the person of VK an instrument with intent to procure a miscarriage of VK ...". The offence was unlawfully procuring a miscarriage — not manslaughter. As it happened, the death of VK resulted from the induced miscarriage, but death was neither the focus of the charge nor an element of the offence. As a result, a dying declaration made by VK was not admissible. It should be noted that, if the accused in *Schwartzenhauer* had been charged in modern times with criminal negligence causing death the declaration would have been admissible because death is a necessary element of that offence.

---

[31] *R. v. Jurtyn*, [1958] O.W.N. 355; see also *R. v. Harrison* (2001), 87 B.C.L.R. (3d) 313 for a current statement of the issues.
[32] *Schwartzenhauer v. R.*, [1935] S.C.R. 367.

I. OFFICIAL STATEMENTS

The *Evidence Acts* provide for the proof of certain government documents. Thus, s. 31(2) of the *Evidence Act* (Ontario) provides that entries in books of account of a municipality are admissible as evidence of the truth of their contents without further proof. This is a specific statutory exception to the hearsay rule. There is, however, a broader common law which provides:[33]

A written report or record of a public official is admissible if the official had first hand knowledge of the reported facts and had a duty to make the record or report.

As early as 1785 the Court notes:[34]

The law reposes such a confidence in public officers that it presumes they will discharge their several trusts with accuracy and fidelity; and therefore, whatever acts they do in discharge of their public duty may be given in evidence and shall be taken to be true, under such degree of caution as the nature and circumstances of each case may appear to require.

While normally the official statements exception to the hearsay rule applies to civil servants, it is not limited to them. A public official may be, for example, a harbour master, or a school teacher, or even an official of a trade organization. The question is what role the declarant plays — is it one related to a governmentally sanctioned role dealing with the public? If so, the declarant is a public official.

---

[33] *R. v. Finestone*, [1953] 2 S.C.R. 107.
[34] *R. v. Aickles* (1785), 1 Leach Cr. L. 390 at 392, 168 E.R. 297.

Chapter 9

EXCLUSION OF OTHERWISE RELEVANT EVIDENCE

COURTS

Whether or not it makes sense to exclude otherwise admissible and relevant evidence depends on the societal role of the court. If the court's role is to determine disputes accurately and efficiently then evidence ought to be excluded only because it is unreliable or excessively time consuming. If, on the other hand, the court's role includes an element of instruction for society as a whole, then evidence, otherwise reliable, but obtained in a fashion repugnant to the court or society can legitimately be excluded.

Until recently the Canadian view was very clearly that the court's job is limited only to dispute resolution. With the advent of a set of constitutionally protected rights, the position changed and Canadian courts now regularly exclude evidence that is otherwise quite reliable because its admission would offend a societal norm.

RIGHT AGAINST SELF-INCRIMINATION

As a general rule, an accused cannot be compelled to give testimony against themselves in a criminal trial. This is clear from both s.11(c) of the *Charter*[1] and s. 5(2) of the *Canada Evidence Act*.[2] Section 11(c) of the Charter provides:

> Any person charged with an offence has the right not to be compelled to be a witness in proceedings against that person in respect of the offence.

This provision applies to an offence, which is broader than a criminal charge, and includes provincial offences.

It is important to note that the right to not testify is not a prohibition on testifying. An accused may give evidence at a criminal trial — it is a question of

---

[1] *Canadian Charter of Rights and Freedoms*, Part I of the *Constitution Act, 1982*, being Schedule B to the *Canada Act 1982* (U.K.), 1982, c. 11.

[2] R.S.C. 1985, c. C-5.

judgment whether to call such evidence and whether such testimony will do more harm than good. An accused, once testifying, may be asked all types of questions dealing with character (say, prior convictions) and, as a result, it may be imprudent to testify. As buttress to the right not to testify, s. 4(6) of the *Canada Evidence Act* provides, "The failure of the person charged ... to testify shall not be made the subject of comment by the judge or by counsel for the prosecution".

Obviously, if upon not testifying the prosecutor told the jury, something like "Now look at the prisoner — if the prisoner could explain surely the prisoner would. What is the prisoner hiding? What does the prisoner not want you to know?", the right not to testify would be insignificant. Thus, the Court comments in the *Gallagher*[3] case, "it is the duty of the Court carefully to protect the accused from damaging insinuations which may not in terms invite a consideration of the prisoner's failure to testify but make indirect and covert allusion of the defendant's silence". The Court may not even imply the accused ought to have taken the stand. But, a (relatively) neutral description of the law setting out the accused right to not testify is proper.[4] The Court may not comment on the accused's failure to testify but may state the law that the accused need not testify. The distinction between stating the law and commenting on the failure to testify is a rather nice one and it is not always clear what falls on what side of the line.

A side issue is whether an appeal court can consider the failure of an accused to testify in deciding whether an appeal is well grounded. It can, although this seems to sit strangely with a right not to testify.[5]

RIGHT TO SILENCE

The *Charter* does not provide a right to silence. The right to not answer questions is deeply ingrained in our legal culture — so much so that many lawyers are surprised the *Charter* is not more explicit in its protection. The Supreme Court of Canada has described the source of the right to silence in the *Chambers*[6] case saying:

> In Canada the right of a suspect not to say anything to the police is not the result of a right of no self-crimination but is merely the exercise by him of the general right enjoyed in this country by anyone to do whatever one pleases, saying what one pleases or choosing not to say certain things, unless obliged to do otherwise by law. It is because no law says that a suspect, save in certain circumstances, must say anything to the police that we say that he has the right to remain silent, which is a positive way of explaining that there is on his part no legal obligation to do otherwise.

---

[3] *R. v. Gallagher*, [1922] 1 W.W.R. 1183 at 1185.
[4] *R. v. McConnell*, [1968] S.C.R. 802.
[5] *R. v. Corbett*, [1975] 2 S.C.R. 275; *R. v. Avon*, [1971] S.C.R. 650.
[6] *R. v. Chambers*, [1990] 2 S.C.R. 1293 at 1315, citing *R. v. Rothman*, [1981] 1 S.C.R. 640 at 683.

The *Hebert*[7] case is interesting in that it illustrates just how seriously the courts take the right to silence, even though it is not expressly enunciated in the *Charter*. In *Hebert* the police tricked the accused, who had claimed his right to silence, into making an inculpatory statement by putting the accused in a cell with a police officer mascarading as a fellow prisoner — needless to say the accused told his new friend all manner of unhelpful things. The Court comments:

> ... the common law confessions rule and the privilege against self-incrimination share a common theme — the right of the individual to choose whether to make a statement to the authorities or to remain silent, coupled with concern with the repute and integrity of the judicial process
>
> ...
>
> The common law rules relating to the right to silence suggest that the essence of the right is the notion that the person whose freedom is placed in question by the judicial process must be given the choice of whether to speak to the authorities or not.

Speaking directly about the trick the police played to get the accused to make the inculpatory statement, the Court held:

> The scope of the right to silence must be defined broadly enough to preserve for the detained person the right to choose whether to speak to the authorities or to remain silent, notwithstanding the fact that he or she is in the superior power of the state. On this view, the scope of the right must extend to exclude tricks which would effectively deprive the suspect of his choice.[8]

Put narrowly, once an accused says "I'm saying nothing, I want to see a lawyer", the state has no further right to obtain a statement from the accused either directly or indirectly (unless after obtaining legal advice the right to silence is waived).

SELF-INCRIMINATION AND THE CHARTER

Unlike the right to silence, the right against self-incrimination is, as mentioned earlier, explicitly set out in the *Charter*. Section 11(c) of the *Charter* says:

> Any person charged with an offence has the right not to be compelled to be a witness in proceedings against that person in respect of the offence.

On its face it seems obvious that s. 11(c) says an accused cannot be forced to testify. The right in s. 11(c) of the *Charter* is reinforced by s. 13 of the *Charter* which provides:

---

[7] *R. v. Hebert*, [1990] 2 S.C.R. 151 at 175.

[8] But note, not all tricks are forbidden. Where police offered gum to an accused who chewed it and threw it away, the police could retrieve the gum for DNA testing purposes: *R. v. Nguyen* (2002), 48 C.R. (5th) 338.

A witness who testifies in any proceedings has the right not to have any incriminating evidence so given used to incriminate that witness in any other proceedings, except in a prosecution for perjury or for giving contradictory evidence.

Section 13 of the *Charter* protects an accused from being forced to testify in a matter in which they are not accused and having that unwilling testimony used against them in a subsequent trial. But what if an accused voluntarily testified in an earlier proceeding? Can that evidence be used against the accused as, say, an admission? The answer appears to be no. The issue was addressed by the Supreme Court of Canada in *R. v. Dubois.*[9] In that case the accused was tried twice for murder. In the first trial, later reversed on appeal, the accused freely testified. During the second trial the accused did not testify, but his evidence from the first trial was read into the record over the accused objection. Ruling the evidence from the first trial inadmissible, the Court held:

> As section 13 guarantees the right of a person against self-incrimination, rather than the rights of a witness giving testimony, it inures to an individual only at the moment an attempt is made to use previous testimony to incriminate its author.

Accordingly, whether or not the prior testimony was given voluntarily is irrelevant to the right against self-incrimination. Of course, one might try to extend the reasoning of *Dubois* to suggest admissions made out of court are also improper. A better view is that such admissions are not testimony and the right against self-incrimination is limited to testimonial statements.

What if the accused testified in an earlier proceeding and now has changed their story? Can the prior inconsistent statement be used in cross-examination? Here the answer is yes — the prior statement is only being used to shake the present testimony and not as testimony.[10] Remember the orthodox position is that such inconsistent statements are not proof of their contents but rather merely evidence of the inconsistency of the witness.

RIGHT TO COUNSEL AND EVIDENTIARY IMPLICATIONS

The Constitution has very considerable impact on evidence in criminal matters. The Canadian Constitution provides, in s. 24(2) of the *Charter*, that:

> Where ... evidence was obtained in a manner that infringed ... this Charter, the evidence shall be excluded if it is established that, having regard to the circumstances, the admission of it in the proceedings would bring the administration of justice into disrepute.

Note carefully, this excludes otherwise admissible evidence but only if (1) it was obtained by a *Charter* violation — there must be a nexus and a close one, and

---

[9]   [1985] 2 S.C.R. 350 at 361.
[10] *R. v. Kuldip*, [1990] 3 S.C.R. 618.

(2) if the admission would bring justice into disrepute. What does the second condition require? Recall the non-*Charter* House of Lords decision in *Chi-Ming* where the Court writes:[11]

> Any civilised system of criminal jurisprudence must accord to the judiciary some means of excluding confessions or admissions obtained by improper methods. This is not only because of the potential unreliability of such statements, but also, and perhaps mainly, because in a civilised society it is vital that persons in custody or charged with offences should not be subject to ill treatment or improper pressure in order to extract confessions.

The Supreme Court of Canada in *Collins*[12] has ruled the question turns on, whether the evidence "could" (not would) bring the administration of justice into disrepute in the eyes of a fair dispassionate person — would such a person say, in effect, "cops or robbers, they're all as one and its a mug's game"?

Bearing all this in mind, consider the *Manninen*[13] case. Manninen was arrested, read his rights and he explicitly asserted his right to counsel. The police, despite this assertion, continued questioning Manninen, eventually obtaining incriminatory materials. The Court noted:

> ... s.10(b) imposes on the police the duty to cease questioning or otherwise attempting to elicit evidence from the detainee until he has had a reasonable opportunity to retain and instruct counsel .... Immediately after the respondent's clear assertion of his right to remain silent and his desire to consult his lawyer, the police officer commenced his questioning as if the respondent had expressed no such desire.

Holding the violation of the right to counsel "wilful and deliberate" and the evidence at issue a "direct consequence of the violation", the Court excluded the incriminating evidence.[14]

---

[11] *R. v. Chi-Ming* (1991), 122 N.R. 307 at 311, quoting *Wong Kam-Ming v. R.* (1980), A.C. 247 (H.L.).
[12] *R. v. Collins*, [1987] 1 S.C.R. 265.
[13] *R. v. Manninen*, [1987] 1 S.C.R. 1233 at 1242, 1243-44.
[14] See also *R. v. Carey* (2001), 42 C.R. (5th) 308 (Ont. S.C.).

Chapter 10

CONFESSIONS

INTRODUCTION

As a general rule, in criminal matters, confessions to public authorities are admissible only upon proof by the prosecutor that the confession was obtained freely and without any pressure on the accused. This rule is, quite obviously, motivated by a fear that coercion will be used to obtain confessions which (a) may be wrong and (b) in any event, may be obtained in violation of society's deeply held views of what is fit and proper. In Roman times slaves could testify only after torture — as *Foxe's Christian Martyrs of the World* shows, even into the sixteenth century torture was not uncommon in England. This history of torture in this century is well known and continuing — it is because of this tragic history that, by the middle of the eighteenth century, the common law began to reject confessions unless made voluntarily.

The rule regarding confessions is broad enough to encompass any statement, whether inculpatory or not. Even an apparently exculpatory statement is subject to the voluntariness requirement. That said, not all statements made by persons accused are confessions. Statements made to people other than authorities are not confessions and even statements made to, say, the police, are not confessions if at the time of the statement the speaker was not yet a suspect or accused. Put briefly, the rule respecting confessions is:

A confession is a statement made by an accused to a person in authority. Such a confession is not admissible in a prosecution of the accused unless the prosecution proves beyond reasonable doubt that the confession was made voluntarily.

FREE AND VOLUNTARY

For a statement, which may be a confession, to be admissible it must be made freely and without the accused being coerced. The question is *subjective* — is this accused making a free and voluntary statement? Thus, it may be that giving the usual warning ("anything you say can and will be used against you") will do for most adults but not for persons of limited capacity.

For example, in *R. v. Beaulieu*[1] the Court rejects a confession made by an accused, even though the customary warning had been given. The Court writes:

> I have studied her demeanor in the box, I have listened carefully to her answers. I am satisfied that her mental development is not very great. It is not sufficient to give a warning and to say that it has been understood. I realize that the warning in the case, and I accept the evidence of the police officers to the extent that the warning was explained but ... it has not been demonstrated that the warning was fully understood by the accused and that all the implications of the statement were understood by her.

The question raised, albeit indirectly, by *Beaulieu* is whether the accused can make a voluntary statement while in a state, permanent or temporary, of mental confusion. The courts have been quite clear that an element of voluntariness is that the speaker must have an operating mind. Thus, someone suffering physical shock,[2] drunkenness[3] or lacking mental capacity[4] cannot make an admissible confession. To establish an operating mind, the prosecutor does not need to show the speaker could decide whether confession was prudent, but, the prosecutor must show, beyond reasonable doubt, that the speaker (a) knew what they were saying (b) knew it could be used against them and (c) comprehended the police warning.[5]

Beyond the "operating mind" requirement, voluntariness requires the confession was not obtained by hope of advantage or fear of prejudice.[6] Lord Salmon stated this test clearly in *D. P. P. v. Ping Lin*:[7]

> The judge's decision is, in reality, a decision on the facts. He has to weigh up the evidence and decide whether he is satisfied that no person in authority has obtained the confession or statement, directly or indirectly, by engendering fear in the accused that he will be worse off if he makes no confession or statement or by exciting hope in the accused that he will be better off if he does make a confession or statement. If the judge is so satisfied, he may admit evidence of the confession or statement. If he is not so satisfied, he must exclude it.

Put simply, before a statement can be said to be free and voluntary, the prosecutor must show, to beyond a reasonable doubt, the accused is in a clear state of mind, knows the statement may be used in evidence and has not been put under any physical or emotional strain so as to influence the accused's thinking.

---

[1]   [1968] 1 C.C.C. 143 at 145 (Alta. C.A.).
[2]   *Ward v. R.*, [1979] 2 S.C.R. 30.
[3]   *Clarkson v. R.*, [1986] 1 S.C.R. 383.
[4]   *R. v. Santinon*, [1973] 3 W.W.R. 113 (B.C.C.A.).
[5]   *R. v. Whittle*, [1994] 2 S.C.R. 114; *R. v. Oliver (No. 2)* (2001), 86 C.R.R. (2d) 304.
[6]   *R. v. Hodgson*, [1998] 2 S.C.R. 449.
[7]   [1975] 3 All E.R. 175 at 187 (H.L.).

WHO IS A PERSON IN AUTHORITY?

A person in authority is anyone an accused reasonably believes is in a position to influence the prosecution of an accused. Thus, a person in authority includes police, prosecutors, jail wardens, owners of property alleged to be stolen, security guards, fire marshals — anyone an accused reasonably believes might influence the prosecution of the criminal case. If the accused reasonably believed this person had power to influence the prosecution then the person qualifies as a person in authority. A functional approach was given in *Newes*[8] by Chief Justice Harvey who wrote:

> … a person in authority within the meaning of the rule is some person whose promise or threat would be likely to influence the accused and induce him to make a statement against his interest from fear or hope.

Thus, the confession rule does not apply[9] if an accused makes statements to someone who is factually in authority but whom the accused does not believe is in authority, — for example, an undercover police officer.[10] By the same token, even if an accused believed someone to be in authority, such belief will not trigger the confession rule unless the belief is reasonable.[11]

THE *VOIR DIRE*

As noted above, once the issue of whether the confession rule applies is raised, the prosecutor must prove, beyond reasonable doubt, that the confession is admissible. Such proof is established in a *voir dire*. A *voir dire* is a trial within a trial — in the case of confessions, the *voir dire* is held to determine whether a confession is voluntary and, therefore admissible. The jury is excluded during the confession *voir dire* and does not hear the evidence taken during the *voir dire*. The evidence heard on a *voir dire* does not form part of the evidence on the trial and it is not repeated later for the jury regardless of whether the confession is admitted. Generally speaking, a *voir dire* ought to be held whenever an issue of a confession is raised unless the accused quite explicitly waives the need for a *voir dire*.[12] Silence or lack of objection is not sufficient as waiver.[13]

The burden of proving a confession is voluntary rests with the prosecution. If the accused wishes, the accused may testify during the *voir dire* but in such event the judge may allow the accused to be questioned on the truth of the statement —

---

[8] *R. v. Newes* (1934), 161 C.C.C. 316 at 317 (Alta. C.A.).
[9] Although the right to silence may serve to exclude the statement made under the *Charter*.
[10] *R. v. Rothman* (1981), 59 C.C.C. (2d) 30 (S.C.C.).
[11] *R. v. Hodgson*, [1998] 2 S.C.R. 449. Of course, a wholly irrational belief might raise other issues of competence.
[12] *R. v. Park*, [1981] S.C.R. 64; *R. v. Nguyen* (2002), 48 C.R. (5th) 338 (Ont. C.A.), but note here, in this specific case, the failure to hold a *voir dire* was harmless.
[13] *R. v. C. (B.)* (1991), 93 Nfld. & P.E.I.R. 324 (Nfld. C.A.).

De Clercq[14] establishes this principle although *De Clercq* has strong dissents by Justices Hall, Spence and Pigeon. The Supreme Court in *De Clercq* held that the truth of a confession might be relevant to its voluntariness. The Privy Council, in *Wong Kam-Ming v. R.*,[15] took a contrary view and would not allow questioning on the truth of the statement sought to be adduced as a confession. It may well be the *De Clercq* decision is subject to reconsideration.

EVIDENCE COLLATERALLY PROVEN TRUE

Why is a confession excluded unless it is shown to be free and voluntary? There are two obvious reasons.

First, it may be that judges consider such evidence to be so frail and suspect that it cannot be given any credit. Thus, in *Warickshall*[16] the Court writes:

> But a confession forced from the mind by flattery of hope, or by the torture of fear comes in so questionable a shape when it is to be considered as evidence of guilt that no credit ought to be given to it; and therefore it is rejected.

This view is squarely in line with the theory of courts being nothing more than rational fact finders.

The alternative view is that involuntary confessions are barred because of the broader societal prohibition on benefiting from prosecutorial misconduct. Lord Hailsham sets out this view clearly in *Wong Kam-Ming*[17] where he writes:

> Any civilised system of criminal jurisprudence must accord to the judiciary some means of excluding confessions or admissions obtained by improper methods. This is not only because of the potential unreliability of such statements, but also, and perhaps mainly, because in a civilised society it is vital that persons in custody or charged with offences should not be subjected to ill treatment or improper pressure in order to extract confessions. It is therefore of very great importance that the courts should continue to insist that before extra-judicial statements can be admitted in evidence the prosecution must be made to prove beyond reasonable doubt that the statement was not obtained in a manner which should be reprobated and was there-fore in the truest sense voluntary.

All this may seem like a pointless policy argument — why care that involuntary confessions are excluded so long as there is a rule? — but it has very real implications. What if an involuntary confession is collaterally proven true? For example, an accused is beaten until saying where the stolen goods were hidden and police then find the stolen goods where the accused said they were to be found. Obviously, such a statement would be an involuntary confession but the part of the statement about the location of the goods was true.

---

[14] *R. v. DeClercq*, [1968] S.C.R. 902.
[15] [1979] 1 All E.R. 939 (P.C.).
[16] *R. v. Warickshall* (1783), 1 Leach 263.
[17] *Wong Kam-Ming v. R.*, [1980] A.C. 247 (P.C.). This is from his dissenting judgment.

If confessions are excluded because they are unreliable and for no other reason then such a verified confession ought to be admitted; in Canadian law, until the *Charter*,[18] such evidence was admitted.[19] The involuntary but verified confession, in total, was not allowed; only so much of the confession as was demonstrated correct was allowed. So, in the stolen goods example the only part of the confession that would go into evidence is the description of where to look for the stolen goods — of course, that is usually plenty to secure a conviction.

What is the law today under the *Charter*? The *Wray* decision, saying involuntary confessions collaterally proven right are partly admissible, is no longer good law. Evidence obtained by violation of the *Charter* (as would have been the case in *Wray*) is to be excluded if its admission would bring the administration of justice into disrepute. More generally, and regardless of the Charter, there is no doubt that the law in Canada now provides an involuntary confession, regardless of whether proven true, cannot be used at all by the prosecution. As the Supreme Court of Canada notes in *Calder*,[20] "involuntary statements may not be used by the Crown for my purpose". The Court emphasized this in *G.(B.)*[21] saying "no use may be made of an inadmissible statement [confession] at any stage whatsoever of the trial".

---

[18] *Canadian Charter of Rights and Freedoms*, Part I of the *Consitution Act, 1982*, being Schedule B to the *Canada Act 1982* (U.K.), 1982, c. 11.
[19] *R. v. Wray*, [1971] S.C.R. 272.
[20] *R. v. Calder*, [1996] 1 S.C.R. 660 at para. 26.
[21] *R. v. G.(B.)*, [1999] 2 S.C.R. 475 at para. 33.

Chapter 11

EVIDENCE OBTAINED ILLEGALLY

ILLEGALLY OBTAINED EVIDENCE

At the outset, we should be clear we are now dealing with evidence obtained as a result of illegal conduct by the State. Such conduct is not necessarily a breach of constitutional rights. As a practical matter, conduct that amounts to illegality is usually unconstitutional conduct — an illegal search of a home is a criminal trespass *and* a breach of the constitutional right to be secure from unreasonable search and seizure. For purposes of our immediate discussion, however, we will assume no constitutional breaches occur as part of the illegal State action. We will deal with such constitutional issues later.

If the role of the court is limited to rational fact finding then, illegality by police ought not to affect admissibility of evidence; recall, an involuntary confession is admissible insofar as its truth is independently confirmed. Put otherwise, if evidence is relevant and material, and there is no reason to doubt its truthfulness, why should illegality in its acquisition affect its admissibility? Two wrongs do not make a right and why should police wrongdoing exclude a criminal's conviction? This view is reflected in *R. v. Hanan*,[1] where the Court writes:

> … the question is not, by what means was the evidence procured; but is, whether the things proved were evidence; and it is not contended that they were not; all that is urged is, that the evidence ought to have been rejected, because it was obtained by means of a trespass — as it is asserted — upon the property of the accused by the police officers engaged in this prosecution. The criminal who wields the "jimmy" or the bludgeon, or uses any other criminally unlawful means or methods, has no right to insist upon being met by the law only when in kid gloves or satin slippers; it is still quite permissible to "set a thief to catch a thief."

Such a view, though overly colourful, is undoubtedly the law of Canada. Except for constitutional breaches, illegality does not taint admissibility of evidence. Generally speaking, the law regarding illegally obtained evidence is the same in both civil and criminal cases.[2] That said, in civil cases, a party may obtain an injunction barring the use of otherwise confidential materials obtained by some

---

[1] (1912), 20 C.C.C. 10 at 16-17 (Ont. C.A.).
[2] *Kuruma, Son of Kaniu v. R.*, [1955] 1 All E.R. 236 (P.C.).

breach of that confidence.[3] Thus, where privileged materials of an employee fell into the hands of the employer during wrongful dismissal litigation, a court was prepared to enjoin the use of those materials by the employer. This limitation does not apply in criminal matters.[4]

WIRETAP EVIDENCE

There is a statutory exception to the principle that illegally obtained evidence is inadmissible. Wiretap evidence[5] is not admissible in a criminal matter unless the prosecutor complies with notice and disclosure requirements prior to seeking to introduce the evidence. The notice and disclosure requirements require the prosecutor provide reasonable notice of all intentions to adduce the evidence together with full particulars of the evidence.[6] Until 1993, the *Criminal Code* provided for the exclusion of wiretap evidence that was not obtained lawfully through judicial preauthorization. At present, and ignoring *Charter* issues,[7] wiretap evidence is admissible if the limited notice and disclosure prerequisites are met.

---

[3] *Ashburton (Lord) v. Pape*, [1913] 2 Ch. 469, [1911-13] All E.R. Rep. 708 (C.A.).
[4] *Butler v. Board of Trade*, [1970] 3 All E.R. 593.
[5] See ss. 184-96 of the *Criminal Code*, R.S.C. 1985, c. C-46 (Appendix A).
[6] *Ibid.*, s. 189(5).
[7] If the wiretap is not judicially preauthorized there is likely to be a breach of the s. 8 *Charter* protection against unreasonable search and seizure.

Chapter 12

THE EXCLUSION REMEDY GENERALLY

CREATION OF REMEDY

In the United States the exclusionary remedy for evidence obtained unconstitutionally is very well established. The exclusionary remedy can be traced to an 1886 decision, *Boyd*,[1] where the United States Supreme Court found that using illegally obtained evidence was akin to forcing someone to testify against themselves. Later, in the 1914 *Weeks*[2] decision, the United States Supreme Court expanded its reasoning saying:

> The tendency of those who execute the criminal law of the country to obtain conviction by means of unlawful seizures should find no sanction in the judgments of the courts. To sanction [such seizures by allowing evidence from them] would be to affirm by judicial decision a manifest neglect, if not an open defiance, of the prohibitions of the Constitution, intended for the protection of the people against such unauthorized action.

There is much logic in this view. However, over time many criticisms of such rigid exclusion emerged, mostly directed at the concern that minor police irregularities could allow serious criminals to go free.

These criticisms led to the exclusion remedy being firmly rejected by Canadian courts when dealing with the Canadian Bill of Rights, passed in 1960.[3] In effect, the Bill of Rights became a dead letter because a breach thereof had no effect on any state authority. Accordingly, when the *Charter* was introduced in the early 1980s, considerable care was taken to ensure it would have an effect and not become just another dead letter. Sections 52 and 24 of the *Constitution Act, 1982*,[4] are key in this regard.

Section 52 makes the *Charter* part of the Constitution and the supreme law of Canada and its provinces. Put otherwise, the *Charter* is superior to, and overrules, any other law.

---

[1]   116 U.S. 616 (1886).
[2]   232 U.S. 383 (1914).
[3]   R.S.C. 1960, c. 44. Other issues, most notably the statutory, as opposed to constitutional, basis of the Bill of Rights impacted on its interpretation.
[4]   Schedule B to the *Canada Act, 1982* (U.K.), 1982, c. 11.

Section 24 is more complex and provides:

Enforcement
24. (1) Anyone whose rights or freedoms, as guaranteed by this Charter, have
been infringed or denied may apply to a court of competent jurisdiction to obtain such remedy as the court considers appropriate and just in the circumstances.

(2) Where, in proceedings under subsection (1), a court concludes that evidence was obtained in a manner that infringed or denied any rights or
freedoms guaranteed by this Charter, the evidence shall be excluded if it is
established that, having regard to all the circumstances, the admission of it
in the proceedings would bring the administration of justice into disrepute.

Subsection (1) is a general power to fashion a remedy — for purposes of exclusion of evidence, only subsection (2) is relevant. Exclusion of evidence can be
made only under s. 24(2);[5] there is no jurisdiction to exclude evidence under s.
24(1).

Exclusion of evidence under s. 24(2) of the *Charter* requires two elements: (1)
the evidence must be obtained in a manner that violated the *Charter* and (2) the
admission of the evidence would bring the administration of justice into disrepute.

The first part of the test requires that there be some alleged *Charter* infringe-
ment. Put otherwise, absent a specific *Charter* breach, there is no basis to seek an
exclusion under the *Charter*. Merely raising an illegality will not trigger the exclusion; only a *Charter* breach will suffice.

The exclusion should be based on a practical consideration of three primary
considerations:[6]

(1) Would the admission of the evidence affect the fairness of the trial?;
(2) How serious was the *Charter* breach?; and
(3) What would the effect of the exclusion be on the repute of the administration of justice?

WHAT DOES "DISREPUTE" MEAN?

What is meant by the word "disrepute"? What is the judge to look to in determining whether the admission of the evidence would bring the administration of
justice into "disrepute"? Justice Lamer wrote in *Collins*:[7]

The concept of disrepute necessarily involves some element of community views,
and the determination of disrepute thus requires the judge to refer to what he con-
ceives to be the views of the community at large. This does not mean that evidence

---

[5] *R. v. Therens*, [1985] 1 S.C.R. 613.
[6] *R. v. Fliss* (2002), S.C.C. 16.
[7] *R. v. Collins*, [1987] 1 S.C.R. 265 at 281-82, quoting Dale Gibson, *The Law of the Charter: General
Principles* (Calgary: Carswell, 1986) at 246.

of the public's perception of the repute of the administration of justice, which ... could be presented in the form of public opinion polls ... , will be determinative of the issue ... The position is different with respect to obscenity, for example, where the court must assess the level of tolerance of the community, whether or not it is reasonable, and may consider public opinion polls ... It would be unwise, in my respectful view, to adopt a similar attitude with respect to the *Charter*. Members of the public generally become conscious of the importance of protecting the rights and freedoms of accused only when they are in some way brought closer to the system either personally or through the experience of friends or family... "The only effective shelter for individuals and unpopular minorities from the shifting winds of public passion," the *Charter* is designed to protect the accused from the majority, so the enforcement of the *Charter* must not be left to that majority.

As noted above, the test for the exclusion of evidence has two parts. There must be a *Charter* breach and then the Court focuses on whether the admission of the evidence into the proceedings "would bring the administration of justice into disrepute".

CAUSATION OR CONNECTION

The English language text of s. 24(2) of the *Charter* ("would bring") suggests the level of likelihood of bringing justice into disrepute must be high upon admission of the impugned evidence. This differs from the French language version which calls for exclusion where admission of the evidence "est susceptible de déconsidérer l'administration de la justice....". This expression, roughly equivalent to the English "*could* bring", is clearly a less demanding standard. It suggests a mere possibility of disrepute. In *Collins*, the Court suggested the standard reflected in the French version was to be used:[8]

> [W]hile both the English text of s. 24(2) and *Rothman* use the words "*would* bring the administration of justice into disrepute", the French versions are very different. The French text of s. 24(2) provides "*est susceptible de* déconsidérer l'administration de la justice", which I would translate as "*could* bring the administration of justice into disrepute". This is supportive of a somewhat lower threshold than the English test. As Dickson, J. (as he then was) wrote in *Hunter v. Southam Inc.*:[9]
>
> > Since the proper approach to the interpretation of the *Canadian Charter of Rights and Freedoms* is a purposive one, before it is possible to assess the reasonableness or unreasonableness of the impact of a search or of a statute authorizing a search, it is first necessary to specify the purpose underlying s. 8; in other words, to delineate the nature of the interests it is meant to protect.

---

[8]   *Supra*, note 6 at 287-288.
[9]   [1984] 2 S.C.R. 145 at 157.

As one of the purposes of s. 24(2) is to protect the right to a fair trial, I would favour
the interpretation of s. 24(2) which better protects that right, the less onerous French
text. Most courts which have considered the issue have also come to this conclusion
.... Section 24(2) should thus be read as "the evidence shall be excluded if it is established that, having regard to all the circumstances, the admission of it in the proceedings *could* bring the administration of justice into disrepute".

More generally, it is unnecessary for the *Charter* breach to lead directly to the
evidence which brings justice into disrepute for s. 24 of the *Charter* to be triggered. A mere temporal link,[10] that is breach before evidence, triggers s. 24 of the
Charter, unless the breach and evidence are clearly remote.[11] As the Court notes
in *R. v. Bartle*:

> Generally speaking, so long as it is not too remotely connected with the violation,
> all evidence obtained as part of the "chain of events" involving the *Charter* breach
> will fall within the scope of s. 24(2).

Nevertheless, the *Stillman*[12] decision allows the admission of evidence, even if
it otherwise forms part of the "chain of events", as long as the State establishes,
on a balance of probabilities, that the evidence would have been inevitably obtained regardless of the breach. It is worth noting that the onus of proof lies with
the State and it is not, even to a balance of probabilities, easy to prove inevitable
discovery.

BURDEN OF PROOF

The party seeking to exclude evidence under s. 24(2) of the *Charter* has the burden of demonstrating the need for exclusion. The Court in *Collins*[13] held, "... the
applicant must make it more probable than not that the admission of the evidence
would bring the administration of justice into disrepute". There is no onus on the
State to establish the admissibility of evidence,[14] however, as mentioned above, if
evidence is otherwise to be excluded and the State still seeks the evidence to be
admitted as being found inevitably despite the breach, the State must show that
inevitability.[15]

---

[10]   *R. v. Strachan*, [1988] 2 S.C.R. 980.
[11]   *R. v. Bartle*, [1994] 3 S.C.R. 173.
[12]   *R. v. Stillman*, [1997] 1 S.C.R. 607.
[13]   *R. v. Collins*, [1987] 1 S.C.R. 265.
[14]   *R. v. Marshall* (1989), 52 C.C.C. (3d) 130 (Ont. C.A.).
[15]   *Stillman, supra*, note 12.

Chapter 13

PROTECTION OF CONFIDENTIAL RELATIONS

PRIVILEGE IN GENERAL

As an exception to the general rule that relevant and material evidence is admissible, sometimes confidential communications, even though relevant and material, are not admissible. The basis of the exclusion is purely societal; no issue of relevance is taken. The confidential communication thus protected is of two types: privileged by class and privileged by case. Those communications privileged by class include solicitor/client, husband/wife and a few others. No investigation into the impact of disclosure in the specific case is made for class privilege. By contrast, regardless of the formal relationship between the parties, case privilege may apply where a truly confidential relationship of value would be harmed by disclosure.

Broadly speaking, exclusion of evidence based on privilege is limited fairly strictly by the court. Speaking of class privilege, the Supreme Court has commented:[1]

> ... class privilege presents many impediments to the proper administration of justice and, for that reason, has not been favoured in Canada ....

Claims of privilege will be restrictively viewed by the Court.

SOLICITOR - CLIENT

Communications between a solicitor and client in a professional capacity are privileged and, subject to a few exceptions, cannot be disclosed except with the consent of the client. The basis for this privilege is clearly set out in *Greenough v. Gaskell*[2] where Lord Brougham writes:

> The foundation of this rule is not difficult to discover ... It is out of regard to the interests of justice, which cannot be upholden, and the administration of justice, which cannot go on without the aid of men skilled in jurisprudence, in the practice of the

---

[1]   *A. (L.L.) v. B. (A.)*, [1995] 4 S.C.R. 536 at 575.
[2]   (1833), 1 My. & K. 98, 39 E.R. 618 (L.C.).

courts, and in those matters affecting rights and obligations which form the subject of all judicial proceedings.

The fact of the communication or the name of the client is not usually privileged — only the contents of the communication is privileged.[3] However, where the mere fact of consulting a lawyer, standing alone, would implicitly disclose the nature of the consultation, the fact of the contact is privileged.[4]

When a client's interest in litigation is transmitted to another party, say by death or bankruptcy, there is some question as to whether the privilege also passes. Thus, can a trustee in bankruptcy waive privilege over statements made by a bankrupt prior to bankruptcy? Does it matter whether the statements relate to business matters or unrelated personal matters (say divorce)? The question is not finally determined but the better answer seems to be that the privilege certainly passes on death to the estate executor or trustee and likely passes to the trustee on bankruptcy.[5]

Communication between a lawyer and a third party made in contemplation of litigation is also privileged, subject to specific disclosure requirements. For example, if a lawyer hires an expert to give a report for trial, the lawyer's discussions with the expert are privileged. If the lawyer wants to call the expert at trial the lawyer has to make disclosure pursuant to civil discovery obligations, but if the report is unhelpful the lawyer can ignore it.

The two concepts described above are what is generally considered to constitute solicitor-client privilege — the first is often called lawyer-client and applies to any professional discussion between a lawyer and client, the second is often called litigation privilege and applies only where litigation is anticipated or pending.

LIMITATIONS ON SOLICITOR-CLIENT PRIVILEGE

There are some limitations on solicitor-client privilege. Not all discussions involving lawyers are privileged.

First, we will consider limits on lawyer-client privilege. The person consulted must be a lawyer in the jurisdiction where the consultation occurs. If an Ontario lawyer is consulted in the United Kingdom about United Kingdom law, the conversation is not privileged. If an Ontario lawyer is consulted in Ontario about United Kingdom law, the privilege applies. The lawyer's agents and employees are covered by the privilege — lawyers often hire translators for foreign-born clients. Anything told to the translator, or the lawyer's student, or secretary or other staff is covered. It is worth noting that independent paralegals are not covered

---

[3]   *Forshaw v. Lewis* (1855), 1 Jur. N.S. 263, 156 E.R. 626.

[4]   *Lavallee Rackel and Heintz v. Canada (Attorney General)* (1998), 160 D.L.R. (4th) 508; *White, Ottenheimer and Baker v. Canada (Attorney General)* (2000), 187 D.L.R. (4th) 581 (Nfld. C.A.).

[5]   *Re Bre-X* (1998), 168 D.L.R. (4th) 215 (Alta. Q.B.); *Lawrence v. Berbrier* 2002 Carswell Ont. 474; *Re Chilcott and Clarkson Co. Ltd.* (1984), 48 O.R. (2d) 545 (Ont. C.A.); *Taberner Investments Ltd. v. Price Waterhouse* (2000), 11 C.P.C. (5th) 111.

by the privilege — a confession (or mere statement) made to a traffic court agent attracts no privilege and the agent could be subpoenaed to produce their file. Also, it is only the communication that is privileged — material evidence is not. If a client tells a lawyer where videotapes of a murder are, counsel cannot disclose this information. If, however, a lawyer goes and gets the videotapes the lawyer cannot conceal them but must turn them over to the State. As Justice Gravely noted in *Murray*, regarding videotapes of crimes alleged to be concealed by counsel:

[The solicitor] did not suggest that confidentiality of the tapes is protected under the umbrella of solicitor-client privilege and no privilege, in my opinion, attaches to this evidence. Solicitor-client privilege protects *communications* between solicitor and client .... These videotapes are not communications. They are, rather, dramatic evidence of crime and pre-existed the solicitor-client relationship.[6]

Privilege also does not apply to advice taken so as to commit a crime. If someone asks about the law without stating why, privilege likely attaches, but if the client seeks advice for the purpose of committing a crime, the privilege does not apply.[7] As Justice Stephen said in the *Cox* case:[8]

The question, therefore, is, whether, if a client applies to a legal adviser for advice intended to facilitate or to guide the client in the commission of a crime or fraud, the legal adviser being ignorant of the purpose for which his advice is wanted, the communication between the two is privileged? We expressed our opinion at the end of the argument that no such privilege existed. If it did, the result would be that a man intending to commit treason or murder might safely take legal advice for the purpose of enabling himself to do so with impunity and that the solicitor to whom the application was made would not be at liberty to give information against his client for the purpose of frustrating his criminal purpose. Consequences so monstrous reduce to an absurdity any principle or rule in which they are involved.

Finally, the solicitor-client privilege is defeated by what has been called "innocence at stake". Thus in *R. v. McClure*[9] the Supreme Court of Canada held that where a lawyer has otherwise privileged information that could assist an innocent accused, that information cannot be privileged, at least as respects the innocent accused. Such otherwise privileged information cannot be used *against* the client who had the communication,[10] however, if it is necessary to demonstrate the innocence of someone wrongfully accused, it will be available. This exception has a fairly long history. As Justice Caulfield noted in 1972:[11]

---

6   *R. v. Murray* (2000), 48 O.R. (3d) 544 at 567 (S.C.).
7   *R. v. Cox* (1884), 48 J.P. 440.
8   *Supra*, note 6, approved in *Solosky v. R.*, [1980] 1 S.C.R. 821; see also, for example, *R. v. Wijesinha*, [1995] 3 S.C.R. 422 and *U.S.A. v. Mammoth Oil Co.*, [1925] 2 D.L.R. 966 (Ont. C.A.).
9   (2001), 151 C.C.C. (3d) 321 (S.C.C.).
10   *R. v. Brown*, 2002 S.C.C. 32.
11   *R. v. Barton*, [1972] 2 All E.R. 1192 at 1994; see also *R. v. Odunbar and Logan* (1982), 68 C.C.C. (2d) 13 (Ont. C.A.).

If there are documents in the possession or control of a solicitor which, on production, help to further the defence of an accused man, then in my judgment no privilege attaches. I cannot conceive that our law would permit a solicitor or other person
to screen from a jury information which, if disclosed to the jury, would perhaps enable a man either to establish his innocence or to resist an allegation made by the
Crown.

The innocence at stake exception applies only when there is no way to put the
innocence to the court except by breaching privilege. Privilege will not be waived
except in the most serious cases where such waiver is required.

Let us now consider litigation privilege.

First, litigation privilege only applies when litigation is pending or at least anticipated. This is very important because accident reports often include very important information and cases can turn on whether such reports are admissible —
recall, for example, such statements are likely admissible against their maker as
an admission and under the hearsay exception. If an accident report was made
before anybody thought of litigation the litigation privilege cannot apply. It is not
enough to say "every accident leads to litigation"; there must be a real apprehen-
sion of concrete litigation — lawyers do not need to be retained at the time, but
their retainer must be expected.[12] As a practical matter, counsel often advise clients to prepare all accident reports in the form of a memorandum to counsel and
mark the document "For Counsel's Instruction and Review".

Second, litigation privilege only applies when a dominant[13] substantial purpose
of the document is "to instruct counsel" or "for counsel's use". The distinction
between the dominant or substantial purpose requirement is more apparent than
real and the better view is that if the document should be created, at least in part,
for litigation, the privilege likely applies.

Finally, if litigation privilege applies, it will not be lost even if the work is
shared with third parties — provided those parties have a common interest with
the disclosing party and that interest is related to the litigation.[14]

OTHER CLASS PRIVILEGES

1. HUSBAND AND WIFE

Generally speaking, except for specific sexual or child abuse offences,[15] a spouse
cannot be required to testify for the Crown against his or her spouse.[16] More

---

[12]   *Goodman & Carr v. Minister of National Revenue*, [1968] 2 O.R. 814 (H.C.).
[13]   *Hill (Litigation guardian of) v. Arcola School Division No. 72* (2000), 179 D.L.R. (4th) 539 (Sask.
       C.A.); *General Accident Assurance Co. v. Chrusz* (2000), 180 D.L.R. (4th) 241 (Ont. C.A.); *Waugh v.
       British Railways Board (H.L.(F.))*, [1980] A.C. 521; *Supercom of California Ltd. v. Sovereign General
       Insurance Co.* (1998), 37 O.R. (3d) 597 (Ont. Gen. Div.).
[14]   *General Accident, supra,* note 13.
[15]   *Canada Evidence Act,* R.S.C. 1985, c. C-5, ss. 4(2), 4(4) (Appendix B).
[16]   *Ibid.,* s. 4(1).

generally, most evidence Acts[17] provide a spousal privilege for communication made during marriage. For these privileges to apply the parties must be legally married; a cohabitation will not suffice to trigger the privilege.

2. STATE PRIVILEGE

Communications made for the purpose of governmental policy-making are privileged. This privilege is not absolute and is subject to weighing before the court.[18] The purpose of the privilege is to allow for free and frank discussion of policy matters at a high government level.

3. JUDGES' PRIVILEGE

Judges cannot be compelled to disclose their discussions or reasoning in coming to a decision.[19] This privilege extends to members of administrative tribunals who, like judges, cannot be compelled to testify regarding their decisions.[20] Jurors are, because of their judicial role, also, normally, not compellable to testify about their deliberations. However, where an issue of juror misconduct is raised, a juror may be called to testify.[21]

4. INFORMANT

Police cannot, except in criminal cases where needed to demonstrate an accused's innocence, be compelled to disclose an informant's name or identity.[22]

GENERAL POLICY TEST

There are some general principles underlying all confidential communication privileges which are usually called the Wigmore criteria:[23]

1. The communications must originate in a *confidence*.
2. This element of *confidentiality must be essential* to the full and satisfactory maintenance of the relation between the parties.

---

[17] See for example, *Evidence Act*, R.S.B.C. 1996, c. 124, s. 8; R.S.O. 1990, c. E.23, s. 11 (Appendix C); *Canada Evidence Act*, s. 4(3) (Appendix B).
[18] *Carey v. Ontario*, [1986] 2 S.C.R. 637.
[19] *MacKeigan (J.A.) v. Royal Commission (Marshall Inquiry)*, [1989] 2 S.C.R. 796; see also the earlier discussion of judges' compellability.
[20] *Ermina v. Minister of Citizenship and Immigration* (1999), 167 D.L.R. (4th) 764 (F.C. T.D.).
[21] *R. v. Budai* (2000), 180 D.L.R. (4th) 565 (B.C.C.A.).
[22] *Humphrey v. Archibald* (1893), 20 O.A.R. 267; *Solicitor General of Canada v. Royal Commission of Inquiry*, [1981] 2 S.C.R. 494.
[23] Here taken from *R. v. Gruenke*, [1991] 3 S.C.R. 263 at 284. It is proof of Dean Wigmore's greatness that two separate policy principles are called the Wigmore criteria. It will be recalled that the exceptions to the hearsay rule are justified by principles also called the Wigmore criteria.

3. The *relation* must be one which in the opinion of the community ought to be sedulously *fostered.*
4. The *injury* that would inure to the relation by the disclosure of the communications must be *greater than the benefit* thereby gained for the correct disposal of litigation.

If a communication not otherwise covered by a class privilege fits with the Wigmore criteria, the court may exclude the communication from evidence.

Privilege will arise on a case by case basis only in very narrow circumstances. The party seeking to establish privilege exists must establish by clear and cogent evidence each element of the Wigmore criteria.[24]

PRIVILEGES NOT EXISTING BY CLASS

There are many privileges not existing by class but commonly assumed to be privileged. These "non-classes" include:

Priest - Penitent
Doctor - Patient
Accountant - Client

These communications are, *prima facie*, not privileged and are admissible unless it is established for this case that the Wigmore criteria apply to exclude the evidence. So, if counsel are faced with a claim of privilege in a confessional, or, perhaps more likely, between a sexual abuse victim and a doctor, counsel has to show the Wigmore criteria apply before an exclusion applies. The court is generally disinclined to grant privilege in anything but the most obvious cases. Speaking in a fairly typical decision, dealing with a claim, for doctor-patient privilege, the Court notes: "The treatment provided...is the focus of the trial and privacy considerations of the doctor-patient relationship must yield to the extent of the litigation process".[25]

In general, the concern of the court for the full disclosure will require disclosure of communications even if it leads to a breach of confidence.

SETTLEMENT DISCUSSIONS

Public policy favours the amicable settlement of civil disputes without trial. As a result, efforts to settle civil disputes are accorded special treatment so as to foster settlement. Thus, Chief Justice Cameron notes:

---

[24] *R. v. Dupont* (1999), 165 D.L.R. (4th) 512 (Que. C.A.).
[25] *Pozdzik v. Wilson* 2002 Carswell Alta. 36, para. 3.

The authorities seem, though not very numerous, to be clear upon the first point, that letters written or communications made without prejudice, or offers made for the sake of buying peace, or to effect a compromise, are inadmissible in evidence. It seemingly being considered against public policy as having a tendency to promote litigation, and to prevent amicable settlements.

All discussions and communications, in a civil context, made for the purpose of resolving a dispute are privileged and cannot be used in evidence. Such communications are often identified by calling them "without prejudice", especially if the communications are written. Admissions during such discussions cannot be used later in court as evidence. The American *Federal Rule of Evidence* 408 describes the exclusion of settlement discussions as follows:

> Evidence of (1) furnishing or offering or promising to furnish, or (2) accepting or offering or promising to accept, a valuable consideration in compromising or attempting to compromise a claim which was disputed as to either validity or amount, is not admissible to prove liability for or invalidity of the claim or its amount. Evidence of conduct or statements made in compromise negotiations is likewise not admissible.

For the settlement privilege to apply the discussions must be designed to lead to settlement — a party cannot put privilege onto letters not intended to lead to settlement by writing "without prejudice".[26] Thus, a letter saying:

> "I am sorry for your injury and I apologize for causing your fall. You lost two days work — I'll pay you $500.00,"

is not barred by settlement privilege. A letter saying:

> "I will give you $500.00 to settle any claim you have as a result of your fall,"

is barred by settlement privilege.[27]

The privilege survives settlement, as respects third parties — an admission made during settlement cannot be used by a third party suing a party who settled.

Two conditions must be met for settlement discussions to remain privileged:

1. a civil dispute must be ongoing or contemplated;[28] and
2. the discussions must be intended as confidential, at least as regards the court.[29]

The application of these conditions seldom leads to difficulties.

---

[26] *Bank of Ottawa v. Stamco Ltd.* (1915), 8 W.W.R. 574 (Sask. T.D.).
[27] A. Best, *Evidence*, 2nd ed. (New York: Aspen Law, 1997) at 20.
[28] *Warren v. Gray Goose Stage Ltd.*, [1937] 1 W.W.R. 465 (Sask. C.A.).
[29] *Podovinikoff v. Montgomery* (1984), 58 B.C.L.R. 204 (C.A.). Accordingly, offers to compromise marked "With Prejudice" are not privileged.

OVERRIDING EXCEPTION TO PRIVILEGES

All privileges are subject to being overridden by the court if the maintenance of the privilege would pose a threat to public safety. Consider, for example, a doctor who, during counselling, learns that a patient is considering causing serious harm to a neighbour. Regardless of whether that doctor-patient communication is privileged on the case by case basis, disclosure of the danger is justified. Where serious harm to an identifiable person exists, privilege is waived, albeit only insofar as is actually necessary to avoid the danger. As the Supreme Court notes, in determining if privilege no longer applies:[30]

> There are three factors to be considered: First, is there a clear risk to an identifiable person or group of persons? Second, is there a risk of serious bodily harm or death? Third, is the danger imminent?

It must be emphasized that the public safety exception applies only to future harm — admissions of past violence, no matter how serious, do not fall within the exception.

---

[30] *Smith v. Jones* (1999), 169 D.L.R. (4th) 387 (S.C.C.).

Chapter 14

OPINION EVIDENCE

INTRODUCTION

Witnesses are asked to testify as to what they themselves said, heard, tasted, perceived. That, in part, is the basis of the hearsay rule — courts want to hear facts, not gossip, and once the court has the facts then the court (judge or jury) can try to work out what those facts mean. Put otherwise, witnesses are not called upon to speculate or make conclusions as to what is the meaning of what they perceived. The determination of what everything means is the province of the trier of fact and the purpose of the trial itself. Briefly put, this is why "opinion evidence" is generally excluded. To allow witnesses to opine as to conclusions would usurp the role of the trier of fact.

The rule against opinion evidence may be stated as:

Opinion evidence, that is conclusions drawn from facts, is inadmissible unless it is (1) an opinion of a layperson that is necessary for a clear understanding of their evidence; or (2) an expert's opinion.

OPINIONS OF LAYPEOPLE

Layperson's opinion evidence is proper where it is rationally based on perception and is needed to understand the evidence of the witness. Phipson notes,[1] "the opinions or beliefs of witnesses who are not experts are admissible ... on grounds of necessity, more direct and positive evidence being often unavailable".

For example, a witness is shown a document and asked "is this your signature?" The answer may be "yes" because the witness remembers signing, but it may also be "I don't recall signing the document, but it certainly is my signature". But that second answer is really an opinion — the witness opines the signature looks like his or hers. Most testimony of laypeople is a mishmash of recalled perception and opinion. A layperson may testify that someone was intoxicated, but that is not something directly perceived but rather something concluded from unstated perceived items. Laypeople cannot testify any other way. The key for a

---

[1] S.L. Phipson, *Phipson on Evidence*, 11th ed. (London: Sweet & Maxwell, 1970) at para. 1313.

laywitness giving an opinion is that the opinion deals with an everyday thing and the witness will not be able to give the testimony any other way.

The Supreme Court in *Graat*[2] restated the lay opinion rule in a way that makes it clear that opinions regarding everyday matters based on personal experience are to be accepted as evidence. The Court noted:

> ... there is little, if any, virtue, in any distinction resting on the tenuous, and frequently false, antithesis between fact and opinion. The line between "fact" and "opinion" is not clear.

Excluding lay opinion, when based on personal experience, serves no purpose and hinders the trier of fact:[3]

> The witnesses had an opportunity for personal observation. They were in a position to give the Court real help.

Typical examples of acceptable lay opinion include intoxication, handwriting, indentification of persons, speed, temperature and time of day.

OPINIONS OF EXPERTS

The reason expert testimony is allowed is because there are certain things a judge or a juror cannot reasonably be expected to understand without the guidance of someone skilled in a recognized field. Thus, one could give a jury all the "facts" about, say, a bridge that collapsed, but the jury would have to be taught engineering before the jury could, by itself, figure out what the facts mean. As the Court notes in *Abbey*:[4]

> An expert's function is precisely this: to provide the judge and jury with a ready-made inference which the judge and jury, due to the technical nature of the facts, are unable to formulate. ... An expert's opinion is admissible to furnish the Court with scientific information which is likely to be outside the experience and knowledge of a judge or jury.

As a result, juries are allowed to hear the opinions of persons with special skills, in recognized areas of expertise, on matters the jury cannot understand without expert advice.

The rule regarding expert testimony can be stated as follows:

If specialized knowledge will assist the trier of fact to understand the evidence or a fact in issue, a witness qualified as an expert by knowledge, skill, experience or training may testify by way of opinion.

---

[2] *R. v. Graat*, [1982] 2 S.C.R. 819 at 835.
[3] *Ibid.*, at 836.
[4] *R. v. Abbey*, [1982] 2 S.C.R. 24 at 42, quoting *Turner* (1974), 60 Crim. App. R. 80, at 83, *per* Lawton L.J.

Phipson[5] states the expert testimony rule thusly:

> The opinions of skilled witnesses are admissible whenever the subject is one upon which competency to form an opinion can only be acquired by a course of special study or experience.

An expert's opinion is admissible only if it is needed to allow the trier of fact to make sense of the evidence.[6] If the trier of fact can properly come to a conclusion without the help of an expert, then such evidence is superfluous and should be excluded.[7] The focus of consideration of allowing expert testimony must be whether the trier of fact needs the assistance an expert can give.

It must be emphasized that expert opinion evidence is allowed as an exception to the general rule against opinion evidence. There is a material risk that the opinion of a highly polished leader in an art or science will be given too much weight. As the Ontario Court of Appeal notes:[8]

> The opinion rule is a general rule of exclusion. Witnesses testify as to facts. As a general rule, they are not allowed to give any opinion about those facts. Opinion evidence is generally *inadmissible*. Opinion evidence is generally excluded because it is a fundamental principle of our system of justice that it is up to the trier of fact to draw inferences from the evidence and to form his or her opinions on the issues in the case. Hence, ..., it is only when the trier of fact is unable to form his or her own conclusions without help that an exception to the opinion rule may be made and expert opinion evidence admitted. It is the expert's precise function to provide the trier of fact with a ready-made inference from the facts which the judge and jury, due to the nature of the facts, are unable to formulate themselves.

Opinion evidence of experts is admissible if necessary to assist the trier of fact. The potential prejudicial effect of the evidence must not outweigh its value to the trier of fact.[9] Accordingly, before admitting expert testimony a court must consider the following questions:[10]

(a) Will the proposed expert opinion evidence enable the trier of fact to appreciate the technicalities of a matter in issue?

(b) Will it provide information which is likely to be outside the experience of the trier of fact?

(c) Is the trier of fact unlikely to form a correct judgment about a matter in issue if unassisted by the expert opinion evidence?

(d) Is the need for the evidence sufficient to overcome its potential prejudicial effect?

---

5 *Supra*, note 1, at para. 1280.
6 *R. v. Mohan*, [1994] 2 S.C.R. 9: "helpfulness" is not the standard; "necessity" is required.
7 *R. v. Marquard*, [1993] 4 S.C.R. 223.
8 *R. v. K.(A.)* (1999), 176 D.L.R. (4th) 665 at 699, citing *R. v. Abbey* (1982), 68 C.C.C. (2d) 394 (S.C.C.) at 409, 138 D.L.R. (3d) 202.
9 *R. v. Parrott*, [2001] 1 S.C.R. 178.
10 *R. v. K.(A.)*, *supra*, note 8 at 707.

BASIS OF EXPERTISE

Obviously, for a person to give expert testimony there must be some basis to call that person an expert. The qualifying of an expert requires proof that (1) this person has some special or peculiar knowledge of their subject and (2) the subject they are expert in is a legitimate area of study. The requirement of special knowledge or skill does not require academic or professional qualifications,[11] although generally experts tend to be academics or professionals. As Chief Justice Falconbridge notes:[12]

> ... it does not matter whether such [expert] knowledge has been acquired by study of scientific works or by practical observation. Hence, one who is an old hunter, and has thus had much experience in the use of firearms, may be as well qualified to testify as to the appearance which a gun recently fired would present as a highly-educated and skilled gunsmith.

The determination of whether an area is one in which expertise is even possible is problematic. Merely because people have devoted time and effort to a topic is not grounds to suggest the topic has value for the court. It is difficult to state an authoritative test, but, broadly put, a topic must have reached a level of general acceptance as being a valid area of human endeavour before it can form the basis of expertise for an expert opinion. Before expert opinion can be accepted, the field of expertise has to have been generally accepted by the scientific, professional or academic community as having achieved a threshold level of reliability. Hallmarks of such reliability include:[13]

- falsifiability;
- peer review and publication;
- acceptance by the relevant academic community;
- a known error rate; and
- existence and maintenance of standards.

Thus, the study of astrobiology, albeit obscure, is likely to be a topic an expert could testify on,[14] whereas UFOology is not likely to be so accepted. Similarly, even in recognized fields, such as history, where there is no general consensus of academic or practical views, evidence cannot be admitted. Thus, the Court in a native lands claim, notes:[15]

---

[11]   *R. v. Wade* (1994), 89 C.C.C. (3d) 39 (Ont. C.A.).
[12]   *Rice v. Sockett* (1912), 27 O.L.R. 410 at 413, quoting *State v. Davis*, 33 S.E. Rev. 449, 55 So. Car. 339 (1899), cited in *Words and Phrases Judicially Defined*, vol. 3, p. 295.
[13]   *R. v. Murrin* (2000), 181 D.L.R. (4th) 320 (B.C.S.C.); see also *Daubert v. Merrell Dow Pharmaceuticals*, 509 U.S. 579 (1993).
[14]   Although it is difficult to think of a case where Martian plant life would be relevant!
[15]   *Delgamuukw v. British Columbia*, [1990] C.N.L.R. 20, 27.

... for purposes of litigation, historians cannot usefully pronounce of matters of broad inference which may be open to serious disagreement or to subsequent revision.

Unless there is a settled, and accepted, expertise, an expert's opinion is inadmissible.

Acceptance of an expert's field seldom poses real problems as the vast majority of experts are called to testify as to matters within traditional academic or professional fields.

Experts are not qualified generally; an expert witness is allowed to opine only within the area in which they are found to have expertise. Best[16] comments:

> Just how specifically a person's experience and training must relate to the topic of testimony is an issue on which trial courts have great discretion. In products liability cases, for example, a manufacturer will often contend that the only truly appropriate witness to testify about safety aspects of its product is someone who has designed that particular type of product. A plaintiff in such a case will often seek to qualify a person with general experience in product design as an expert. Obviously, if courts held that an expert must be someone who has worked on the specific type of product that allegedly harmed the plaintiff, the supply of experts would be reduced. On the other hand, if courts are extremely permissive in allowing generalists to testify as experts, or in allowing witnesses with expertise in one field to generalize and apply it to other fields, the value of the expert testimony will be considerably weakened.

Often several experts must be called to provide testimony covering all areas for which opinion evidence is needed since a single expert does not have a broad enough expertise. The federal and provincial evidence Acts[17] limit the number of experts who may be called at trial without leave of the court, although such limits are set high enough to ensure they are seldom met. The limits are intended to save court time and acknowledge that cases are not to be decided on the basis of how many expert witnesses each side calls.

FACTUAL BASIS OF EXPERT TESTIMONY

An expert gives an opinion as to the interpretation of facts — almost invariably (doctors doing a physical exam are the only common exception) experts have no direct knowledge of the facts they base their opinions on. The expert did not see the bridge collapse or the gun fire. In order to determine if the opinion is of any value, the facts it is based on must be described and proven. As Phipson notes,[18] "where the opinion of experts is based on reports of facts, those facts ... must be proved independently".

---

[16] A. Best, *Evidence*, 2nd ed. (New York: Aspen Law, 1997) at 163.
[17] *Canada Evidence Act*, R.S.C. 1985, c. C-5, s. 7 (Appendix B) and, for example, *Manitoba Evidence Act*, R.S.M. 1987, c. E150, s. 25; *Evidence Act*, R.S.N.B. 1973, c. E-11, s. 23; Ontario *Evidence Act*, R.S.O. 1990, c. E.23, s. 12 (Appendix C).
[18] *Supra*, note 1 at para. 1280.

Accordingly, expert testimony is usually given by way of a hypothetical question that sets out the facts the expert's opinion is based on. This allows the trier of fact to decide if the expert's testimony is worth anything. After all, if the expert's opinion is based on facts not accepted by the trier of fact, the opinion is of little or no value. The usual form of question is thus.

"Now, if we assume a, b and c to be facts, what, if any, opinion do you have about d?"

If the court rejects a, b or c, it can judge the expert's view accordingly. Furthermore, cross-examination is made possible — the expert can be asked, "what if, instead of a, b, and c, x, y and z were true"? All this said, the hypothetical question is not required if previous evidence clearly shows the factual basis of the opinion.[19]

The factual basis for an expert's opinion sometimes causes a concern for hearsay. Specifically, what if the expert's opinion is based on out-of-court assertions that are not otherwise proven? Considerable debate has surrounded this issue, but it appears the best analysis is that, provided otherwise acceptable, an expert's testimony, even if partially based on unproven hearsay, remains admissible, albeit subject to less weight.[20] Obviously, whenever possible, it is prudent to prove all of the factual bases of an expert's opinion.[21]

OPINION EVIDENCE AND ULTIMATE ISSUE

Occasionally expert testimony is objected to as being directed to the "ultimate issue" of the dispute. The concern is that an expert opinion on the very issue the court is to decide tends to usurp the role of the court as decision-maker.[22] Such concerns are not determinative in modern Canadian law. As the Court notes in *R. v. B. (R.H.)*:[23]

> While care must be taken to ensure that the judge or jury, and not the expert, makes the final decision on all issues in the case, it has long been accepted that expert evidence on matters of fact should not be excluded simply because it suggests answers to issues which are at the core of the dispute before the Court.

At most, the ultimate issue rule amounts to a principle that ought to govern a court's consideration of an expert's opinion.

---

[19]   *R. v. Bleta*, [1964] S.C.R. 561.
[20]   *R. v. Lavallee*, [1990] 1 S.C.R. 852.
[21]   *R. v. Abbey*, [1982] 2 S.C.R. 24.
[22]   *North Cheshire and Manchester Brewery Co. v. Manchester Brewery Co.*, [1899] A.C. 83 (H.L.).
[23]   *R. v. B. (R.H.)* (1994), 29 C.R. (4th) 113 at 114 (S.C.C.).

Chapter 15

EVIDENCE OF CHARACTER

CHARACTER OF AN ACCUSED

Evidence of bad character is not admissible to prove an accused committed a criminal act.[1] Best notes:[2]

> In evidence law, "character" means the type of person someone is — honest, dishonest, generous, selfish, friendly, nasty, careless, cautious, hot-headed, or calm, for example. A basic rule (with some exceptions) is that evidence of a person's character may not be introduced to support an inference that the person acted on a specific occasion in conformity with that character.

That said, an accused may adduce evidence of a community reputation for good character.[3] If an accused adduces such evidence of good character, the State may rebut it by cross-examining about incidents in the accused's past.[4]

An accused seeking to show good character may call evidence of general reputation in the community.[5] The personal opinion of the witness as to the accused's character is not properly put in evidence,[6] although the witness may describe specific acts of good conduct in giving testimony.[7]

In responding to evidence of good character the State may call (1) general evidence of bad character[8] (although a witness's personal opinion of the accused's character is inadmissible[9]) (2) evidence of similar acts[10] or (3) cross-examine the accused about specific past disreputable acts.[11]

---

[1] *R. v. G. (S.G.)*, [1997] 2 S.C.R. 716. Such evidence is permitted to determine if an offender is a dangerous offender; see s. 757 of the *Criminal Code*, R.S.C. 1985, c. C-46 (Appendix A).
[2] A. Best, *Evidence*, 2nd ed. (New York: Aspen Law, 1997) at 29.
[3] *R. v. Kootenay* (1994), 27 C.R. (4th) 376 (Alta. C.A.).
[4] *R. v. McNamara* (1981), 56 C.C.C. (2d) 193 (Ont. C.A.).
[5] *R. v. Mohan*, [1994] 2 S.C.R. 9.
[6] *R. v. Clarke* (1998), 129 C.C.C. (3d) 1 (Ont. C.A.); *R. v. Demyen* (1976), 31 C.C.C. (2d) 383 (Sask. C.A.).
[7] *R. v. Mohan*, *supra*, note 5.
[8] *R. v. McNamara*, *supra*, note 4.
[9] *R. v. Tilley* (1953), 17 C.R. 1 (Ont. C.A.).
[10] *R. v. McFadden* (1981), 28 C.R. (3d) 33 (B.C.C.A.).
[11] *R. v. McNamara*, *supra*, note 4. See also s. 666 of the *Criminal Code* (Appendix A).

The question of character of an accused was dealt with extensively in *McFadden*,[12] a decision of the British Columbia Court of Appeal. The Court notes:

> On the other hand, character (in the sense of general reputation and an actual moral disposition ...) cannot be an issue in a criminal case unless the accused makes it an issue by leading evidence of his good character. Logically, knowledge of the character of a person would assist in determining whether he is the type of person who would, or who would not, do the particular act, and evidence of the character of an accused should be admissible, therefore, when the doing of any act is in issue. Logic notwithstanding, the prosecution may not adduce evidence of the bad character of an accused unless the accused does put his character in issue. Some of the reasons commonly advanced for this principle are confusion of issues, unfair surprise and unfair, or undue, prejudice ....

> The purpose of evidence of good character is to show that the accused is a person who is not likely to have committed the act with which he is charged, and also to enhance his credibility. An accused may adduce evidence of good character: (1) by calling witnesses; (2) by cross-examining Crown witnesses on the subject; and (3) by giving testimony. Normally, he may lead evidence of good character by adducing evidence only of his general reputation, not by adducing evidence of specific acts which might tend to establish his character. The Crown may call evidence of bad character in rebuttal, but such evidence also must relate only to general reputation... An accused may put his character in issue in the course of giving his testimony, not by giving evidence of his general reputation, but by making assertions which tend to show that he is a person of good character, particularly with regard to the aspect of his character which is in issue. Obviously, the Crown may rebut this testimony by calling evidence of bad character, but may the Crown call evidence only of general reputation, or may the Crown call evidence other than the evidence of general reputation? In some circumstances, the Crown may call evidence of specific incidents in rebutting evidence of good character. For example, ... the Crown could prove previous convictions as evidence of bad character. The Crown may also adduce similar fact evidence to rebut evidence of good character .... There may be other circumstances in which the Crown may lead evidence of specific instances in rebuttal of the testimony of good character.

It is essential to be clear that evidence tending to show an accused in a negative light is not, because of that tendency, inadmissible. Calling evidence to dispute good character does not breach the prohibition on seeking to prove an accused guilty by the use of bad character evidence. The rule "excluding such evidence applies only where the sole purpose of evidence touching on character is to show the accused is the type of person likely to have committed the offence".[13] Evidence called for another reason does not breach the prohibition.

---

[12] *Supra*, note 10 at 37-38.
[13] *R. v. Lamirande* 2002 Carswell Man. 151 (C.A.) at para. 69; see also *R. v. B. (F.F.)* [1993] 1 S.C.R. 697 and *R. v. G. (S.G.)*, [1997] 2 S.C.R. 716.

CHARACTER OF NON-PARTIES

In an assault case, can an accused say the victim is generally known as a violent person and so self-defence is plausible? And can the State then adduce evidence the victim was generally known as a peaceable person and so unlikely to have precipitated violence? Yes[14] and yes.[15]

There is no limit, other than relevance and materiality, to proving character of third parties. And such character can be proven by reference to specific acts of charity or violence and not only by general community reputation.[16] But, note, if the character of the victim is put in question it is a short step to suggesting the accused is of good character and if that step is taken, even by accident, the State may adduce evidence of bad character. If such evidence exists it may be devastating.

The character of a victim of crime is, as mentioned, relevant to make a claim of, say, self-defence, more likely justified.[17] This is true regardless of whether the accused knew of the victim's propensity for violence or not. As Justice Martin notes in *Scopelliti*:[18]

> I agree, of course, that evidence of previous acts of violence by the deceased, not known to the accused, must be confined to evidence of previous acts of violence which may legitimately and reasonably assist the jury in arriving at a just verdict with respect to the accused's claim of self-defence.

Since there is a danger that evidence of a victim's bad character will be misused, the evidence must be treated carefully and its probative value carefully weighed. Justice Martin continues:[19]

> Since evidence of prior acts of violence by the deceased is likely to arouse feelings of hostility against the deceased, there must inevitably be some element of discretion in the determination whether the proffered evidence has sufficient probative value for the purpose for which it is tendered to justify its admission. Moreover, great care must be taken to ensure that such evidence, if admitted, is not misused.

Courts will be loath to restrict the right of an accused to call material and relevant evidence, even when that evidence may have some prejudicial effect. Thus, the Supreme Court of Canada notes, "the prejudice must substantially outweigh the value of the evidence before a judge can exclude evidence relevant to a defence allowed by law".[20]

---

[14] *R. v. Dubois* (1976), 30 C.C.C. (2d) 412 (Ont. C.A.).
[15] *R. v. Soares* (1987), 34 C.C.C. (3d) 403 (Ont. C.A.).
[16] *R. v. Yaeck* (1991), 10 C.R. (4th) 1 (Ont. C.A.); *R. v. Varga* (2001), 150 D.A.C. 358.
[17] Consent, in sexual matters, has been limited by ss. 273.1 and 273.2 of the *Criminal Code* (Appendix A).
[18] *R. v. Scopelliti* (1981), 34 O.R. (2d) 524 at 538 (Ont. C.A.).
[19] *Ibid.*, at 538-39.
[20] *R. v. Seaboyer* (1991), 7 C.R. (4th) 117 at 139 (S.C.C.).

COMPLAINANTS IN SEXUAL OFFENCES

Historically, there has been a significant concern that defence counsel in sexual assault cases abused their ability to cross-examine complainants regarding character. The fear was that profoundly intrusive examinations exploring the sexual history of the complainant discouraged proper prosecution, were of no assistance to the court and needlessly humiliated complainants in sexual assault cases.

Recognizing these concerns, Parliament amended the *Criminal Code* and created a "rape shield" provision. Section 276 of the *Criminal Code*, which applies to relevant evidence disclosing the sexual experiences of a complainant, provides for the exclusion of such evidence unless its probative value is substantially outweighed by the need to ensure a fair trial. Specifically, s. 276 provides:

276.(1) In proceedings in respect of an offence [dealing with sexual impropriety] evidence that the complainant has engaged in sexual activity, whether with the accused or with any other person, is not admissible to support an inference that, by reason of the sexual nature of that activity, the complainant
(a)   is more likely to have consented to the sexual activity that forms the subject-matter of the charge; or
(b)   is less worthy of belief.

(2) In proceedings in respect of an offence referred to in subsection (1), no evidence shall be adduced by or on behalf of the accused that the complainant has engaged in sexual activity other than the sexual activity that forms the subject-matter of the charge, whether with the accused or with any other person, unless the judge, provincial court judge or justice determines, ... that the evidence
(a)   is of specific instances of sexual activity;
(b)   is relevant to an issue at trial; and
(c)   has significant probative value that is not substantially outweighed by the danger of prejudice to the proper administration of justice.

(3) In determining whether evidence is admissible under subsection (2), the judge, provincial court judge or justice shall take into account
(a)   the interests of justice, including the right of the accused to make a full answer and defence;
(b)   society's interest in encouraging the reporting of sexual assault offences;
(c)   whether there is a reasonable prospect that the evidence will assist in arriving at a just determination in the case;
(d)   the need to remove from the fact-finding process any discriminatory belief or bias;
(e)   the risk that the evidence may unduly arouse sentiments of prejudice, sympathy or hostility in the jury;
(f)   the potential prejudice to the complainant's personal dignity and right of privacy;
(g)   the right of the complainant and of every individual to personal security and to the full protection and benefit of the law; and
(h)   any other factor that the judge, provincial court judge or justice considers relevant.

In addition, general sexual reputation cannot be used to prove a complainant unworthy of belief. Section 277 of the *Criminal Code* provides:

... evidence of sexual reputation, whether general or specific, is not admissible for the purpose of challenging or supporting the credibility of the complainant.

In holding evidence relating to the sexual activity of a complainant to a higher standard than other complainants, the courts have not become blind to evidence that could demonstrate innocence. As the Supreme Court of Canada notes in *Darrach*:[21]

Section 276 is designed to prevent the use of evidence of prior sexual activity for improper purposes. The requirement of "significant probative value" serves to exclude evidence of trifling relevance that, even though not used to support the two forbidden inferences, would still endanger the "proper administration of justice." The Court has recognized that there are inherent "damages and disadvantages presented by the admission of such evidence".

The court, in applying the "rape shield" law balances the rights of both the complainant and the accused.

PROPENSITY AND EXPERT TESTIMONY

If a particular state of mind or mental capacity is grossly abnormal, but the subject of a particular field of expertise, an expert may offer opinion as to whether or not the accused has that mental capacity. In theory this is not proof of bad character but rather a psychiatric fact, just as proof of a physiological fact is admissible. There is a fine line between, for instance, a mere disposition for violence (which is not the subject of expert evidence) and a peculiar psychiatric tendency (which may be the subject of such evidence). As the Court notes in *Robertson*:[22]

In my view, psychiatric evidence with respect to disposition or its absence is admissible on behalf of the defence, if relevant to an issue in the case, where the disposition in question constitutes a characteristic feature of an abnormal group falling within the range of study of the psychiatrist, and from whom the jury can, therefore, receive appreciable assistance with respect to a matter outside the knowledge of persons who have not made a special study of the subject. A *mere* disposition for violence, however, is not so uncommon as to constitute a feature characteristic of an abnormal group falling within the special field of study of the psychiatrist and permitting psychiatric evidence to be given of the absence of such disposition in the accused.

---

[21] *R. v. Darrach* (2000), 148 C.C.C. (3d) 97 at 119, citing *R. v. Seaboyer, supra*, note 20.
[22] *R. v. Robertson* (1975), 21 C.C.C. (2d) 385 at 429-30 (Ont. C.A.).

Expert testimony of an accused's mental state is proper but only if relevant to an issue other than mere propensity.[23] One way to look at the issue is to ask whether the evidence could be properly analogized to testimony regarding a physiological fact — is it similar to evidence that, say, the killer was left-handed? If the analogy between physiologic and psychiatric fact is close, then, subject to prejudicial effect overwhelming probative value,[24] the expert evidence is admissible.

PROPENSITY AND PREJUDICE

As can be seen by the admission of propensity evidence where such evidence is analogous to a physiological fact, there is no blanket rejection of propensity where its probative value is very high.[25] The determination of admission is based on a balancing of probative value and prejudicial effect. Justice Cory notes,[26] "evidence of propensity or disposition may be relevant to the crime charged, but it is usually inadmissible because its slight probative value is ultimately outweighed by its highly prejudicial effect". To similar effect is the decision in *R. v. B. (C.R.)* noting:[27]

> While the language of some of the assertions of the exclusionary rule admittedly might be taken to suggest that mere disposition evidence can <u>never</u> be admissible, the preponderant view prevailing in Canada is the view taken by the majority in *Boardman* — evidence of propensity, while generally inadmissible, may exceptionally be admitted where the probative value of the evidence in relation to an issue in question is so high that it displaces the heavy prejudice which will inevitably inure to the accused where evidence of prior immoral or illegal acts is presented to the jury. [Emphasis in original]

Only where probative value is very high will the prejudicial effect of propensity evidence be outweighed.

---

[23] *R. v. Pascoe* (1997), 5 C.R. (5th) 341 (Ont. C.A.).
[24] *Ibid.*
[25] *R. v. Handy* 2002 S.C.C. 56 at paras. 59-68.
[26] *R. v. Arp* (1998), 20 C.R. (5th) 1 at para. 40.
[27] [1990] 1 S.C.R. 717 at 730-731.

Chapter 16

SIMILAR FACT EVIDENCE AND CREDIBILITY

CHARACTER AND PSYCHIATRIC PROPENSITY

In order to prove a case, the plaintiff/prosecutor must demonstrate the facts alleged and cannot show the defendant/accused is a "bad person" and therefore more likely than not to be liable.[1] An accused is on trial for their acts and not their character. The general rule is set out in *Makin*:[2]

> It is undoubtedly not competent for the prosecution to adduce evidence tending to shew that the accused has been guilty of criminal acts other than those covered by the indictment, for the purpose of leading to the conclusion that the accused is a person likely from his criminal conduct or character to have committed the offence for which he is being tried. On the other hand, the mere fact that the evidence adduced tends to shew the commission of other crimes does not render it inadmissible if it be relevant to an issue before the jury, and it may be so relevant if it bears upon the question whether the acts alleged to constitute the crime charged in the indictment were designed or accidental, or to rebut a defence which would otherwise be open to the accused.

The key is that evidence of similar acts can be admitted, even though it may incidentally show bad character, if it is otherwise relevant. You can prove guilt, and thereby incidentally show bad character; what you cannot do is prove bad character and thereby prove guilt. The rule against similar facts, except in exceptional cases, is not new. As Chief Justice Holt commented, when faced with alleged similar facts in 1692:[3]

> "Are you going to arraign his whole life? Away, away, that ought not to be; that is nothing to the matter."

Thus in *Makin*, a dead baby was the subject of a charge of murder. The Makins were "baby farmers". They took unwanted children into their care in return for money. The body of a baby was found buried in their garden. The burial was clearly irregular, but this standing alone was not necessarily proof of murder —

---

[1] See, for example, *R. v. G. (S.G.)*, [1997] 2 S.C.R. 716 at 730.
[2] *Makin v. Attorney General for New South Wales*, [1894] A.C. 57 at 65 (P.C.).
[3] *Harrison's Trial* (1692), 12 How. St. Tr. 833 at 864.

nothing about the body showed murder. The State adduced evidence of at least nine more dead babies buried on the accused's property — the evidence of the other dead babies did show the accused was very wicked, but the legal basis of allowing proof of the other dead babies was to rebut accidental death. One infant may die accidentally, even two, but not ten and counting.

In an important article on "Similar Facts"[4] Lord Hoffman wrote:

> This evidence [of all the other babies] was relevant on account of the statistical improbability that a number of children which the Makins had at various times had in their care would all have died of natural causes. From this it followed that they were likely to have been murdered and once this stage of reasoning had been reached it was a short step to concluding the Makins had murdered them. But it is fair to say that in the *Makin* case, the similar fact evidence was not used to show that the accused were the sort of people likely to have committed the offence. On the contrary, any view of the character of the Makins is derived from the conclusion they are guilty and not vice versa.

Put somewhat differently, Justice Iacobucci notes:[5]

> ... evidence which tends to show bad character or a criminal disposition on the part of the accused is admissible if (1) relevant to some other issue beyond disposition or character, or (2) *the probative value outweighs the prejudicial effect.* [Emphasis added.]

The concern about similar facts arises from the perception that the prejudicial effect of allowing this type of evidence may overwhelm any probative value the evidence has. As Justice Dickson noted:[6]

> ... the Crown should not adduce evidence of other similar acts unless it appears from what was said at the time of arrest or from the evidence presented by the Crown at trial or from the cross-examination of Crown witnesses or from the evidence of defence witnesses that the defence which the evidence of similar acts is intended to refute is really in issue; otherwise the accused may be gravely prejudiced by evidence introduced ostensibly to meet a possible defence but in truth to bolster the case for the Crown.

The dangers of admitting evidence of past conduct are well known to Canadian courts:[7]

> Nobody is charged with having a "general" disposition or propensity for theft or violence or whatever. The exclusion thus generally prohibits character evidence to be used as circumstantial proof of conduct, i.e., to allow an inference from the "similar facts" that the accused has the propensity or disposition to do the type of

---

4   (1975), 91 L.Q. Rev. 193.
5   *R. v. B. (F.F.)*, [1993] 1 S.C.R. 697 at 731.
6   In dissent in *R. v. Leblanc*, [1977] 1 S.C.R. 339 at 348.
7   *R. v. Handy* 2002 S.C.C. 56 at para. 31, citing Great Britain Law Commission, Consultation Paper No. 141, *Evidence in Criminal Proceedings: Previous Misconduct of a Defendant* (1996) at §7.2.

acts charged and is therefore guilty of the offence. The danger is that the jury might be confused by the multiplicity of incidents and put more weight than is logically justified on the ex-wife's testimony ("reasoning prejudice") or by convicting based on bad personhood ("moral prejudice").

The real question to be asked is whether the probative value of the evidence sought to be adduced outweighs the prejudicial effect of admitting the similar facts. As the Supreme Court notes in *Arp*:[8]

> ... in considering whether similar fact evidence should be admitted the basic and fundamental question that must be determined is whether the probative value of the evidence outweighs its prejudicial effect.

Since evidence of prior actions can easily be given too much weight, the balance between probative value and prejudicial effect is of great significance. Another element of prejudice is the difficulty a defendant may have responding to the "similar facts". As Justice Binnie notes in a case where the Crown sought to adduce evidence of numerous prior acts:[9]

> From the [accused's] point of view, introduction of the similar fact evidence radically changed the trial. He was on trial for one incident, to which he pleaded not guilty, but was instead confronted with eight different incidents, of which seven were not the subject matter of any charge.

An accused can be overwhelmed by the attempt to disprove similar facts — such prejudice can be very real.

HOW SIMILAR IS SIMILAR?

Now, how "similar" must "similar facts" be to the case at bar? It is hard to give a fixed rule, but a phrase often used by the Court is "striking similarity". Thus, in *R. v. Rosenberg*[10] Judge Graburn wrote:

> While it is true that common sense and the law do not require perfect similarity and the dissimilarities do not rule out evidence of similar facts, ... I am not satisfied that the similarities here are so striking ... that it would be an affront to common sense to exclude the evidence. I say this particularly in the context that ordinarily a person is only required to defend the charge against him.

The *Drysdale*[11] case is a good example of evidence that was not similar enough. The accused was charged with murdering a child. The Crown adduced

---

[8]   *R. v. Arp* (1999), 166 D.L.R. (4th) 296 at 315; see also *R. v. B.(L.)* (1997), 116 C.C.C. (3d) 481 (Ont. C.A.); *R. v. F.(D.S.)*, [1999] 169 D.L.R. (4th) 639 (Ont. C.A.).
[9]   *R. v. Handy* 2002 S.C.C. 56 at para. 25.
[10]   (1978), 42 C.C.C. (3d) 49 at 55 (Ont. Co. Ct.).
[11]   *R. v. Drysdale*, [1969] 2 C.C.C. 141 (Man. C.A.).

evidence that showed the accused was an awful man — he even beat up dogs — but not evidence of killing other children. The court rejected, on appeal, all the evidence of dissimilar events which showed the wickedness of the accused. The bad character of an accused is not relevant, but similar acts can show, among other things, identity. The similarity must be to a high degree,[12] although the standard to apply to the main inference from similar fact evidence is to a balance of probability.[13] The onus to establish that the probative value of the similar fact evidence outweighs its prejudicial effect rests with the Crown, albeit to a civil standard. Unless that onus is met, a court may not admit similar fact evidence. Thus, the Supreme Court notes, in *Handy*,[14]

> "... similar fact evidence [is] *prima facie* inadmissible and ... the Crown did not discharge the onus of establishing on a balance of probabilities that its probative value outweighed its undoubted prejudice.
>
> ....
>
> A trial judge has no discretion to admit similar fact evidence whose prejudicial effect outweighs its probative value.

The admission of similar fact evidence is all a matter of degree — perhaps the best thing to do is consider if coincidence is reasonable as a hypothesis. As the Supreme Court has noted:[15]

> ... a principled approach to the admission of similar fact evidence will in all cases rest on the finding that the accused's involvement in the alleged similar acts or counts is unlikely to be the product of coincidence. This conclusion ensures that the evidence has sufficient probative force to be admitted....

A bad man may have a family member murdered by a stranger — but if he strangles young girls in a particular way and then is accused of doing it again coincidence seems implausible.

CIVIL CASES

The similar fact rule also applies in civil cases. The element of prejudice is less important but the concept is the same — a civil case is limited to the facts in issue, not history, and unless there is some reason to believe similar prior acts have probative value exceeding prejudicial effect, the prior circumstances are not admissible. That said, it is easier to adduce evidence of similar facts in a civil case than in a criminal matter. Broadly put, the risk of unfair prejudice is lower in a

---

12   *R. v. Arp* (1998), 20 C.R. (5th) 1 (S.C.C.).
13   *Ibid.*
14   *R. v. Handy* 2002 S.C.C. 56 at paras. 151 and 153.
15   *Arp, supra*, note 12 at 20.

civil case and so the danger of a flawed decision is reduced. Thus, the Court notes:[16]

> Evidence of similar facts is admissible when it is logically probative or relevant to a material issue in the case, and it is not unduly oppressive or unfair to the other side.

In the civil context, similar fact evidence ought generally to be admitted, unless so to do would be unfair or oppressive.[17]

The "Barber's Itch" case is the classic civil similar facts case. In *Hales v. Kerr*[18] a customer went to a barber and got a shave. During the shave he was nicked and developed a disease called barber's itch. The disease is passed, among other ways, by unclean razors. As a result, the plaintiff lost work and had to see doctors thereby incurring medical expenses and the like. The customer sued and called other customers who also caught barber's itch after being shaved at the barbershop. The barber denied the disease came from his shop and said the testimony of the other customers was excluded by the similar facts rule — the Court disagreed. It wrote:

> It is not legitimate to charge a man with an act of negligence on a day in October and to ask a jury to infer that he was negligent on that day because he was negligent on every day in September. The defendant may have mended his ways before the day named in October; moreover, he does not come to trial prepared to meet all the allegations of previous negligence. There are many reasons why such evidence is not admissible on such an issue. But where the issue is that the defendant pursues a course of conduct which is dangerous to his neighbours it is legitimate to shew that his conduct has been a source of danger on other occasions, and it is a legitimate inference that, having caused injury on those occasions, it has caused injury in the plaintiff's case also. No doubt in a trial at *nisi prius* the judge must exercise great care and caution in the admission of such evidence as this, so as to avoid prejudicing the defendant's case. In the present case I think the evidence of the two witnesses Cheverton and Currie was admissible on the ground that it went to establish a dangerous practice carried on in the defendant's establishment.

Evidence of similar facts both prior to and subsequent to the acts forming the basis of the dispute can be admitted. Such facts can prove motivation or intention.[19]

---

[16] *Durrani v. Augier* (2000), 190 D.L.R. (4th) 183 at 192 (Ont. S.C.J.), citing J. Sopinka, S. Lederman and A. Bryant, *The Law of Evidence*, 2nd ed. (Markham, Ont.: Butterworths, 1999) at 602.

[17] *N.(K.) v. Alberta* (1999), 174 D.L.R. (4th) 366 (Alta. Q.B.); but see *Statton v. Johnson* (1999), 172 D.L.R. (4th) 535 at 554 (B.C.C.A.) where the Court held that, even in civil cases, only where "the objective impossibility of coincidence is established" does similar fact evidence have "sufficient probative value to be admitted".

[18] [1908] 2 K.B. 601 at 604-05.

[19] S.L. Phipson, *Phipson on Evidence*, 11th ed. (London: Sweet & Maxwell, 1970) at para. 502.

Chapter 17

CREDIBILITY

COLLATERAL FACTS RULE

The collateral facts rule prohibits evidence the sole purpose of which is to contradict a witness's testimony regarding a collateral fact.[1] A collateral fact is a fact that is neither relevant nor material. Put otherwise, if a question is put to a witness regarding a fact that does not impact on an issue in the lawsuit, the answer to that question, regardless of what the answer is, cannot be challenged by extrinsic evidence.[2] The rule can be stated as follows:

No extrinsic evidence may be called to contradict a witness on matters solely raised to challenge the witness's credibility.

The purpose of the collateral facts rule is to limit evidence called to that which is truly of assistance to the court.[3]

CROSS-EXAMINING ON PRIOR STATEMENT

There are two ways a prior statement of a witness can be used.

First, a statement by a party may be adduced by an opponent to prove its truth. This is merely the admission exception to the hearsay rule:

As a general rule, anything a party says may be used against that party even though it is hearsay.

So, if you have a party opposite in the witness box and they say X, you can call evidence that that party once said Y and you can rely on Y for its truth. The prior statement is used to prove its truth.

Second, you can use a prior inconsistent statement to cross-examine a witness. In such cases, the prior statement is not admitted to prove its truth (unless it is adopted by the witness) but only to show the witness's testimony is unreliable.

---

[1]   *R. v. Mulvihill* (1914), 22 C.C.C. 354 (B.C.C.A.).
[2]   *R. v. Steinberg*, [1931] S.C.R. 421.
[3]   *R. v. B.(A.R.)* (1998), 18 C.R. (5th) 241 (Ont. C.A.).

Note the very limited use of such prior statement — the statement is not evidence of the facts contained therein — the statement is only evidence of testimonial weakness. The prior statement can remove the present testimony's effect but not more.

A prior inconsistent statement may also be admissible as proof of its contents, even if not adopted by the witness, if the criteria of necessity and reliability are met.[4] This is merely a special example of the general acceptance of hearsay not otherwise admissible on a case by case basis. A common practice of police is to videotape, under oath, the initial statement of a complainant. If the complainant is unavailable, or ultimately refuses to testify,[5] the statement *may* be admissible to prove its truth.

PRIOR CRIMINAL CONVICTIONS

The prior criminal convictions of any witness are relevant insofar as they impact on credibility. This is true of accused as witnesses as well as any other witness.[6] An accused may not be convicted on the basis they were a bad person. Thus, in theory anyway, the accused's criminal past is only relevant for credibility and nothing else. Of course, as a practical matter, once the record is before the court, the past conduct and character will colour the case and make a conviction more likely.

As a tactical matter, if you represent an accused with a criminal past you probably do not want to allow the accused to testify because the criminal record can be devastating. But what if you have to call the accused, what can you do?

Counsel can ask the court not to allow the State to cross-examine on prior convictions. The court may exclude them on a prejudicial effect/probative value test. At the very least, you can ask the court to make the limited use of convictions very clear to the jury. The court has the discretion to exclude evidence of prior convictions in appropriate cases.[7] Such exclusion of prior convictions is proper only where the risk of prejudice exceeds the probative value of the prior convictions, especially as regards credibility.[8]

In summary, an accused who elects to testify can be cross-examined on prior convictions like any other witness. The purpose of such cross-examination is to weaken credibility, so the convictions of an accused are relevant only when the accused testifies — evidence of those prior convictions cannot go in unless the accused testifies.

---

[4]   *R. v. B. (K.G.)*, [1993] 1 S.C.R. 740.
[5]   Often an issue in spousal abuse cases.
[6]   *Morris v. R.*, [1979] 1 S.C.R. 405.
[7]   *R. v. Corbett*, [1988] 1 S.C.R. 670.
[8]   *R. v. Charland* (1996), 2 C.R. (5th) 318 (Alta. C.A.), aff'd 12 C.R. (5th) 226 (S.C.C.); *R. v. Gibson* (2001), 153 C.C.C. (3d) 465 (B.C.C.A.).

IMPEACHING YOUR OWN WITNESS

The general rule against impeaching your own witness comes from *Wright v. Beckett*[9] which says:

> A party never shall be permitted to produce general evidence to discredit his own witness, for that would be to enable him to destroy the witness if he spoke against him, and to make him a good witness if he spoke for him, with the means in his hands of destroying his credit if he spoke for him.

Nevertheless, at common law, it is very clear that you can contradict your own witness, but you cannot call evidence going solely to the witness's credibility. This rule is applied pragmatically — you can raise issues related to your witness's character to deal with an issue likely to arise on cross-examination. Thus, if you call a drug dealer as a witness to a car accident you can ask about the drug dealing in chief so that it doesn't come as a shock in cross-examination. What you cannot do is attack the witness if they give unhelpful testimony. Thus, if you anticipated the drug dealer would say "the light was green" but he actually says "the light was red" you cannot then discredit the witness by drawing attention to the witness's character defects.

The key is that by calling a witness you are asking the court to accept their testimony as honestly given — it may be mistaken, but you suggest it is honest. Put otherwise, if the witness is unworthy of belief why are they being called?

SUPPORTING CREDIBILITY

A prior consistent statement of a witness is generally inadmissible.[10] It proves nothing except that a witness has not changed their story. This last point gives rise to the exception — a prior consistent statement can be adduced to rebut an allegation of recent fabrication.

Specifically, if a witness's account of some incident or set of facts is challenged (directly or implicitly) as being of recent invention, the party calling the witness is allowed to rebut that challenge by showing that at some earlier time the witness made a statement to the same effect.[11] Now, the earlier statement must have been made contemporaneously with the event or at a time sufficiently early to be inconsistent with the suggestion it is of late invention[12] — the earlier statement is adduced solely to prove consistency. The earlier statement itself is not evidence of the truth of its contents.[13]

It is improper to call evidence solely for the purpose of bolstering the credibility of a witness. Such evidence violates the rule against oath helping. The

---

[9] (1834), 1 Mood & Rob. 414.
[10] *R. v. Keeler*, [1977] 36 C.C.C. (2d) 9 (Alta. C.A.); *R. v. R. (A.E.)* (2001), 151 O.A.C. 105.
[11] *R. v. Evans*, [1993] 2 S.C.R. 629; *R. v. V. (J.M.)*, 2001 B.C.C.A. 627.
[12] *R. v. O'Connor* (1995), 100 C.C.C. (3d) 285 (Ont. C.A.).
[13] *R. v. Kliman* (1996), 47 C.R. (4th) 137 (B.C.C.A.).

determination of whether a witness is or is not telling the truth lies within the province of the trier of fact and no evidence in this regard is proper. As the Court in *Marquard* notes:[14]

> It is fundamental that the ultimate conclusion as to the credibility or truthfulness of a particular witness is for the trier of fact ....

Accordingly, a party is not permitted to produce general evidence to support or bolster the credit of their witness.

POLYGRAPHS, LIE DETECTORS AND TRUTH SERUMS

Polygraphs, lie detectors and truth serums are all directed as mechanical techniques to bolster the credibility of witnesses. General evidence called solely to bolster a witness's credibility is improper — this is just the rule against oath-helping. Similarly, the repetition of statements given while subject to polygraphs, lie detectors or truth serums that are consistent with present testimony amount to nothing more than prior consistent statements. Finally, there is very real doubt as to the accuracy of truth measuring techniques. For all these reasons, the admission of the results of polygraphs, lie detectors or truth serums has been rejected by the courts.[15] Similarly, evidence that a witness offered to take a lie detector test is rejected as amounting to oath-helping.[16]

As a side point, just because a lie detector test's results are not admissible does *not* mean the interview itself is inadmissible. Thus, the transcript of a lie detector interview is admissible on the same basis as any other question and answer session. An accused asked to take a lie detector test cannot do so without risk as, subject to the confession rule, any statements made during the test can be used against the accused as an admission.

CORROBORATION

At one time, corroboration was a central feature of evidence law. Presently, corroboration is, absent a few statutory provisions,[17] limited to a principle of reasoning that ought to be put by the court to the trier of fact. Basically, whenever a case rests on the testimony of potentially untrustworthy witnesses (say, co-conspirators

---

[14] *R. v. Marquard* (1993), 108 D.L.R. (4th) 46 at 50 (S.C.C.); see also *R. v. Béland*, [1987] 2 S.C.R. 398.
[15] *Béland, supra*, note 14; *R. v. Phillion*, [1978], 37 C.R.N.S. 361 (S.C.C.).
[16] *R. v. Bedgood* (1990), 80 C.R. (3d) 227 (N.S.C.A.); but see *R. v. B.* (1997), 104 O.A.C. 81 where the desire to take a lie detector test was taken to be a valid proof of a lack of guilty mind.
[17] For example, s. 47(3) of the *Criminal Code*, R.S.C. 1985, c. C-46 (Appendix A) provides:
      No person shall be convicted of high treason or treason on the evidence of only one witness, unless the evidence of that witness is corroborated in a material particular by evidence that implicates the accused.
      Corroboration, as a rule of evidence, is rapidly becoming historical interest only. Significant provisions requiring corroboration are rare.

in a narcotics prosecution), a judge is prudent to advise the jury to consider the risks of accepting such testimony.[18]

Corroboration is some independent evidence that affects a party and connects the party with the cause or offence. Specifically, it must be evidence that confirms (in some fashion) not only that a cause exists or has occurred but also that the party in dispute is connected to it. It need only go to a single material point and it is enough that it tends to show the cause exists and a party is connected to it. In a sexual assault of a young child, for example, corroboration might be found from torn clothing with traces of a blood type of the accused — this does not prove the liability of the defendant but tends to support it.

---

[18] *Vetrovec v. R.*, [1982] 1 S.C.R. 811.

Chapter 18

THE BEST EVIDENCE RULE

INTRODUCTION

The modern form of the best evidence rule is little more than a shadow of the original rule, which, at its height, formed one of the foundations of the law of evidence. In the eighteenth century, the best evidence rule was described as follows:[1]

> The judges and sages of the law have laid it down that there is but one general rule of evidence, *the best that the nature of the case will admit.*

Note, the form of the eighteenth century rule does not exclude secondary evidence, say, copies of original documents, if the primary evidence is unavailable. The rule was limited to the (very sensible) proposition that the court ought to be given the best available evidence. Speaking of the case of written documents, the Court in *MacDonnell*,[2] comments as follows:

> ... if you want to get at the contents of a written document, the proper way is, to produce it, if you can.

Properly limited, the statement of law in *MacDonnell* is still good law.[3] Proof of the contents of a written document ought to be made by production of the original document. This, highly limited, rule is the modern form of the best evidence rule:[4]

> ... it is now well established that any application of the best evidence rule is confined to cases in which it can be shown that the party has the original and could produce it but does not.

---

[1] *Omychund v. Barker* (1744), 26 E.R. 15 (L.C.).
[2] *MacDonnell v. Evans* (1852), 138 E.R. 742.
[3] Although some courts have gone so far as to suggest the rule is defunct entirely. Thus, *R. v. Penny* 2000 Carswell Nfld. 208, citing *Garton v. Hunter* (1969) 1 All E.R. 451 adopts the following passage:
>   Nowadays we do not confine ourselves to the best evidence. We admit all relevant evidence. The goodness or badness of the evidences goes only to weight and not admissibility.
>   See also *R. v. Galarce* (1983), 35 C.R. (3d) 268 (Sask. Q.B.).
[4] *R. v. Wayte* (1982), 76 Cr. App. Rep. 110.

Speaking of the modern rule, the Court in *Governor of Pentonville*[5] writes:

> What is meant by a party having a document available in his hands? We would say that it means a party who has the original of the document with him in court, or could have it in court without any difficulty. In such a case, if he refuses to produce the original... the court would infer the worst. The copy should be excluded.

Additionally, where a copy, rather than an original, is produced, the court will reject the copy and apply the best evidence rule, only where there is a legitimate dispute as to the contents of the document.[6] The need for a "legitimate dispute" suggests some duty is cast upon the party opposing the copy's admission to say the copy is doubtful. The American *Federal Rules of Evidence* set out the requirement thusly:[7]

> To prove the content of a writing, recording, or photograph, the original writing, recording, or photograph is required, except as otherwise provided in these rules or by Act of Congress.
>
>   ...
>
> A duplicate is admissible to the same extent as an original unless (1) a genuine question is raised as to the authenticity of the original or (2) in the circumstances it would be unfair to admit the duplicate in lieu of the original.

LIMITATIONS OF RULE

The best evidence rule deals with the contents of documents, not the existence or identification of documents. Thus, in *Pelrine v. Arron*,[8] the Court, in allowing proof of copies, said:

> [The] evidence is objected to as not admissible by reason of the "best evidence rule". It seems to me, however, that [the] evidence, in essence, concerned the existence of cheques rather than proof of their contents.

Where the existence as opposed to the context of a document is relevant, proof of that existence is not subject to the best evidence rule. The best evidence rule applies to the contents of documents. Documents, in this context, is to be read expansively and includes audio and video tapes.[9]

Of course, accepting that tapes can be documents makes the question of what is an original and what is a copy not as straightforward as might be thought. As the Court noted in *Hall*:[10]

---

[5]   *R. v. Governor of Pentonville Prison, Ex p. Osman (No. 3)*, [1989] 3 All E.R. 701 at (Q.B.D.); see also *R. v. Penny, supra*, note 3 at para. 42.
[6]   *R. v. Cotroni*, [1979] 2 S.C.R. 256.
[7]   FED. R. EVID. 1002 and 1003.
[8]   (1969), 3 D.L.R. (3d) 713 at 724 (N.S.C.A.).
[9]   *R. v. Cotroni, supra*, note 6.
[10] *R. v. Hall* 1998 Carswell BC 2139.

Several Courts of Appeal have ruled carbon copies are admissible as originals, even if they are not the top white copy.

Similarly, courts have considered photocopies, video cassettes and computer printouts in the context of originals or copies.[11] More broadly speaking, it may be said the best evidence rule does not apply at all to anything other than written documents and has no application to videotapes, photographs or similar items.[12]

WHEN IS SECONDARY EVIDENCE ADMISSIBLE?

If the best evidence rule applies, certain exceptions to the rule exist allowing the proof of a document by secondary evidence. If the original has been lost or destroyed[13] evidence from a copy may be admitted.[14] In such a case the copy must be verified as a true copy that contains the same terms as the original.[15] Parol evidence of a lost or destroyed document is also admissible.[16] When a document is unavailable for court because the original is in the hands of a party outside the process of the court or who cannot be compelled to produce the original, secondary evidence of the document's contents is proper.[17] Similarly, if a document is in the hands of a person subject to compulsory production to the court, but that person does not comply with their obligation to produce, the document may be proven by secondary evidence.[18] American Federal Rule of Evidence 1004 sets out the admission of secondary evidence as follows:

> The original is not required, and other evidence of the contents of a writing, recording, or photograph is admissible if —
>
> (1) Originals lost or destroyed. All originals are lost or have been destroyed, unless the proponent lost or destroyed them in bad faith; or
> (2) Original not obtainable. No original can be obtained by any available judicial process or procedure; or
> (3) Original in possession of opponent. At a time when an original was under the control of the party against whom offered, that party was put on notice, by the pleadings or otherwise, that the contents would be a subject of proof at the hearing, and that party does not produce the original at the hearing; or
> (4) Collateral matters. The writing, recording, or photograph is not closely related to a controlling issue.

---

[11] *R. v. Wayte* (1982), 76 Cr. App. R. [photocopies]; *R. v. Caughlin* (1987), 18 B.C.L.R. (2d) 186 (Co. Ct.) [video]; *R. v. Bicknell* (1988), 41 C.C.C. (3d) 545 (B.C.C.A.) [computer printouts].
[12] *Penny, supra*, note 3.
[13] *R. v. Betterest Vinyl Manufacturing Ltd.* (1989), 42 B.C.L.R. (2d) 198 (C.A.).
[14] *R. v. Wayte* (1982) 76 Cr. App. R. 110 (C.A.).
[15] *R. v. Collins* (1960), 44 Cr. App. R. 170 (C.A.).
[16] *R. v. Collins, supra*, note 15.
[17] *R. v. Nowaz* (1976), 3 All E.R. 5 (C.A.); *Dennison v. Gahans*, [1946] 1 D.L.R. 72 (NB. Ch. D.).
[18] *Cyr v. DeRosier* (1910), 40 N.B.R. 373 (C.A.).

The American rule, while not identical to Canadian practice, is very similar and could well be adopted as a legitimate statement of the common law principle.

FUTURE OF THE BEST EVIDENCE RULE

As a rule of reasoning and advocacy, the principle that a document's contents are best proven by the original document is unquestionable. Nevertheless, such a position suggests only that less weight should be given to copies of documents, rather than suggesting copies of documents ought to be excluded. Objections based on the best evidence rule are rare in Canadian courts and the future of the best evidence rule is doubtful. As the Court notes in *Governor of Pentonville Prison*:[19]

> ... this court would be more than happy to say goodbye to the best evidence rule. We accept that it served an important purpose in the days of parchment and quill pens. But, since the invention of carbon paper and, still more, the photocopier and the telefacsimile machine, that purpose has largely gone. Where there is an allegation of forgery the court will obviously attach little, if any, weight to anything other than the original; so also if the copy produced in court is illegible. But to maintain a general exclusionary rule for these limited purposes is, in our view, hardly justifiable.

---

[19]   *Supra*, note 5 at 728.

Chapter 19

FORENSIC EVIDENCE

REQUIREMENTS OF FORENSIC EVIDENCE

The ability to prove forensic evidence depends upon a number of other areas of evidence. First, there has to be proof establishing that the evidence adduced in court can be traced back to the place where whatever incident is at issue took place. Second, there usually has to be an expert who can interpret the meaning of the forensic evidence for the jury. For example, suppose a bullet casing is to be adduced in a murder trial — in order for the casing to be admitted, the party seeking adduction must show that (1) the casing was found at the murder site and (2) the casing is relevant to some issue at trial. In all likelihood, the proof the casing was found at the murder site can be established by a police witness who can identify the casing as that found at the crime scene. The meaning of the bullet case, however, will likely require expert evidence to interpret and explain it.

CHAIN OF CONTINUITY

Broadly speaking, it is unnecessary to set out the chain of continuity or possession in order to have an exhibit admitted into evidence. So long as a witness can say the evidence tendered is the same evidence as at a relevant earlier time, the evidence is admissible and failure to prove continuity goes only to weight. Thus, in *R. v. Penny*[1] the Court notes:

> The proof of continuity (chain of possession) of exhibits, i.e. "perfecting the exhibit," goes to weight and not admissibility. In other words, so long as one witness is able to identify and prove the tendered exhibit by testifying that it is the "same" item that the witness had previously handled, the failure to prove an unbroken chain of possession of the exhibit bears on weight and not admissibility.

To similar effect is the *Donald*[2] case, where the New Brunswick Court of Appeal held an item seized from an accused could be adduced if it were (a) relevant and (b) there was some basis, on sworn evidence, to suppose the item seized was

---

[1] 2000 Carswell Nfld. 208, para. 45.
[2] *R. v. Donald* (1958), 28 C.R. 206.

the item adduced — proof of continuity is unnecessary, although, as an advocacy point it may be prudent.

PREREQUISITES TO ADMISSION

Sometimes, forensic evidence does not need an expert to explain its significance. Photographs, videotapes and audiotapes fall into this category of evidence with self-evident significance. As the Nova Scotia Court of Appeal notes:[3]

> A photograph can often more clearly and accurately portray or describe persons, places or things than a witness can by oral evidence. They are not subject to the difficulty inherent in oral evidence of absorbing and relating the mass of detail and then remembering it.

A similar analysis applies to videotapes and audiotapes. As Justice Cory notes in *Nikolovski*:[4]

> The video camera on the other hand is never subject to stress. Through tumultuous events it continues to record accurately and dispassionately all that comes before it.

The conditions precedent to the admission of photographs, videotapes and audiotapes are fairly straightforward and were set out by the Nova Scotia Court of Appeal in *Creemer*[5] as follows:

> All the cases dealing with the admissibility of photographs go to show that such admissibility depends on (1) their accuracy in truly representing the facts; (2) their fairness and absence of any intention to mislead; (3) their verification on oath by a person capable to do so.

EVIDENCE REQUIRING EXPERT OPINION

Beyond evidence the significance of which is obvious, some forensic evidence must be explained by experts in order to have meaning for the trier of fact. The significance of such evidence can be overwhelming.[6] Nevertheless, the principles upon which expert evidence is admitted are the customary governing expert evidence.

---

[3]   *R. v. Smith (G.A.)* (1986), 71 N.S.R. (2d) 229 at 237 (C.A.).
[4]   *R. v. Nikolovski* (1996), 111 C.C.C. (3d) 403 at 412 (S.C.C.).
[5]   *R. v. Creemer and Cormier* [1968] 1 C.C.C. 14 at 22; followed by many cases including *R. v. Baptiste* 2000 Carswell Ont. 1566 (OSCL); *Burke v. Leung* 1996 Carswell BC 922 (B.C.S.C.); *R. v. Harder* (1980), 21 A.R. 102 (C.A.).
[6]   For example, see *R. v. McCullough* (2000), 142 C.C.C. (3d) 149 (Ont. C.A.).

OPINIONS OF EXPERTS

Expert testimony is allowed because there are certain things a judge or a juror cannot reasonably be expected to understand without the guidance of someone skilled in a recognized field. Thus, one could give a jury all the "facts" about, say, a bridge that has collapsed but it would require teaching the jury to be engineers before the jury could, by itself, figure out what the facts mean. As the Court notes in *Abbey*:[7]

> A expert's function is precisely this: to provide the judge and jury with a ready-made inference which the judge and jury, due to the technical nature of the facts, are unable to formulate. ... An expert's opinion is admissible to furnish the Court with scientific information which is likely to be outside the experience and knowledge of a judge or jury.

As a result, juries are allowed to hear the opinions of persons with special skills, in recognized areas of expertise, on matters the jury cannot understand without expert advice.

The rule regarding expert testimony can be stated as follows:

> If specialized knowledge will assist the trier of fact to understand the evidence or a fact in issue, a witness qualified as an expert by knowledge, skill, experience or training may testify by way of opinion.

An expert's opinion is admissible only if it is needed to allow the trier of fact to make sense of the evidence.[8] If the trier of fact can properly come to a conclusion without the help of an expert, then such evidence is superfluous and should be excluded.[9] The focus of consideration of allowing expert testimony must be whether the trier of fact needs the assistance an expert can give. Only where strictly necessary will expert evidence be allowed.

Opinion evidence of experts is admissible if necessary to assist the trier of fact. The potential prejudicial effect of the evidence must not outweigh its value to the trier of fact. That said, police experts are seldom challenged on their qualifications. Accordingly, before admitting expert testimony a court must consider the following questions:[10]

(a) Will the proposed expert opinion evidence enable the trier of fact to appreciate the technicalities of a matter in issue?

(b) Will it provide information which is likely to be outside the experience of the trier of facts?

(c) Is the trier of fact unlikely to form a correct judgment about a matter in issue if unassisted by the expert opinion evidence?

---

[7] *R. v. Abbey*, [1982] 2 S.C.R. 24.
[8] *R. v. Mohan*, [1994] 2 S.C.R. 9: "helpfulness" is not the standard, "necessity" is required.
[9] *R. v. Marquard*, [1993] 4 S.C.R. 223.
[10] *R. v. K. (A.)*, (1999) 176 D.L.R. (4th) 665 at 707.

(d)   Is the need for the evidence sufficient to overcome its potential prejudicial effect?

Proof of specific types of evidence, say DNA or fingerprints, depend on ensuring the expert is properly qualified and has the evidentiary basis for an opinion.[11]

---

[11]   For specific types of evidence see J. Gibson, *Criminal Law: Evidence, Practice and Procedure* (Toronto: Carswell, 1988) and, for a general review of pathological issues, F. Jaffe, *Guide to Pathological Evidence for Lawyers and Police Officers*, 3rd ed. (Toronto: Carswell, 1991).

Appendix A

CRIMINAL CODE

R.S.C. 1985, c. C-46
An Act respecting the Criminal Law

Part I

General

8. (1) **Application to territories** — The provisions of this Act apply throughout Canada except

(a)   in the Yukon Territory, in so far as they are inconsistent with the *Yukon Act*,

(b)   in the Northwest Territories, in so far as they are inconsistent with the *Northwest Territories Act*; and

(c)   in Nunavut, in so far as they are inconsistent with the *Nunavut Act*.

(2) **Application of criminal law of England** — The criminal law of England that was in force in a province immediately before April 1, 1955 continues in force in the province except as altered, varied, modified or affected by this Act or any other Act of the Parliament of Canada.

(3) **Common law principles continued** — Every rule and principle of the common law that renders any circumstance a justification or excuse for an act or a defence to a charge continues in force and applies in respect of proceedings for an offence under this Act or any other Act of Parliament except in so far as they are altered by or are inconsistent with this Act or any other Act of Parliament.

[1993, c. 28, Sch. III, s. 26 (in force April 1, 1999).]

Part VI

Invasion Of Privacy

Interception of Communications

184. (1) **Interception** — Every one who, by means of any electro-magnetic, acoustic, mechanical or other device, wilfully intercepts a private communication is guilty of an indictable offence and liable to imprisonment for a term not exceeding five years.

(2) **Saving provision** — Subsection (1) does not apply to

(a) a person who has the consent to intercept, express or implied, of the originator of the private communication or of the person intended by the originator thereof to receive it;

(b) a person who intercepts a private communication in accordance with an authorization or pursuant to section 184.4 or any person who in good faith aids in any way another person who the aiding person believes on reasonable grounds is acting with an authorization or pursuant to section 184.4;

(c) a person engaged in providing a telephone, telegraph or other communication service to the public who intercepts a private communication,

(i) if the interception is necessary for the purpose of providing the service,

(ii) in the course of service observing or random monitoring necessary for the purpose of mechanical or service quality control checks, or

(iii) if the interception is necessary to protect the person's rights or property directly related to providing the service; or

(d) an officer or servant of Her Majesty in right of Canada who engages in radio frequency spectrum management, in respect of a private communication intercepted by that officer or servant for the purpose of identifying, isolating or preventing an unauthorized or interfering use of a frequency or of a transmission.

(3) [Repealed, 1993, c. 40, s. 3 (in force August 1, 1993)]

[1993, c. 40, s. 3 (in force August 1, 1993).]

184.1 (1) **Interception to prevent bodily harm** — An agent of the state may intercept, by means of any electro-magnetic, acoustic, mechanical or other device, a private communication if

(a) either the originator of the private communication or the person intended by the originator to receive it has consented to the interception;

(b) the agent of the state believes on reasonable grounds that there is a risk of bodily harm to the person who consented to the interception; and

(c) the purpose of the interception is to prevent the bodily harm.

(2) **Admissibility of intercepted communication** — The contents of a private communication that is obtained from an interception pursuant to subsection (1) are inadmissible as evidence except for the purposes of proceedings in which actual, attempted or threatened bodily harm is alleged, including proceedings in respect of an application for an authorization under this Part or in respect of a search warrant or a warrant for the arrest of any person.

(3) **Destruction of recordings and transcripts** — The agent of the state who intercepts a private communication pursuant to subsection (1) shall, as soon as is practicable in the circumstances, destroy any recording of the private communication that is obtained from an interception pursuant to subsection (1), any full or partial transcript of the recording and any notes made by that agent of the private communication if nothing in the private communication suggests that bodily harm, attempted bodily harm or threatened bodily harm has occurred or is likely to occur.

(4) **Definition of "agent of the state"** — For the purposes of this section, "agent of the state" means
   (a)   a peace officer; and
   (b)   a person acting under the authority of, or in cooperation with, a peace officer.

[1993, c. 40, s. 4 (in force August 1, 1993).]

184.2 (1) **Interception with consent** — A person may intercept, by means of any electro-magnetic, acoustic, mechanical or other device, a private communication where either the originator of the private communication or the person intended by the originator to receive it has consented to the interception and an authorization has been obtained pursuant to subsection (3).

(2) **Application for authorization** — An application for an authorization under this section shall be made by a peace officer, or a public officer who has been appointed or designated to administer or enforce any federal or provincial law and whose duties include the enforcement of this or any other Act of Parliament, *ex parte* and in writing to a provincial court judge, a judge of a superior court of criminal jurisdiction or a judge as defined in section 552, and shall be accompanied by an affidavit, which may be sworn on the information and belief of that peace officer or public officer or of any other peace officer or public officer, deposing to the following matters:
   (a)   that there are reasonable grounds to believe that an offence against this or any other Act of Parliament has been or will be committed;
   (b)   the particulars of the offence;
   (c)   the name of the person who has consented to the interception;
   (d)   the period for which the authorization is requested; and
   (e)   in the case of an application for an authorization where an authorization has previously been granted under this section or section 186, the particulars of the authorization.

(3) **Judge to be satisfied** — An authorization may be given under this section if the judge to whom the application is made is satisfied that
   (a)   there are reasonable grounds to believe that an offence against this or any other Act of Parliament has been or will be committed;
   (b)   either the originator of the private communication or the person intended by the originator to receive it has consented to the interception; and
   (c)   there are reasonable grounds to believe that information concerning the offence referred to in paragraph (a) will be obtained through the interception sought.

(4) **Content and limitation of authorization** — An authorization given under this section shall
   (a)   state the offence in respect of which private communications may be intercepted;
   (b)   state the type of private communication that may be intercepted;
   (c)   state the identity of the persons, if known, whose private communications are to be intercepted, generally describe the place at which private communications may be intercepted, if a general description of that place

can be given, and generally describe the manner of interception that may be used;

(d)   contain the terms and conditions that the judge considers advisable in the public interest; and

(e)   be valid for the period, not exceeding sixty days, set out therein.

[1993, c. 40, s. 4 (in force August 1, 1993).]

Interception of Communications

184.3 (1) **Application by means of telecommunication** — Notwithstanding section 184.2, an application for an authorization under subsection 184.2(2) may be made *ex parte* to a provincial court judge, a judge of a superior court of criminal jurisdiction or a judge as defined in section 552, by telephone or other means of telecommunication, if it would be impracticable in the circumstances for the applicant to appear personally before a judge.

(2) **Application** — An application for an authorization made under this section shall be on oath and shall be accompanied by a statement that includes the matters referred to in paragraphs 184.2(2)(a) to (e) and that states the circumstances that make it impracticable for the applicant to appear personally before a judge.

(3) **Recording** — The judge shall record, in writing or otherwise, the application for an authorization made under this section and, on determination of the application, shall cause the writing or recording to be placed in the packet referred to in subsection 187(1) and sealed in that packet, and a recording sealed in a packet shall be treated as if it were a document for the purposes of section 187.

(4) **Oath** — For the purposes of subsection (2), an oath may be administered by telephone or other means of telecommunication.

(5) **Alternative to oath** — An applicant who uses a means of telecommunication that produces a writing may, instead of swearing an oath for the purposes of subsection (2), make a statement in writing stating that all matters contained in the application are true to the knowledge or belief of the applicant and such a statement shall be deemed to be a statement made under oath.

(6) **Authorization** — Where the judge to whom an application is made under this section is satisfied that the circumstances referred to in paragraphs 184.2(3)(a) to (c) exist and that the circumstances referred to in subsection (2) make it impracticable for the applicant to appear personally before a judge, the judge may, on such terms and conditions, if any, as are considered advisable, give an authorization by telephone or other means of telecommunication for a period of up to thirty-six hours.

(7) **Giving authorization** — Where a judge gives an authorization by telephone or other means of telecommunication, other than a means of telecommunication that produces a writing,

(a)   the judge shall complete and sign the authorization in writing, noting on its face the time, date and place at which it is given;

(b)   the applicant shall, on the direction of the judge, complete a facsimile of the authorization in writing, noting on its face the name of the judge who gave it and the time, date and place at which it was given; and

(c)   the judge shall, as soon as is practicable after the authorization has been given, cause the authorization to be placed in the packet referred to in subsection 187(1) and sealed in that packet.

(8) **Giving authorization where telecommunication produces writing** — Where a judge gives an authorization by a means of telecommunication that produces a writing, the judge shall

(a)   complete and sign the authorization in writing, noting on its face the time, date and place at which it is given;

(b)   transmit the authorization by the means of telecommunication to the applicant, and the copy received by the applicant shall be deemed to be a facsimile referred to in paragraph (7)(b); and

(c)   as soon as is practicable after the authorization has been given, cause the authorization to be placed in the packet referred to in subsection 187(1) and sealed in that packet.

[1993, c. 40, s. 4 (in force August 1, 1993).]

184.4 Interception in exceptional circumstances — A peace officer may intercept, by means of any electro-magnetic, acoustic, mechanical or other device, a private communication where

(a)   the peace officer believes on reasonable grounds that the urgency of the situation is such that an authorization could not, with reasonable diligence, be obtained under any other provision of this Part;

(b)   the peace officer believes on reasonable grounds that such an interception is immediately necessary to prevent an unlawful act that would cause serious harm to any person or to property; and

(c)   either the originator of the private communication or the person intended by the originator to receive it is the person who would perform the act that is likely to cause the harm or is the victim, or intended victim, of the harm.

[1993, c. 40, s. 4 (in force August 1, 1993).]

184.5 (1) Interception of radio-based telephone communications — Every person who intercepts, by means of any electro-magnetic, acoustic, mechanical or other device, maliciously or for gain, a radio-based telephone communication, if the originator of the communication or the person intended by the originator of the communication to receive it is in Canada, is guilty of an indictable offence and liable to imprisonment for a term not exceeding five years.

(2) **Other provisions to apply** — Section 183.1, subsection 184(2) and sections 184.1 to 190 and 194 to 196 apply, with such modifications as the circumstances require, to interceptions of radio-based telephone communications referred to in subsection (1).

[1993, c. 40, s. 4 (in force August 1, 1993).]

184.6 One application for authorization sufficient — For greater certainty, an application for an authorization under this Part may be made with respect to both private communications and radio-based telephone communications at the same time.

[1993, c. 40, s. 4 (in force August 1, 1993).]

185. (1) **Application for authorization** — An application for an authorization to be given under section 186 shall be made *ex parte* and in writing to a judge of a superior court of criminal jurisdiction or a judge as defined in section 552 and shall be signed by the Attorney General of the province in which the application is made or the Solicitor General of Canada or an agent specially designated in writing for the purposes of this section by

(a)   the Solicitor General of Canada personally or the Deputy Solicitor General of Canada personally, if the offence under investigation is one in respect of which proceedings, if any, may be instituted at the instance of the Government of Canada and conducted by or on behalf of the Attorney General of Canada; or

(b)   the Attorney General of a province personally or the Deputy Attorney General of a province personally, in any other case, and shall be accompanied by an affidavit, which may be sworn on the information and belief of a peace officer or public officer deposing to the following matters:

(c)   the facts relied on to justify the belief that an authorization should be given together with particulars of the offence;

(d)   the type of private communication proposed to be intercepted;

(e)   the names, addresses and occupations, if known, of all persons, the interception of whose private communications there are reasonable grounds to believe may assist the investigation of the offence, a general description of the nature and location of the place, if known, at which private communications are proposed to be intercepted and a general description of the manner of interception proposed to be used;

(f)   the number of instances, if any, on which an application has been made under this section in relation to the offence and a person named in the affidavit pursuant to paragraph (e) and on which the application was withdrawn or no authorization was given, the date on which each application was made and the name of the judge to whom each application was made;

(g)   the period for which the authorization is requested; and

(h)   whether other investigative procedures have been tried and have failed or why it appears they are unlikely to succeed or that the urgency of the matter is such that it would be impractical to carry out the investigation of the offence using only other investigative procedures.

(1.1) **Exception for criminal organizations and terrorist groups** — Notwithstanding paragraph (1)(h), that paragraph does not apply where the application for an authorization is in relation to

(a)   an offence under section 467.11, 467.12 or 467.13;

(b)   an offence committed for the benefit of, at the direction of or in association with a criminal organization; or

(c)   a terrorism offence.

(2) **Extension of period for notification** — An application for an authorization may be accompanied by an application, personally signed by the Attorney General of the province in which the application for the authorization is made or the Solicitor General of Canada if the application for the authorization is made by him or on his behalf, to substitute for the period mentioned in subsection 196(1) such longer period not exceeding three years as is set out in the application.

(3) **Where extension to be granted** — Where an application for an authorization is accompanied by an application referred to in subsection (2), the judge to whom the applications are made shall first consider the application referred to in subsection (2) and where, on the basis of the affidavit in support of the application for the authorization and any other affidavit evidence submitted in support of the application referred to in subsection (2), the judge is of the opinion that the interests of justice warrant the granting of the application, he shall fix a period, not exceeding three years, in substitution for the period mentioned in subsection 196(1).

(4) **Where extension not granted** — Where the judge to whom an application for an authorization and an application referred to in subsection (2) are made refuses to fix a period in substitution for the period mentioned in subsection 196(1) or where the judge fixes a period in substitution therefor that is less than the period set out in the application referred to in subsection (2), the person appearing before the judge on the application for the authorization may withdraw the application for the authorization and thereupon the judge shall not proceed to consider the application for the authorization or to give the authorization and shall return to the person appearing before him on the application for the authorization both applications and all other material pertaining thereto.

[1993, c. 40, s. 5 (in force August 1, 1993); 1997, c. 23, s. 4 (in force May 2, 1997); 1997, c. 18, s. 8 (in force June 16, 1997); 2001, c. 32, s. 5 (in force January 7, 2002); 2001, c. 41, ss. 6, 133 (s. 6 in force December 24, 2001; s. 133 in force January 7, 2002).]

186. (1) **Judge to be satisfied** — An authorization under this section may be given if the judge to whom the application is made is satisfied

    (a)   that it would be in the best interests of the administration of justice to do so; and

    (b)   that other investigative procedures have been tried and have failed, other investigative procedures are unlikely to succeed or the urgency of the matter is such that it would be impractical to carry out the investigation of the offence using only other investigative procedures.

(1.1) **Exception for criminal organizations and terrorism offences** — Notwithstanding paragraph (1)(b), that paragraph does not apply where the judge is satisfied that the application for an authorization is in relation to

    (a)   an offence under section 467.11, 467.12 or 467.13;

    (b)   an offence committed for the benefit of, at the direction of or in association with a criminal organization; or

    (c)   a terrorism offence.

(2) **Where authorization not to be given** — No authorization may be given to intercept a private communication at the office or residence of a solicitor, or at any other place ordinarily used by a solicitor and by other solicitors for the purpose

of consultation with clients, unless the judge to whom the application is made is satisfied that there are reasonable grounds to believe that the solicitor, any other solicitor practising with him, any person employed by him or any other such solicitor or a member of the solicitor's household has been or is about to become a party to an offence.

(3) **Terms and conditions** — Where an authorization is given in relation to the interception of private communications at a place described in subsection (2), the judge by whom the authorization is given shall include therein such terms and conditions as he considers advisable to protect privileged communications between solicitors and clients.

(4) **Content and limitation of authorization** — An authorization shall
(a)   state the offence in respect of which private communications may be intercepted;
(b)   state the type of private communication that may be intercepted;
(c)   state the identity of the persons, if known, whose private communications are to be intercepted, generally describe the place at which private communications may be intercepted, if a general description of that place can be given, and generally describe the manner of interception that may be used;
(d)   contain such terms and conditions as the judge considers advisable in the public interest; and
(e)   be valid for the period, not exceeding sixty days, set out therein.

(5) **Persons designated** — The Solicitor General of Canada or the Attorney General, as the case may be, may designate a person or persons who may intercept private communications under authorizations.

(5.1) **Installation and removal of device** — For greater certainty, an authorization that permits interception by means of an electro-magnetic, acoustic, mechanical or other device includes the authority to install, maintain or remove the device covertly.

(5.2) **Removal after expiry of authorization** — On an *ex parte* application, in writing, supported by affidavit, the judge who gave an authorization referred to in subsection (5.1) or any other judge having jurisdiction to give such an authorization may give a further authorization for the covert removal of the electro-magnetic, acoustic, mechanical or other device after the expiry of the original authorization
(a)   under any terms or conditions that the judge considers advisable in the public interest; and
(b)   during any specified period of not more than sixty days.

(6) **Renewal of authorization** — Renewals of an authorization may be given by a judge of a superior court of criminal jurisdiction or a judge as defined in section 552 on receipt by him of an *ex parte* application in writing signed by the Attorney General of the province in which the application is made or the Solicitor General of Canada or an agent specially designated in writing for the purposes of section 185 by the Solicitor General of Canada or the Attorney General, as the

case may be, accompanied by an affidavit of a peace officer or public officer deposing to the following matters:

(a) the reason and period for which the renewal is required;

(b) full particulars, together with times and dates, when interceptions, if any, were made or attempted under the authorization, and any information that has been obtained by any interception; and

(c) the number of instances, if any, on which, to the knowledge and belief of the deponent, an application has been made under this subsection in relation to the same authorization and on which the application was withdrawn or no renewal was given, the date on which each application was made and the name of the judge to whom each application was made, and supported by such other information as the judge may require.

(7) **Renewal** — A renewal of an authorization may be given if the judge to whom the application is made is satisfied that any of the circumstances described in subsection (1) still obtain, but no renewal shall be for a period exceeding sixty days.

[1993, c. 40, s. 6 (in force August 1, 1993); 1997, c. 23, s. 5 (in force May 2, 1997); 1999, c. 5, s. 5 (in force May 1, 1999); 2001, c. 32, s. 6 (in force January 7, 2002); 2001, c. 41, ss. 61, 133 (s. 6.1) in force December 24, 2001; s. 133 in force January 7, 2002).]

186.1 Time limitation in relation to criminal organizations and terrorism offences — Notwithstanding paragraphs 184.2(4)(e) and 186(4)(e) and subsection 186(7), an authorization or any renewal of an authorization may be valid for one or more periods specified in the authorization exceeding sixty days, each not exceeding one year, where the authorization is in relation to

(a) an offence under section 467.11, 467.12 or 467.13;

(b) an offence committed for the benefit of, at the direction of or in association with a criminal organization; or

(c) a terrorism offence.

[1997, c. 23, s. 6 (in force May 2, 1997); 2001, c. 32, s. 7 (in force January 7, 2002); 2001, c. 41, ss. 7, 133 (s. 7 in force December 24, 2001; s. 133 in force January 7, 2002).]

187. (1) Manner in which application to be kept secret — All documents relating to an application made pursuant to any provision of this Part are confidential and, subject to subsection (1.1), shall be placed in a packet and sealed by the judge to whom the application is made immediately on determination of the application, and that packet shall be kept in the custody of the court in a place to which the public has no access or in such other place as the judge may authorize and shall not be dealt with except in accordance with subsections (1.2) to (1.5).

(1.1) **Exception** — An authorization given under this Part need not be placed in the packet except where, pursuant to subsection 184.3(7) or (8), the original authorization is in the hands of the judge, in which case that judge must place it in the packet and the facsimile remains with the applicant.

(1.2) **Opening for further application** — The sealed packet may be opened and its contents removed for the purpose of dealing with an application for a further authorization or with an application for renewal of an authorization.

(1.3) **Opening on order of judge** — A provincial court judge, a judge of a superior court of criminal jurisdiction or a judge as defined in section 552 may order that the sealed packet be opened and its contents removed for the purpose of copying and examining the documents contained in the packet.

(1.4) **Opening on order of trial judge** — A judge or provincial court judge before whom a trial is to be held and who has jurisdiction in the province in which an authorization was given may order that the sealed packet be opened and its contents removed for the purpose of copying and examining the documents contained in the packet if

(a)   any matter relevant to the authorization or any evidence obtained pursuant to the authorization is in issue in the trial; and

(b)   the accused applies for such an order for the purpose of consulting the documents to prepare for trial.

(1.5) **Order for destruction of documents** — Where a sealed packet is opened, its contents shall not be destroyed except pursuant to an order of a judge of the same court as the judge who gave the authorization.

(2) **Order of judge** — An order under subsection (1.2), (1.3), (1.4) or (1.5) made with respect to documents relating to an application made pursuant to section 185 or subsection 186(6) or 196(2) may only be made after the Attorney General or the Solicitor General by whom or on whose authority the application for the authorization to which the order relates was made has been given an opportunity to be heard.

(3) **Idem** — An order under subsection (1.2), (1.3), (1.4) or (1.5) made with respect to documents relating to an application made pursuant to subsection 184.2(2) or section 184.3 may only be made after the Attorney General has been given an opportunity to be heard.

(4) **Editing of copies** — Where a prosecution has been commenced and an accused applies for an order for the copying and examination of documents pursuant to subsection (1.3) or (1.4), the judge shall not, notwithstanding those subsections, provide any copy of any document to the accused until the prosecutor has deleted any part of the copy of the document that the prosecutor believes would be prejudicial to the public interest, including any part that the prosecutor believes could

(a)   compromise the identity of any confidential informant;

(b)   compromise the nature and extent of ongoing investigations;

(c)   endanger persons engaged in particular intelligence-gathering techniques and thereby prejudice future investigations in which similar techniques would be used; or

(d)   prejudice the interests of innocent persons.

(5) **Accused to be provided with copies** — After the prosecutor has deleted the parts of the copy of the document to be given to the accused under subsection (4), the accused shall be provided with an edited copy of the document.

(6) **Original documents to be returned** — After the accused has received an edited copy of a document, the prosecutor shall keep a copy of the original document, and an edited copy of the document and the original document shall be returned to the packet and the packet resealed.

(7) **Deleted parts** — An accused to whom an edited copy of a document has been provided pursuant to subsection (5) may request that the judge before whom the trial is to be held order that any part of the document deleted by the prosecutor be made available to the accused, and the judge shall order that a copy of any part that, in the opinion of the judge, is required in order for the accused to make full answer and defence and for which the provision of a judicial summary would not be sufficient, be made available to the accused.

[R.S., 1985, c. 27 (1st Supp.), s. 24 (in force December 4, 1985); 1993, c. 40, s. 7 (in force August 1, 1993).]

188. (1) **Applications to specially appointed judges** — Notwithstanding section 185, an application made under that section for an authorization may be made *ex parte* to a judge of a superior court of criminal jurisdiction, or a judge as defined in section 552, designated from time to time by the Chief Justice, by a peace officer specially designated in writing, by name or otherwise, for the purposes of this section by

    (a)   the Solicitor General of Canada, if the offence is one in respect of which proceedings, if any, may be instituted by the Government of Canada and conducted by or on behalf of the Attorney General of Canada, or

    (b)   the Attorney General of a province, in respect of any other offence in the province,

if the urgency of the situation requires interception of private communications to commence before an authorization could, with reasonable diligence, be obtained under section 186.

(2) **Authorizations in emergency** — Where the judge to whom an application is made pursuant to subsection (1) is satisfied that the urgency of the situation requires that interception of private communications commence before an authorization could, with reasonable diligence, be obtained under section 186, he may, on such terms and conditions, if any, as he considers advisable, give an authorization in writing for a period of up to thirty-six hours.

(3) [Repealed, 1993, c. 40, s. 8 (in force August 1, 1993)]

(4) **Definition of "Chief Justice"** — In this section, "Chief Justice" means

    (a)   in the Province of Ontario, the Chief Justice of the Ontario Court;

    (b)   in the Province of Quebec, the Chief Justice of the Superior Court;

    (c)   in the Provinces of Nova Scotia and British Columbia, the Chief Justice of the Supreme Court;

    (d)   in the Provinces of New Brunswick, Manitoba, Saskatchewan and Alberta, the Chief Justice of the Court of Queen's Bench;

    (e)   in the Provinces of Prince Edward Island and Newfoundland, the Chief Justice of the Supreme Court, Trial Division; and

    (f)   in the Yukon Territory, the Northwest Territories and Nunavut, the senior judge within the meaning of subsection 22(3) of the Judges Act.

(5) **Inadmissibility of evidence** — The trial judge may deem inadmissible the evidence obtained by means of an interception of a private communication pursuant to a subsequent authorization given under this section, where he finds that the application for the subsequent authorization was based on the same facts, and involved the interception of the private communications of the same person or

persons, or related to the same offence, on which the application for the original authorization was based.

[R.S., 1985, c. 27 (1st Supp.), ss. 25, 185 (Sch. III, item 6)(F) (in force December 4, 1985); 1985, c. 27 (2nd Supp.), s. 10 (Sch., items 6(7) and (8)); 1990, c. 17, s. 10 (in force September 1, 1990); 1992, c. 1, s. 58 (1) (Sch. I, item 4) (in force February 28, 1992); 1992, c. 51, s. 35 (in force January 30, 1993); 1993, c. 28, s. 78 (Sch. III, item 29), this amendment was repealed before it came into force by 1999, c. 3, s. 12 (Sch. item 6), c. 40, s. 8 (in force August 1, 1993); 1999, c. 3, s. 28 (in force April 1, 1999)]

188.1 (1) **Execution of authorizations** — Subject to subsection (2), the interception of a private communication authorized pursuant to section 184.2, 184.3, 186 or 188 may be carried out anywhere in Canada.

(2) **Execution in another province** — Where an authorization is given under section 184.2, 184.3, 186 or 188 in one province but it may reasonably be expected that it is to be executed in another province and the execution of the authorization would require entry into or upon the property of any person in the other province or would require that an order under section 487.02 be made with respect to any person in that other province, a judge in the other province may, on application, confirm the authorization and when the authorization is so confirmed, it shall have full force and effect in that other province as though it had originally been given in that other province.

[1993, c. 40, s. 9 (in force August 1, 1993).]

188.2 No civil or criminal liability — No person who acts in accordance with an authorization or under section 184.1 or 184.4 or who aids, in good faith, a person who he or she believes on reasonable grounds is acting in accordance with an authorization or under one of those sections incurs any criminal or civil liability for anything reasonably done further to the authorization or to that section.

[1993, c. 40, s. 9 (in force August 1, 1993).]

189. (1) [Repealed, 1993, c. 40, s. 10 (in force August 1, 1993)];

(2) [Repealed, 1993, c. 40, s. 10 (in force August 1, 1993)];

(3) [Repealed, 1993, c. 40, s. 10 (in force August 1, 1993)];

(4) [Repealed, 1993, c. 40, s. 10 (in force August 1, 1993)]

(5) **Notice of intention to produce evidence** — The contents of a private communication that is obtained from an interception of the private communication pursuant to any provision of, or pursuant to an authorization given under, this Part shall not be received in evidence unless the party intending to adduce it has given to the accused reasonable notice of the intention together with

    (a)   a transcript of the private communication, where it will be adduced in the form of a recording, or a statement setting out full particulars of the private communication, where evidence of the private communication will be given *viva voce*; and

    (b)   a statement respecting the time, place and date of the private communication and the parties thereto, if known.

(6) **Privileged evidence** — Any information obtained by an interception that, but for the interception, would have been privileged remains privileged and inadmissible as evidence without the consent of the person enjoying the privilege.

[1993, c. 40, s. 10 (in force August 1, 1993).]

190. Further particulars — Where an accused has been given notice pursuant to subsection 189(5), any judge of the court in which the trial of the accused is being or is to be held may at any time order that further particulars be given of the private communication that is intended to be adduced in evidence.

191. (1) **Possession, etc.** — Every one who possesses, sells or purchases any electromagnetic, acoustic, mechanical or other device or any component thereof knowing that the design thereof renders it primarily useful for surreptitious interception of private communications is guilty of an indictable offence and liable to imprisonment for a term not exceeding two years.

(2) **Exemptions** — Subsection (1) does not apply to

(a) a police officer or police constable in possession of a device or component described in subsection (1) in the course of his employment;

(b) a person in possession of such a device or component for the purpose of using it in an interception made or to be made in accordance with an authorization;

(b.1) a person in possession of such a device or component under the direction of a police officer or police constable in order to assist that officer or constable in the course of his duties as a police officer or police constable;

(c) an officer or a servant of Her Majesty in right of Canada or a member of the Canadian Forces in possession of such a device or component in the course of his duties as such an officer, servant or member, as the case may be; and

(d) any other person in possession of such a device or component under the authority of a licence issued by the Solicitor General of Canada.

(3) **Terms and conditions of licence** — A licence issued for the purpose of paragraph (2)(d) may contain such terms and conditions relating to the possession, sale or purchase of a device or component described in subsection (1) as the Solicitor General of Canada may prescribe.

[R.S., 1985, c. 27 (1st Supp.), s. 26 (in force December 4, 1985).]

192. (1) **Forfeiture** — Where a person is convicted of an offence under section 184 or 191, any electro-magnetic, acoustic, mechanical or other device by means of which the offence was committed or the possession of which constituted the offence, on the conviction, in addition to any punishment that is imposed, may be ordered forfeited to Her Majesty whereupon it may be disposed of as the Attorney General directs.

(2) **Limitation** — No order for forfeiture shall be made under subsection (1) in respect of telephone, telegraph or other communication facilities or equipment owned by a person engaged in providing telephone, telegraph or other communication service to the public or forming part of the telephone, telegraph or other communication service or system of that person by means of which an offence under section 184 has been committed if that person was not a party to the offence.

193. (1) **Disclosure of information** — Where a private communication has been intercepted by means of an electro-magnetic, acoustic, mechanical or other device without the consent, express or implied, of the originator thereof or of the person intended by the originator thereof to receive it, every one who, without the express consent of the originator thereof or of the person intended by the originator thereof to receive it, wilfully

(a)   uses or discloses the private communication or any part thereof or the substance, meaning or purport thereof or of any part thereof, or

(b)   discloses the existence thereof,

is guilty of an indictable offence and liable to imprisonment for a term not exceeding two years.

(2) **Exemptions** — Subsection (1) does not apply to a person who discloses a private communication or any part thereof or the substance, meaning or purport thereof or of any part thereof or who discloses the existence of a private communication

(a)   in the course of or for the purpose of giving evidence in any civil or criminal proceedings or in any other proceedings in which the person may be required to give evidence on oath;

(b)   in the course of or for the purpose of any criminal investigation if the private communication was lawfully intercepted;

(c)   in giving notice under section 189 or furnishing further particulars pursuant to an order under section 190;

(d)   in the course of the operation of

(i)   a telephone, telegraph or other communication service to the public, or

(ii)   a department or an agency of the Government of Canada,

if the disclosure is necessarily incidental to an interception described in paragraph 184(2)(c) or (d);

(e)   where disclosure is made to a peace officer or prosecutor in Canada or to a person or authority with responsibility in a foreign state for the investigation or prosecution of offences and is intended to be in the interests of the administration of justice in Canada or elsewhere; or

(f)   where the disclosure is made to the Director of the Canadian Security Intelligence Service or to an employee of the Service for the purpose of enabling the Service to perform its duties and functions under section 12 of the *Canadian Security Intelligence Service Act.*

(3) **Publishing of prior lawful disclosure** — Subsection (1) does not apply to a person who discloses a private communication or any part thereof or the substance, meaning or purport thereof or of any part thereof or who discloses the existence of a private communication where that which is disclosed by him was, prior to the disclosure, lawfully disclosed in the course of or for the purpose of giving evidence in proceedings referred to in paragraph (2)(a).

[R.S., 1985, c. 30 (4th Supp.), s. 45 (in force October 1, 1988); 1993, c. 40, s. 11 (in force August 1, 1993).]

193.1 (1) Disclosure of information received from interception of radio-based telephone communications — Every person who wilfully uses or discloses a radio-based telephone communication or who wilfully discloses the existence of such a communication is guilty of an indictable offence and liable to imprisonment for a term not exceeding two years, if

(a)   the originator of the communication or the person intended by the originator of the communication to receive it was in Canada when the communication was made;

(b)   the communication was intercepted by means of an electromagnetic, acoustic, mechanical or other device without the consent, express or implied, of the originator of the communication or of the person intended by the originator to receive the communication; and

(c)   the person does not have the express or implied consent of the originator of the communication or of the person intended by the originator to receive the communication.

(2) **Other provisions to apply** — Subsections 193(2) and (3) apply, with such modifications as the circumstances require, to disclosures of radio-based telephone communications.

[1993, c. 40, s. 12 (in force August 1, 1993).]

194. (1) **Damages** — Subject to subsection (2), a court that convicts an accused of an offence under section 184, 184.5, 193 or 193.1 may, on the application of a person aggrieved, at the time sentence is imposed, order the accused to pay to that person an amount not exceeding five thousand dollars as punitive damages.

(2) **No damages where civil proceedings commenced** — No amount shall be ordered to be paid under subsection (1) to a person who has commenced an action under Part II of the *Crown Liability Act*.

(3) **Judgment may be registered** — Where an amount that is ordered to be paid under subsection (1) is not paid forthwith, the applicant may, by filing the order, enter as a judgment, in the superior court of the province in which the trial was held, the amount ordered to be paid, and that judgment is enforceable against the accused in the same manner as if it were a judgment rendered against the accused in that court in civil proceedings.

(4) **Moneys in possession of accused may be taken** — All or any part of an amount that is ordered to be paid under subsection (1) may be taken out of moneys found in the possession of the accused at the time of his arrest, except where there is a dispute respecting ownership of or right of possession to those moneys by claimants other than the accused.

[1993, c. 40, s. 13 (in force August 1, 1993).]

195. (1) **Annual report** — The Solicitor General of Canada shall, as soon as possible after the end of each year, prepare a report relating to

(a)   authorizations for which he and agents to be named in the report who were specially designated in writing by him for the purposes of section 185 made application, and

(b)   authorizations given under section 188 for which peace officers to be named in the report who were specially designated by him for the purposes of that section made application,

and interceptions made thereunder in the immediately preceding year.

(2) **Information respecting authorizations** — The report referred to in subsection (1) shall, in relation to authorizations and interceptions made thereunder, set out

(a) the number of applications made for authorizations;

(b) the number of applications made for renewal of authorizations;

(c) the number of applications referred to in paragraphs (a) and (b) that were granted, the number of those applications that were refused and the number of applications referred to in paragraph (a) that were granted subject to terms and conditions;

(d) the number of persons identified in an authorization against whom proceedings were commenced at the instance of the Attorney General of Canada in respect of

  (i) an offence specified in the authorization,

  (ii) an offence other than an offence specified in the authorization but in respect of which an authorization may be given, and

  (iii) an offence in respect of which an authorization may not be given;

(e) the number of persons not identified in an authorization against whom proceedings were commenced at the instance of the Attorney General of Canada in respect of

  (i) an offence specified in such an authorization,

  (ii) an offence other than an offence specified in such an authorization but in respect of which an authorization may be given, and

  (iii) an offence other than an offence specified in such an authorization and for which no such authorization may be given,

  and whose commission or alleged commission of the offence became known to a peace officer as a result of an interception of a private communication under an authorization;

(f) the average period for which authorizations were given and for which renewals thereof were granted;

(g) the number of authorizations that, by virtue of one or more renewals thereof, were valid for more than sixty days, for more than one hundred and twenty days, for more than one hundred and eighty days and for more than two hundred and forty days;

(h) the number of notifications given pursuant to section 196;

(i) the offences in respect of which authorizations were given, specifying the number of authorizations given in respect of each of those offences;

(j) a description of all classes of places specified in authorizations and the number of authorizations in which each of those classes of places was specified;

(k) a general description of the methods of interception involved in each interception under an authorization;

(l) the number of persons arrested whose identity became known to a peace officer as a result of an interception under an authorization;

(m) the number of criminal proceedings commenced at the instance of the Attorney General of Canada in which private communications obtained by interception under an authorization were adduced in evidence and the number of those proceedings that resulted in a conviction; and

(n)   the number of criminal investigations in which information obtained as a result of the interception of a private communication under an authorization was used although the private communication was not adduced in evidence in criminal proceedings commenced at the instance of the Attorney General of Canada as a result of the investigations.

(3) **Other information** — The report referred to in subsection (1) shall, in addition to the information referred to in subsection (2), set out

(a)   the number of prosecutions commenced against officers or servants of Her Majesty in right of Canada or members of the Canadian Forces for offences under section 184 or 193; and

(b)   a general assessment of the importance of interception of private communications for the investigation, detection, prevention and prosecution of offences in Canada.

(4) **Report to be laid before Parliament** — The Solicitor General of Canada shall cause a copy of each report prepared by him under subsection (1) to be laid before Parliament forthwith on completion thereof, or if Parliament is not then sitting, on any of the first fifteen days next thereafter that Parliament is sitting.

(5) **Report by Attorneys General** — The Attorney General of each province shall, as soon as possible after the end of each year, prepare and publish or otherwise make available to the public a report relating to

(a)   authorizations for which he and agents specially designated in writing by him for the purposes of section 185 made application, and

(b)   authorizations given under section 188 for which peace officers specially designated by him for the purposes of that section made application,

and interceptions made thereunder in the immediately preceding year setting out, with such modifications as the circumstances require, the information described in subsections (2) and (3).

[R.S., 1985, c. 27 (1st Supp.), s. 27 (in force December 4, 1985).]

196. (1) **Written notification to be given** — The Attorney General of the province in which an application under subsection 185(1) was made or the Solicitor General of Canada if the application was made by or on behalf of the Solicitor General of Canada shall, within ninety days after the period for which the authorization was given or renewed or within such other period as is fixed pursuant to subsection 185(3) or subsection (3) of this section, notify in writing the person who was the object of the interception pursuant to the authorization and shall, in a manner prescribed by regulations made by the Governor in Council, certify to the court that gave the authorization that the person has been so notified.

(2) **Extension of period for notification** — The running of the ninety days referred to in subsection (1), or of any other period fixed pursuant to subsection 185(3) or subsection (3) of this section, is suspended until any application made by the Attorney General or the Solicitor General to a judge of a superior court of criminal jurisdiction or a judge as defined in section 552 for an extension or a subsequent extension of the period for which the authorization was given or renewed has been heard and disposed of.

(3) **Where extension to be granted** — Where the judge to whom an application referred to in subsection (2) is made, on the basis of an affidavit submitted in support of the application, is satisfied that

(a) the investigation of the offence to which the authorization relates, or

(b) a subsequent investigation of an offence listed in section 183 commenced as a result of information obtained from the investigation referred to in paragraph (a),

is continuing and is of the opinion that the interests of justice warrant the granting of the application, the judge shall grant an extension, or a subsequent extension, of the period, each extension not to exceed three years.

(4) **Application to be accompanied by affidavit** — An application pursuant to subsection (2) shall be accompanied by an affidavit deposing to

(a) the facts known or believed by the deponent and relied on to justify the belief that an extension should be granted; and

(b) the number of instances, if any, on which an application has, to the knowledge or belief of the deponent, been made under that subsection in relation to the particular authorization and on which the application was withdrawn or the application was not granted, the date on which each application was made and the judge to whom each application was made.

(5) **Exception for criminal organizations and terrorist groups** — Notwithstanding subsections (3) and 185(3), where the judge to whom an application referred to in subsection (2) or 185(2) is made, on the basis of an affidavit submitted in support of the application, is satisfied that the investigation is in relation to

(a) an offence under section 467.11, 467.12 or 467.13;

(b) an offence committed for the benefit of, at the direction of or in association with a criminal organization; or

(c) a terrorism offence.

and is of the opinion that the interests of justice warrant the granting of the application, the judge shall grant an extension, or a subsequent extension, of the period, but no extension may exceed three years.

[R.S., 1985, c. 27 (1st Supp.), s. 28 (in force December 4, 1985); 1993, c. 40, s. 14 (in force August 1, 1993); 1997, c. 23, s. 7 (in force May 2, 1997); 2001, c. 32, s. 8 (in force January 7, 2002); 2002, c. 41, ss. 8, 133 (s. 8 in force December 24, 2001; s. 133 in force January 7, 2002).]

Part VIII

Offences Against The Person And Reputation

Assaults

273.1 (1) **Meaning of "consent"** — Subject to subsection (2) and subsection 265(3), "consent" means, for the purposes of sections 271, 272 and 273, the voluntary agreement of the complainant to engage in the sexual activity in question.

(2) **Where no consent obtained** — No consent is obtained, for the purposes of sections 271, 272 and 273, where

(a) the agreement is expressed by the words or conduct of a person other than the complainant;

(b)   the complainant is incapable of consenting to the activity;
(c)   the accused induces the complainant to engage in the activity by abusing a position of trust, power or authority;
(d)   the complainant expresses, by words or conduct, a lack of agreement to engage in the activity; or
(e)   the complainant, having consented to engage in sexual activity, expresses, by words or conduct, a lack of agreement to continue to engage in the activity.

(3) **Subsection (2) not limiting** — Nothing in subsection (2) shall be construed as limiting the circumstances in which no consent is obtained.
[1992, c. 38, s. 1 (in force August 15, 1992).]

273.2 Where belief in consent not a defence — It is not a defence to a charge under section 271, 272 or 273 that the accused believed that the complainant consented to the activity that forms the subject-matter of the charge, where
(a)   the accused's belief arose from the accused's
    (i)   self-induced intoxication, or
    (ii)   recklessness or wilful blindness; or
(b)   the accused did not take reasonable steps, in the circumstances known to the accused at the time, to ascertain that the complainant was consenting.
[1992, c. 38, s. 1 (in force August 15, 1992).]

274. Corroboration not required — Where an accused is charged with an offence under section 151, 152, 153, 155, 159, 160, 170, 171, 172, 173, 212, 271, 272 or 273, no corroboration is required for a conviction and the judge shall not instruct the jury that it is unsafe to find the accused guilty in the absence of corroboration.
[R.S., 1985, c. 19 (3rd Supp.), s. 11 (in force January 1, 1988).]

275. Rules respecting recent complaint abrogated — The rules relating to evidence of recent complaint are hereby abrogated with respect to offences under sections 151, 152, 153, 155 and 159, subsections 160(2) and (3), and sections 170, 171, 172, 173, 271, 272 and 273.
[R.S., 1985, c. 19 (3rd Supp.), s. 11 (in force January 1, 1988).]

276. (1) **Evidence of complainant's sexual activity** — In proceedings in respect of an offence under section 151, 152, 153, 155 or 159, subsection 160(2) or (3) or section 170, 171, 172, 173, 271, 272 or 273, evidence that the complainant has engaged in sexual activity, whether with the accused or with any other person, is not admissible to support an inference that, by reason of the sexual nature of that activity, the complainant
(a)   is more likely to have consented to the sexual activity that forms the subject-matter of the charge; or
(b)   is less worthy of belief.

(2) **Idem** — In proceedings in respect of an offence referred to in subsection (1), no evidence shall be adduced by or on behalf of the accused that the complainant has engaged in sexual activity other than the sexual activity that forms the subject-matter of the charge, whether with the accused or with any other person,

unless the judge, provincial court judge or justice determines, in accordance with the procedures set out in sections 276.1 and 276.2, that the evidence

(a) is of specific instances of sexual activity;

(b) is relevant to an issue at trial; and

(c) has significant probative value that is not substantially outweighed by the danger of prejudice to the proper administration of justice.

(3) **Factors that judge must consider** — In determining whether evidence is admissible under subsection (2), the judge, provincial court judge or justice shall take into account

(a) the interests of justice, including the right of the accused to make a full answer and defence;

(b) society's interest in encouraging the reporting of sexual assault offences;

(c) whether there is a reasonable prospect that the evidence will assist in arriving at a just determination in the case;

(d) the need to remove from the fact-finding process any discriminatory belief or bias;

(e) the risk that the evidence may unduly arouse sentiments of prejudice, sympathy or hostility in the jury;

(f) the potential prejudice to the complainant's personal dignity and right of privacy;

(g) the right of the complainant and of every individual to personal security and to the full protection and benefit of the law; and

(h) any other factor that the judge, provincial court judge or justice considers relevant.

[R.S., 1985, c. 27 (1st Supp.), s. 203; R.S. 1985, c. 19 (3rd Supp.), s. 12; 1992, c. 38, s. 2 (in force August 15, 1992).]

276.1 (1) **Application for hearing** — Application may be made to the judge, provincial court judge or justice by or on behalf of the accused for a hearing under section 276.2 to determine whether evidence is admissible under subsection 276(2).

(2) **Form and content of application** — An application referred to in subsection (1) must be made in writing and set out

(a) detailed particulars of the evidence that the accused seeks to adduce, and

(b) the relevance of that evidence to an issue at trial,

and a copy of the application must be given to the prosecutor and to the clerk of the court.

(3) **Jury and public excluded** — The judge, provincial court judge or justice shall consider the application with the jury and the public excluded.

(4) **Judge may decide to hold hearing** — Where the judge, provincial court judge or justice is satisfied

(a) that the application was made in accordance with subsection (2),

(b) that a copy of the application was given to the prosecutor and to the clerk of the court at least seven days previously, or such shorter interval as the judge, provincial court judge or justice may allow where the interests of justice so require, and

(c)   that the evidence sought to be adduced is capable of being admissible under subsection 276(2),

the judge, provincial court judge or justice shall grant the application and hold a hearing under section 276.2 to determine whether the evidence is admissible under subsection 276(2).

[1992, c. 38, s. 2 (in force August 15, 1992).]

276.2 (1) **Jury and public excluded** — At a hearing to determine whether evidence is admissible under subsection 276(2), the jury and the public shall be excluded.

(2) **Complainant not compellable** — The complainant is not a compellable witness at the hearing.

(3) **Judge's determination and reasons** — At the conclusion of the hearing, the judge, provincial court judge or justice shall determine whether the evidence, or any part thereof, is admissible under subsection 276(2) and shall provide reasons for that determination, and

(a)   where not all of the evidence is to be admitted, the reasons must state the part of the evidence that is to be admitted;

(b)   the reasons must state the factors referred to in subsection 276(3) that affected the determination; and

(c)   where all or any part of the evidence is to be admitted, the reasons must state the manner in which that evidence is expected to be relevant to an issue at trial.

(4) **Record of reasons** — The reasons provided under subsection (3) shall be entered in the record of the proceedings or, where the proceedings are not recorded, shall be provided in writing.

[1992, c. 38, s. 2 (in force August 15, 1992).]

276.3 (1) **Publication prohibited** — No person shall publish in a newspaper, as defined in section 297, or in a broadcast, any of the following:

(a)   the contents of an application made under section 276.1;

(b)   any evidence taken, the information given and the representations made at an application under section 276.1 or at a hearing under section 276.2;

(c)   the decision of a judge, provincial court judge or justice under subsection 276.1(4), unless the judge, provincial court judge or justice, after taking into account the complainant's right of privacy and the interests of justice, orders that the decision may be published; and

(d)   the determination made and the reasons provided under section 276.2, unless

(i)   that determination is that evidence is admissible, or

(ii)   the judge, provincial court judge or justice, after taking into account the complainant's right of privacy and the interests of justice, orders that the determination and reasons may be published.

(2) **Offence** — Every person who contravenes subsection (1) is guilty of an offence punishable on summary conviction.

[1992, c. 38, s. 2 (in force August 15, 1992).]

276.4 Judge to instruct jury re use of evidence — Where evidence is admitted at trial pursuant to a determination made under section 276.2, the judge shall instruct the jury as to the uses that the jury may and may not make of that evidence.

[1992, c. 38, s. 2 (in force August 15, 1992).]

276.5 Appeal — For the purposes of sections 675 and 676, a determination made under section 276.2 shall be deemed to be a question of law.

[1992, c. 38, s. 2 (in force August 15, 1992).]

278.1 Definition of "record" — For the purposes of sections 278.2 to 278.9, "record" means any form of record that contains personal information for which there is a reasonable expectation of privacy and includes, without limiting the generality of the foregoing, medical, psychiatric, therapeutic, counselling, education, employment, child welfare, adoption and social services records, personal journals and diaries, and records containing personal information the production or disclosure of which is protected by any other Act of Parliament or a provincial legislature, but does not include records made by persons responsible for the investigation or prosecution of the offence.

[1997, c. 30, s. 1 (in force May 12, 1997).]

278.2 (1) Production of record to accused — No record relating to a complainant or a witness shall be produced to an accused in any proceedings in respect of

(a)   an offence under section 151, 152, 153, 153.1, 155, 159, 160, 170, 171, 172, 173, 210, 211, 212, 213, 271, 272 or 273,

(b)   an offence under section 144, 145, 149, 156, 245 or 246 of the Criminal Code, chapter C-34 of the Revised Statutes of Canada, 1970, as it read immediately before January 4, 1983, or

(c)   an offence under section 146, 151, 153, 155, 157, 166 or 167 of the Criminal Code, chapter C-34 of the Revised Statutes of Canada, 1970, as it read immediately before January 1, 1988,

or in any proceedings in respect of two or more offences that include an offence referred to in any of paragraphs (a) to (c), except in accordance with sections 278.3 to 278.91.

(2) **Application of provisions** — Section 278.1, this section and sections 278.3 to 278.91 apply where a record is in the possession or control of any person, including the prosecutor in the proceedings, unless, in the case of a record in the possession or control of the prosecutor, the complainant or witness to whom the record relates has expressly waived the application of those sections.

(3) **Duty of prosecutor to give notice** — In the case of a record in respect of which this section applies that is in the possession or control of the prosecutor, the prosecutor shall notify the accused that the record is in the prosecutor's possession but, in doing so, the prosecutor shall not disclose the record's contents.

[1997, c. 30, s. 1 (in force May 12, 1997); 1998, c. 9, s. 3 (in force June 30, 1998).]

278.3 (1) **Application for production** — An accused who seeks production of a record referred to in subsection 278.2(1) must make an application to the judge before whom the accused is to be, or is being, tried.

(2) **No application in other proceedings** — For greater certainty, an application under subsection (1) may not be made to a judge or justice presiding at any other proceedings, including a preliminary inquiry.

(3) **Form and content of application** — An application must be made in writing and set out

(a) particulars identifying the record that the accused seeks to have produced and the name of the person who has possession or control of the record; and

(b) the grounds on which the accused relies to establish that the record is likely relevant to an issue at trial or to the competence of a witness to testify.

(4) **Insufficient grounds** — Any one or more of the following assertions by the accused are not sufficient on their own to establish that the record is likely relevant to an issue at trial or to the competence of a witness to testify:

(a) that the record exists;

(b) that the record relates to medical or psychiatric treatment, therapy or counselling that the complainant or witness has received or is receiving;

(c) that the record relates to the incident that is the subject-matter of the proceedings;

(d) that the record may disclose a prior inconsistent statement of the complainant or witness;

(e) that the record may relate to the credibility of the complainant or witness;

(f) that the record may relate to the reliability of the testimony of the complainant or witness merely because the complainant or witness has received or is receiving psychiatric treatment, therapy or counselling;

(g) that the record may reveal allegations of sexual abuse of the complainant by a person other than the accused;

(h) that the record relates to the sexual activity of the complainant with any person, including the accused;

(i) that the record relates to the presence or absence of a recent complaint;

(j) that the record relates to the complainant's sexual reputation; or

(k) that the record was made close in time to a complaint or to the activity that forms the subject-matter of the charge against the accused.

(5) **Service of application and subpoena** — The accused shall serve the application on the prosecutor, on the person who has possession or control of the record, on the complainant or witness, as the case may be, and on any other person to whom, to the knowledge of the accused, the record relates, at least seven days before the hearing referred to in subsection 278.4(1) or any shorter interval that the judge may allow in the interests of justice. The accused shall also serve a subpoena issued under Part XXII in Form 16.1 on the person who has possession or control of the record at the same time as the application is served.

(6) **Service on other persons** — The judge may at any time order that the application be served on any person to whom the judge considers the record may relate.

[1997, c. 30, s. 1 (in force May 12, 1997).]

278.4 (1) **Hearing *in camera*** — The judge shall hold a hearing *in camera* to determine whether to order the person who has possession or control of the record to produce it to the court for review by the judge.

(2) **Persons who may appear at hearing** — The person who has possession or control of the record, the complainant or witness, as the case may be, and any other person to whom the record relates may appear and make submissions at the hearing, but they are not compellable as witnesses at the hearing.

(3) **Costs** — No order for costs may be made against a person referred to in subsection (2) in respect of their participation in the hearing.

[1997, c. 30, s. 1 (in force May 12, 1997).]

278.5 (1) **Judge may order production of record for review** — The judge may order the person who has possession or control of the record to produce the record or part of the record to the court for review by the judge if, after the hearing referred to in subsection 278.4(1), the judge is satisfied that

   (a)   the application was made in accordance with subsections 278.3(2) to (6);
   (b)   the accused has established that the record is likely relevant to an issue at trial or to the competence of a witness to testify; and
   (c)   the production of the record is necessary in the interests of justice.

(2) **Factors to be considered** — In determining whether to order the production of the record or part of the record for review pursuant to subsection (1), the judge shall consider the salutary and deleterious effects of the determination on the accused's right to make a full answer and defence and on the right to privacy and equality of the complainant or witness, as the case may be, and any other person to whom the record relates. In particular, the judge shall take the following factors into account:

   (a)   the extent to which the record is necessary for the accused to make a full answer and defence;
   (b)   the probative value of the record;
   (c)   the nature and extent of the reasonable expectation of privacy with respect to the record;
   (d)   whether production of the record is based on a discriminatory belief or bias;
   (e)   the potential prejudice to the personal dignity and right to privacy of any person to whom the record relates;
   (f)   society's interest in encouraging the reporting of sexual offences;
   (g)   society's interest in encouraging the obtaining of treatment by complainants of sexual offences; and
   (h)   the effect of the determination on the integrity of the trial process.

[1997, c. 30, s. 1 (in force May 12, 1997).]

278.6 (1) **Review of record by judge** — Where the judge has ordered the production of the record or part of the record for review, the judge shall review it in the absence of the parties in order to determine whether the record or part of the record should be produced to the accused.

(2) **Hearing *in camera*** — The judge may hold a hearing *in camera* if the judge considers that it will assist in making the determination.

(3) **Provisions re hearing** — Subsections 278.4(2) and (3) apply in the case of a hearing under subsection (2).

[1997, c. 30, s. 1 (in force May 12, 1997).]

278.7 (1) **Judge may order production of record to accused** — Where the judge is satisfied that the record or part of the record is likely relevant to an issue at trial or to the competence of a witness to testify and its production is necessary in the interests of justice, the judge may order that the record or part of the record that is likely relevant be produced to the accused, subject to any conditions that may be imposed pursuant to subsection (3).

(2) **Factors to be considered** — In determining whether to order the production of the record or part of the record to the accused, the judge shall consider the salutary and deleterious effects of the determination on the accused's right to make a full answer and defence and on the right to privacy and equality of the complainant or witness, as the case may be, and any other person to whom the record relates and, in particular, shall take the factors specified in paragraphs 278.5(2)(a) to (h) into account.

(3) **Conditions on production** — Where the judge orders the production of the record or part of the record to the accused, the judge may impose conditions on the production to protect the interests of justice and, to the greatest extent possible, the privacy and equality interests of the complainant or witness, as the case may be, and any other person to whom the record relates, including, for example, the following conditions:

(a)   that the record be edited as directed by the judge;

(b)   that a copy of the record, rather than the original, be produced;

(c)   that the accused and counsel for the accused not disclose the contents of the record to any other person, except with the approval of the court;

(d)   that the record be viewed only at the offices of the court;

(e)   that no copies of the record be made or that restrictions be imposed on the number of copies of the record that may be made; and

(f)   that information regarding any person named in the record, such as their address, telephone number and place of employment, be severed from the record.

(4) **Copy to prosecutor** — Where the judge orders the production of the record or part of the record to the accused, the judge shall direct that a copy of the record or part of the record be provided to the prosecutor, unless the judge determines that it is not in the interests of justice to do so.

(5) **Record not to be used in other proceedings** — The record or part of the record that is produced to the accused pursuant to an order under subsection (1) shall not be used in any other proceedings.

(6) **Retention of record by court** — Where the judge refuses to order the production of the record or part of the record to the accused, the record or part of the

record shall, unless a court orders otherwise, be kept in a sealed package by the court until the later of the expiration of the time for any appeal and the completion of any appeal in the proceedings against the accused, whereupon the record or part of the record shall be returned to the person lawfully entitled to possession or control of it.

[1997, c. 30, s. 1 (in force May 12, 1997).]

278.8 (1) **Reasons for decision** — The judge shall provide reasons for ordering or refusing to order the production of the record or part of the record pursuant to subsection 278.5(1) or 278.7(1).

(2) **Record of reasons** — The reasons referred to in subsection (1) shall be entered in the record of the proceedings or, where the proceedings are not recorded, shall be provided in writing.

[1997, c. 30, s. 1 (in force May 12, 1997).]

278.9 (1) **Publication prohibited** — No person shall publish in a newspaper, as defined in section 297, or in a broadcast, any of the following:

(a)　the contents of an application made under section 278.3;

(b)　any evidence taken, information given or submissions made at a hearing under subsection 278.4(1) or 278.6(2); or

(c)　the determination of the judge pursuant to subsection 278.5(1) or 278.7(1) and the reasons provided pursuant to section 278.8, unless the judge, after taking into account the interests of justice and the right to privacy of the person to whom the record relates, orders that the determination may be published.

(2) **Offence** — Every person who contravenes subsection (1) is guilty of an offence punishable on summary conviction.

[1997, c. 30, s. 1 (in force May 12, 1997).]

TAKE NOTE On the expiration of three years after the coming into force of this Act [278.1 to 278.91], the provisions contained herein shall be referred to such committee of the House of Commons, of the Senate or of both Houses of Parliament as may be designated or established by Parliament for that purpose.

[1997, c. 30, s. 3.1(1)]

Part XV

Special Procedure And Powers

General Powers of Certain Officials

486. (1) **Exclusion of public in certain cases** — Any proceedings against an accused shall be held in open court, but where the presiding judge, provincial court judge or justice, as the case may be, is of the opinion that it is in the interest of public morals, the maintenance of order or the proper administration of justice, or that it is necessary to prevent injury to international relations or national defence or national security, to exclude all or any members of the public from the court room for all or part of the proceedings, he may so order.

(1.1) **Protection of child witnesses** — For the purposes of subsections (1) and (2.3) and for greater certainty, the "proper administration of justice" includes ensuring that the interests of witnesses under the age of eighteen years are safeguarded in proceedings in which the accused is charged with a sexual offence, an offence against any of sections 271, 272 and 273 or an offence in which violence against the person is alleged to have been used, threatened or attempted.

(1.2) **Support person** — In proceedings referred to in subsection (1.1), the presiding judge, provincial court judge or justice may, on application of the prosecutor or a witness who, at the time of the trial or preliminary hearing, is under the age of fourteen years or who has a mental or physical disability, order that a support person of the witness' choice be permitted to be present and to be close to the witness while testifying.

(1.3) **Witness not to be a support person** — The presiding judge, provincial court judge or justice shall not permit a witness in the proceedings referred to in subsection (1.1) to be a support person unless the presiding judge, provincial court judge or justice is of the opinion that the proper administration of justice so requires.

(1.4) **No communication while testifying** — The presiding judge, provincial court judge or justice may order that the support person and the witness not communicate with each other during the testimony of the witness.

(1.5) **Protection of justice system participants** — For the purposes of subsection (1) and for greater certainty, the "proper administration of justice" includes ensuring the protection of justice system participants who are involved in the proceedings.

(2) **Reasons to be stated** — Where an accused is charged with an offence mentioned in section 274 and the prosecutor or the accused makes an application for an order under subsection (1), the presiding judge, provincial court judge or justice, as the case may be, shall, if no such order is made, state, by reference to the circumstances of the case, the reason for not making an order.

(2.1) **Testimony outside court room** — Notwithstanding section 650, where an accused is charged with an offence under section 151, 152, 153, 155 or 159, subsection 160(2) or (3), or section 163.1, 170, 171, 172, 173, 210, 211, 212, 213, 266, 267, 268, 271, 272 or 273 and the complainant or any witness, at the time of the trial or preliminary inquiry, is under the age of eighteen years or is able to communicate evidence but may have difficulty doing so by reason of a mental or physical disability, the presiding judge or justice, as the case may be, may order that the complainant or witness testify outside the court room or behind a screen or other device that would allow the complainant or witness not to see the accused, if the judge or justice is of the opinion that the exclusion is necessary to obtain a full and candid account of the acts complained of from the complainant or witness.

(2.101) **Testimony outside court room** — Notwithstanding section 650, where an accused is charged with an offence referred to in subsection (2.102), the presiding judge or justice, as the case may be, may order that any witness testify

(a)   outside the court room, if the judge or justice is of the opinion that the order is necessary to protect the safety of the witness; and

(b)   outside the court room or behind a screen or other device that would allow the witness not to see the accused, if the judge or justice is of the opinion that the order is necessary to obtain a full and candid account from the witness.

(2.102) **Offences** — The offences for the purposes of subsection (2.101) are

(a)   an offence under section 423.1, 467.11, 467.12 or 467.13, or a serious offence committed for the benefit of, at the direction of, or in association with, a criminal organization;

(b)   a terrorism offence;

(c)   an offence under subsection 16(1) or (2), 17(1), 19(1), 20(1) or 22(1) of the *Security of Information Act*; and

(d)   an offence under subsection 21(1) or section 23 of the *Security of Information Act* that is committed in relation to an offence referred to in paragraph (c).

(2.11) **Same procedure for opinion** — Where the judge or justice is of the opinion that it is necessary for the complainant or witness to testify in order to determine whether an order under subsection (2.1) or (2.101) should be made in respect of that complainant or witness, the judge or justice shall order that the complainant or witness testify pursuant to that subsection.

(2.2) **Condition of exclusion** — A complainant or witness shall not testify outside the court room pursuant to subsection (2.1), (2.101) or (2.11) unless arrangements are made for the accused, the judge or justice and the jury to watch the testimony of the complainant or other witness by means of closed-circuit television or otherwise and the accused is permitted to communicate with counsel while watching the testimony.

(2.3) **Accused not to cross-examine child witness** — In proceedings referred to in subsection (1.1), the accused shall not personally cross-examine a witness who at the time of the proceedings is under the age of eighteen years, unless the presiding judge, provincial court judge or justice is of the opinion that the proper administration of justice requires the accused to personally conduct the cross-examination and, if the accused is not personally conducting the cross-examination, the presiding judge, provincial court judge or justice shall appoint counsel for the purpose of conducting the cross-examination.

(3) **Order restricting publication** — Subject to subsection (4), the presiding judge or justice may make an order directing that the identity of a complainant or a witness and any information that could disclose the identity of the complainant or witness shall not be published in any document or broadcast in any way, when an accused is charged with

(a)   any of the following offences:

(i)   an offence under section 151, 152, 153, 153.1, 155, 159, 160, 170, 171, 172, 173, 210, 211, 212, 213, 271, 272, 273, 346 or 347,

(ii) an offence under section 144, 145, 149, 156, 245 or 246 of the *Criminal Code*, chapter C-34 of the Revised Statutes of Canada, 1970, as it read immediately before January 4, 1983, or

(iii) an offence under section 146, 151, 153, 155, 157, 166 or 167 of the *Criminal Code*, chapter C-34 of the Revised Statutes of Canada, 1970, as it read immediately before January 1, 1988; or

(b) two or more offences being dealt with in the same proceeding, at least one of which is an offence referred to in any of subparagraphs (a)(i), (ii) and (iii).

(3.1) **Limitation** — An order made under subsection (3) does not apply in respect of the disclosure of information in the course of the administration of justice where it is not the purpose of the disclosure to make the information known in the community.

(4) **Mandatory order on application** — The presiding judge or justice shall

(a) at the first reasonable opportunity, inform any witness under the age of eighteen years and the complainant to proceedings in respect of an offence mentioned in subsection (3) of the right to make an application for an order under subsection (3); and

(b) on application made by the complainant, the prosecutor or any such witness, make an order under that subsection.

(4.1) **Ban on publication, etc.** — A judge or justice may, in any proceedings against an accused other than in respect of an offence set out in subsection (3), make an order directing that the identity of a victim or witness — or, in the case of an offence referred to in subsection (4.11), the identity of a justice system participant who is involved in the proceedings — or any information that could disclose their identity, shall not be published in any document or broadcast in any way, if the judge or justice is satisfied that the order is necessary for the proper administration of justice.

(4.11) **Offences** — The offences for the purposes of subsection (4.1) are

(a) an offence under section 423.1 or a criminal organization offence;

(b) a terrorism offence;

(c) an offence under subsection 16(1) or (2), 17(1), 19(1), 20(1) or 22(1) of the *Security of Information Act*; and

(d) an offence under subsection 21(1) or section 23 of the *Security of Information Act* that is committed in relation to an offence referred to in paragraph (c).

(4.2) **Order restricting publication** — An order made under subsection (4.1) does not apply in respect of the disclosure of information in the course of the administration of justice if it is not the purpose of the disclosure to make the information known in the community.

(4.3) **Application** — An order under subsection (4.1) may be made on the application of the prosecutor, a victim or a witness. The application must be made to the presiding judge or justice or, if the judge or justice has not been determined, to a judge of a superior court of criminal jurisdiction in the judicial district where the proceedings will take place.

(4.4) **Contents of application** — The application must be in writing and set out the grounds on which the applicant relies to establish that the order is necessary for the proper administration of justice.

(4.5) **Notice of application** — The applicant shall provide notice of the application to the prosecutor, the accused and any other person affected by the order that the judge or justice specifies.

(4.6) **Hearing may be held** — The judge or justice may hold a hearing to determine whether an order under subsection (4.1) should be made, and the hearing may be in private.

(4.7) **Factors to be considered** — In determining whether to make an order under subsection (4.1), the judge or justice shall consider

(a)   the right to a fair and public hearing;

(b)   whether there is a real and substantial risk that the victim or witness would suffer significant harm if their identity were disclosed;

(c)   whether the victim or witness needs the order for their security or to protect them from intimidation or retaliation;

(d)   society's interest in encouraging the reporting of offences and the participation of victims and witnesses;

(e)   whether effective alternatives are available to protect the identity of the victim or witness;

(f)   the salutary and deleterious effects of the proposed order;

(g)   the impact of the proposed order on the freedom of expression of those affected by it; and

(h)   any other factor that the judge or justice considers relevant.

(4.8) **Conditions** — An order made under subsection (4.1) may be subject to any conditions that the judge or justice thinks fit.

(4.9) **Publication of application prohibited** — Unless the presiding judge or justice refuses to make an order under subsection (4.1), no person shall publish in any document or broadcast in any way

(a)   the contents of an application referred to in subsection (4.3);

(b)   any evidence taken, information given, or submissions made at a hearing under subsection (4.6); or

(c)   any other information that could identify the person to whom the application relates as a victim or witness in the proceedings.

(5) **Failure to comply with order** — Every person who fails to comply with an order made under subsection (3) or (4.1) is guilty of an offence punishable on summary conviction.

(6) [Repealed, R.S., 1985, c. 19 (3rd Supp.), s. 14]

[R.S., 1985, c. 27 (1st Supp.), s. 203 (in force December 4, 1985); 1985, c. 19 (3rd Supp.), s. 14 (in force January 1, 1988); 1985, c. 23 (4th Supp.), s. 1 (in force October 1, 1988); 1992, c. 1, s. 60 (Sch. I, item 32)(F) (in force February 28, 1992); 1992, c. 21, s. 9 (in force June 30, 1992); 1993, c. 45, s. 7 (in force August 1, 1993); 1997, c. 16, s. 6 (in force May 26, 1997); 1999, c. 25, s. 2 (in force December 1, 1999); 2001, c. 32, s. 29 (in force January 7, 2002); 2001, c. 41, ss. 16, 34, 133 (ss. 16, 34 in force December 24, 2001; s. 133 in force January 7, 2002).]

Part XX
Procedure In Jury Trials And General Provisions

Corroboration

659. Children's evidence — Any requirement whereby it is mandatory for a court to give the jury a warning about convicting an accused on the evidence of a child is abrogated.

[R.S., 1985, c. 19 (3rd Supp.), s. 15 (in force January 1, 1988); 1993, c. 45, s. 9 (in force August 1, 1993).]

Previous Convictions

666. Evidence of character — Where, at a trial, the accused adduces evidence of his good character, the prosecutor may, in answer thereto, before a verdict is returned, adduce evidence of the previous conviction of the accused for any offences, including any previous conviction by reason of which a greater punishment may be imposed.

Part XXI
Appeals—Indictable Offences

Powers of the Court of Appeal

686. (1) **Powers** — On the hearing of an appeal against a conviction or against a verdict that the appellant is unfit to stand trial or not criminally responsible on account of mental disorder, the court of appeal
- (a) may allow the appeal where it is of the opinion that
  - (i) the verdict should be set aside on the ground that it is unreasonable or cannot be supported by the evidence,
  - (ii) the judgment of the trial court should be set aside on the ground of a wrong decision on a question of law, or
  - (iii) on any ground there was a miscarriage of justice;
- (b) may dismiss the appeal where
  - (i) the court is of the opinion that the appellant, although he was not properly convicted on a count or part of the indictment, was properly convicted on another count or part of the indictment,
  - (ii) the appeal is not decided in favour of the appellant on any ground mentioned in paragraph (a),
  - (iii) notwithstanding that the court is of the opinion that on any ground mentioned in subparagraph (a)(ii) the appeal might be decided in favour of the appellant, it is of the opinion that no substantial wrong or miscarriage of justice has occurred, or
  - (iv) notwithstanding any procedural irregularity at trial, the trial court had jurisdiction over the class of offence of which the appellant was

convicted and the court of appeal is of the opinion that the appellant suffered no prejudice thereby;

(c) may refuse to allow the appeal where it is of the opinion that the trial court arrived at a wrong conclusion respecting the effect of a special verdict, may order the conclusion to be recorded that appears to the court to be required by the verdict and may pass a sentence that is warranted in law in substitution for the sentence passed by the trial court; or

(d) may set aside a conviction and find the appellant unfit to stand trial or not criminally responsible on account of mental disorder and may exercise any of the powers of the trial court conferred by or referred to in section 672.45 in any manner deemed appropriate to the court of appeal in the circumstances.

(e) [Repealed, 1991, c. 43, s. 9 (in force February 4, 1992)]

(2) **Order to be made** — Where a court of appeal allows an appeal under paragraph (1)(a), it shall quash the conviction and

(a) direct a judgment or verdict of acquittal to be entered; or

(b) order a new trial.

(3) **Substituting verdict** — Where a court of appeal dismisses an appeal under subparagraph (1)(b)(i), it may substitute the verdict that in its opinion should have been found and

(a) affirm the sentence passed by the trial court; or

(b) impose a sentence that is warranted in law or remit the matter to the trial court and direct the trial court to impose a sentence that is warranted in law.

(4) **Appeal from acquittal** — If an appeal is from an acquittal or verdict that the appellant or respondent was unfit to stand trial or not criminally responsible on account of mental disorder, the court of appeal may

(a) dismiss the appeal; or

(b) allow the appeal, set aside the verdict and

(i) order a new trial, or

(ii) except where the verdict is that of a court composed of a judge and jury, enter a verdict of guilty with respect to the offence of which, in its opinion, the accused should have been found guilty but for the error in law, and pass a sentence that is warranted in law, or remit the matter to the trial court and direct the trial court to impose a sentence that is warranted in law.

(5) **New trial under Part XIX** — Subject to subsection (5.01), if an appeal is taken in respect of proceedings under Part XIX and the court of appeal orders a new trial under this Part, the following provisions apply:

(a) if the accused, in his notice of appeal or notice of application for leave to appeal, requested that the new trial, if ordered, should be held before a court composed of a judge and jury, the new trial shall be held accordingly;

(b) if the accused, in his notice of appeal or notice of application for leave to appeal, did not request that the new trial, if ordered, should be held before a court composed of a judge and jury, the new trial shall, without further election by the accused, be held before a judge or provincial court judge, as the case may be, acting under Part XIX, other than a judge or provincial court judge who tried the accused in the first instance, unless the court of appeal directs that the new trial be held before the judge or provincial court judge who tried the accused in the first instance;

(c)   if the court of appeal orders that the new trial shall be held before a court composed of a judge and jury, the new trial shall be commenced by an indictment in writing setting forth the offence in respect of which the new trial was ordered; and

(d)   notwithstanding paragraph (a), if the conviction against which the accused appealed was for an offence mentioned in section 553 and was made by a provincial court judge, the new trial shall be held before a provincial court judge acting under Part XIX, other than the provincial court judge who tried the accused in the first instance, unless the court of appeal directs that the new trial be held before the provincial court judge who tried the accused in the first instance.

(5.01) **New trial under Part XIX — Nunavut** — If an appeal is taken in respect of proceedings under Part XIX and the Court of Appeal of Nunavut orders a new trial under Part XXI, the following provisions apply:

(a)   if the accused, in the notice of appeal or notice of application for leave to appeal, requested that the new trial, if ordered, should be held before a court composed of a judge and jury, the new trial shall be held accordingly;

(b)   if the accused, in the notice of appeal or notice of application for leave to appeal, did not request that the new trial, if ordered, should be held before a court composed of a judge and jury, the new trial shall, without further election by the accused, and without a further preliminary inquiry, be held before a judge, acting under Part XIX, other than a judge who tried the accused in the first instance, unless the Court of Appeal of Nunavut directs that the new trial be held before the judge who tried the accused in the first instance;

(c)   if the Court of Appeal of Nunavut orders that the new trial shall be held before a court composed of a judge and jury, the new trial shall be commenced by an indictment in writing setting forth the offence in respect of which the new trial was ordered; and

(d)   despite paragraph (a), if the conviction against which the accused appealed was for an indictable offence mentioned in section 553, the new trial shall be held before a judge acting under Part XIX, other than the judge who tried the accused in the first instance, unless the Court of Appeal of Nunavut directs that the new trial be held before the judge who tried the accused in the first instance.

(5.1) **Election if new trial a jury trial** — Subject to subsection (5.2), if a new trial ordered by the court of appeal is to be held before a court composed of a judge and jury,

(a)   the accused may, with the consent of the prosecutor, elect to have the trial heard before a judge without a jury or a provincial court judge;

(b)	the election shall be deemed to be a re-election within the meaning of subsection 561(5); and

(c)	subsection 561(5) applies, with such modifications as the circumstances require, to the election.

(5.2) **Election if new trial a jury trial – Nunavut** — If a new trial ordered by the Court of Appeal of Nunavut is to be held before a court composed of a judge and jury, the accused may, with the consent of the prosecutor, elect to have the trial heard before a judge without a jury. The election shall be deemed to be a re-election within the meaning of subsection 561.1(1), and subsection 561.1(6) applies, with any modifications that the circumstances require, to the election.

(6) **Where appeal allowed against verdict of unfit to stand trial** — Where a court of appeal allows an appeal against a verdict that the accused is unfit to stand trial, it shall, subject to subsection (7), order a new trial.

(7) **Appeal court may set aside verdict of unfit to stand trial** — Where the verdict that the accused is unfit to stand trial was returned after the close of the case for the prosecution, the court of appeal may, notwithstanding that the verdict is proper, if it is of the opinion that the accused should have been acquitted at the close of the case for the prosecution, allow the appeal, set aside the verdict and direct a judgment or verdict of acquittal to be entered.

(8) **Additional powers** — Where a court of appeal exercises any of the powers conferred by subsection (2), (4), (6) or (7), it may make any order, in addition, that justice requires.

[R.S., 1985, c. 27 (1st Supp.), ss. 145, 203 (in force December 4, 1985); 1991, c. 43, s. 9 (Sch., item 8) (in force February 4, 1992);1997, c. 18, s. 98 (in force June 16, 1997); 1999, c. 3, s. 52 (in force April 1, 1999); 1999, c. 5, s. 26 (in force May 1, 1999).]

Part XXII
Procuring Attendance

Videotaped Evidence

715.1 Evidence of complainant or witness — In any proceeding relating to an offence under section 151, 152, 153, 155 or 159, subsection 160(2) or (3), or section 163.1, 170, 171, 172, 173, 210, 211, 212, 213, 266, 267, 268, 271, 272 or 273, in which the complainant or other witness was under the age of eighteen years at the time the offence is alleged to have been committed, a videotape made within a reasonable time after the alleged offence, in which the complainant or witness describes the acts complained of, is admissible in evidence if the complainant or witness, while testifying, adopts the contents of the videotape.

[R.S., 1985, c. 19 (3rd Supp.), s. 16 (in force January 1, 1988); 1997, c. 16, s. 7 (in force May 26, 1997).]

Part XXIV
Dangerous Offenders And Long-Term Offenders

Dangerous Offenders

757. Evidence of character — Without prejudice to the right of the offender to tender evidence as to his or her character and repute, evidence of character and repute may, if the court thinks fit, be admitted on the question of whether the offender is or is not a dangerous offender or a long-term offender.

[1997, c. 17, s. 5 (in force August 1, 1997).]

Appendix B

CANADA EVIDENCE ACT

R.S.C. 1985, c. C-5

An Act respecting witnesses and evidence

1. Short title — This Act may be cited as the *Canada Evidence Act*.

Part I

Application

2. Application — This Part applies to all criminal proceedings and to all civil proceedings and other matters whatever respecting which Parliament has jurisdiction.

[R.S., c. E-10, s. 2]

Witnesses

3. Interest or crime — A person is not incompetent to give evidence by reason of interest or crime.

[R.S. c. E-10, s. 3]

4. Accused and spouse — (1) Every person charged with an offence, and, except as otherwise provided in this section, the wife or husband, as the case may be, of the person so charged, is a competent witness for the defence, whether the person so charged is charged solely or jointly with any other person.

(2) **Idem** — The wife or husband of a person charged with an offence against subsection 50(1) of the *Young Offenders Act* or with an offence against any of sections 151, 152, 153, 155 or 159, subsection 160(2) or (3), or sections 170 to 173, 179, 212, 215, 218, 271 to 273, 280 to 283, 291 to 294 or 329 of the *Criminal Code*, or an attempt to commit any such offence, is a competent and compellable witness for the prosecution without the consent of the person charged.

(3) **Communications during marriage** — No husband is compellable to disclose any communication made to him by his wife during their marriage, and no wife is compellable to disclose any communication made to her by her husband during their marriage.

(4) **Offences against young persons** — The wife or husband of a person charged with an offence against any of sections 220, 221, 235, 236, 237, 239, 240,

266, 267, 268 or 269 of the *Criminal Code* where the complainant or victim is under the age of fourteen years is a competent and compellable witness for the prosecution without the consent of the person charged.

(5) **Saving** — Nothing in this section affects a case where the wife or husband of a person charged with an offence may at common law be called as a witness without the consent of that person.

(6) **Failure to testify** — The failure of the person charged, or of the wife or husband of that person, to testify shall not be made the subject of comment by the judge or by counsel for the prosecution.

[R.S. 1985, c. 19 (3rd Supp.), s. 17]

5. (1) **Incriminating questions** —No witness shall be excused from answering any question on the ground that the answer to the question may tend to criminate him, or may tend to establish his liability to a civil proceeding at the instance of the Crown or of any person.

(2) **Answer not admissible against witness** — Where with respect to any question a witness objects to answer on the ground that his answer may tend to criminate him, or may tend to establish his liability to a civil proceeding at the instance of the Crown or of any person, and if but for this Act, or the Act of any provincial legislature, the witness would therefore have been excused from answering the question, then although the witness is by reason of this Act or the provincial Act compelled to answer, the answer so given shall not be used or admissible in evidence against him in any criminal trial or other criminal proceeding against him thereafter taking place, other than a prosecution for perjury in the giving of that evidence or for the giving of contradictory evidence.

[S.C. 1997, c. 18, s. 116]

6. (1) **Evidence of person with physical disability** — If a witness has difficulty communicating by reason of a physical disability, the court may order that the witness be permitted to give evidence by any means that enables the evidence to be intelligible.

(2) **Evidence of person with mental disability** — If a witness with a mental disability is determined under section 16 to have the capacity to give evidence and has difficulty communicating by reason of a disability, the court may order that the witness be permitted to give evidence by any means that enables the evidence to be intelligible.

(3) **Inquiry** — The court may conduct an inquiry to determine if the means by which a witness may be permitted to give evidence under subsection (1) or (2) is necessary and reliable.

[S.C. 1998, c. 9, s. 1]

6.1 Identification of accused — For greater certainty, a witness may give evidence as to the identity of an accused whom the witness is able to identify visually or in any other sensory manner.

[added, S.C. 1998, c. 9, s. 1]

7. Expert witnesses — Where, in any trial or other proceeding, criminal or civil, it is intended by the prosecution or the defence, or by any party, to examine as witnesses professional or other experts entitled according to the law or practice to give opinion evidence, not more than five of such witnesses may be called on either side without the leave of the court or judge or person presiding.

8. Handwriting comparison — Comparison of a disputed writing with any writing proved to the satisfaction of the court to be genuine shall be permitted to be made by witnesses, and such writings, and the evidence of witnesses respecting those writings, may be submitted to the court and jury as proof of the genuineness or otherwise of the writing in dispute.

9. (1) **Adverse witnesses** — A party producing a witness shall not be allowed to impeach his credit by general evidence of bad character, but if the witness, in the opinion of the court, proves adverse, the party may contradict him by other evidence, or, by leave of the court, may prove that the witness made at other times a statement inconsistent with his present testimony, but before the last mentioned proof can be given the circumstances of the supposed statement, sufficient to designate the particular occasion, shall be mentioned to the witness, and he shall be asked whether or not he did make the statement.

(2) **Previous statements by witness not proved adverse** — Where the party producing a witness alleges that the witness made at other times a statement in writing, reduced to writing, or recorded on audio tape or video tape or otherwise, inconsistent with the witness' present testimony, the court may, without proof that the witness is adverse, grant leave to that party to cross-examine the witness as to the statement and the court may consider the cross-examination in determining whether in the opinion of the court the witness is adverse.

[S.C. 1994, c. 44, s. 85]

10. (1) **Cross-examination as to previous statements** — On any trial a witness may be cross-examined as to previous statements that the witness made in writing, or that have been reduced to writing, or recorded on audio tape or video tape or otherwise, relative to the subject-matter of the case, without the writing being shown to the witness or the witness being given the opportunity to listen to the audio tape or view the video tape or otherwise take cognizance of the statements, but, if it is intended to contradict the witness, the witness' attention must, before the contradictory proof can be given, be called to those parts of the statement that are to be used for the purpose of so contradicting the witness, and the judge, at any time during the trial, may require the production of the writing or tape or other medium for inspection, and thereupon make such use of it for the purposes of the trial as the judge thinks fit.

(2) **Deposition of witness in criminal investigation** — A deposition of a witness, purporting to have been taken before a justice on the investigation of a criminal charge and to be signed by the witness and the justice, returned to and produced from the custody of the proper officer shall be presumed, in the absence of evidence to the contrary, to have been signed by the witness.

[1994, c. 44, s. 86 (in force February 15, 1985).]

11. Cross-examination as to previous oral statements — Where a witness, on cross-examination as to a former statement made by him relative to the subject-matter of the case and inconsistent with his present testimony, does not distinctly admit that he did make the statement, proof may be given that he did in fact make it, but before that proof can be given the circumstances of the supposed statement, sufficient to designate the particular occasion, shall be mentioned to the witness, and he shall be asked whether or not he did make the statement.

12. (1) **Examination as to previous convictions** — A witness may be questioned as to whether the witness has been convicted of any offence, excluding any offence designated as a contravention under the *Contraventions Act*, but including such an offence where the conviction was entered after a trial on an indictment.

(1.1) **Proof of previous convictions** — If the witness either denies the fact or refuses to answer, the opposite party may prove the conviction.

(2) **How conviction proved** — A conviction may be proved by producing

(a)   a certificate containing the substance and effect only, omitting the formal part, of the indictment and conviction, if it is for an indictable offence, or a copy of the summary conviction, if it is for an offence punishable on summary conviction, purporting to be signed by the clerk of the court or other officer having the custody of the records of the court in which the conviction, if on indictment, was had, or to which the conviction, if summary, was returned; and

(b)   proof of identity.

[S.C. 1992, c. 47, s. 66]

Oaths and Solemn Affirmations

13. Who may administer oaths — Every court and judge, and every person having, by law or consent of parties, authority to hear and receive evidence, has power to administer an oath to every witness who is legally called to give evidence before that court, judge or person.

14. (1) **Solemn affirmation by witness instead of oath** — A person may, instead of taking an oath, make the following solemn affirmation:

I solemnly affirm that the evidence to be given by me shall be the truth, the whole truth and nothing but the truth.

(2) **Effect** — Where a person makes a solemn affirmation in accordance with subsection (1), his evidence shall be taken and have the same effect as if taken under oath.

[S.C. 1994, c. 44, s. 87]

15. (1) **Solemn affirmation by deponent** — Where a person who is required or who desires to make an affidavit or deposition in a proceeding or on an occasion on which or concerning a matter respecting which an oath is required or is lawful, whether on the taking of office or otherwise, does not wish to take an oath, the court or judge, or other officer or person qualified to take affidavits or depositions, shall permit the person to make a solemn affirmation in the words following, namely, "I,......., do solemnly affirm, etc.", and that solemn affirmation has the same force and effect as if that person had taken an oath.

(2) **Effect** — Any witness whose evidence is admitted or who makes a solemn affirmation under this section or section 14 is liable to indictment and punishment for perjury in all respects as if he had been sworn.

[S.C. 1994, c. 44, s. 88]

16. (1) **Witness whose capacity is in question** — Where a proposed witness is a person under fourteen years of age or a person whose mental capacity is challenged, the court shall, before permitting the person to give evidence, conduct an inquiry to determine

  (a) whether the person understands the nature of an oath or a solemn affirmation; and
  (b) whether the person is able to communicate the evidence.

(2) **Testimony under oath or solemn affirmation** — A person referred to in subsection (1) who understands the nature of an oath or a solemn affirmation and is able to communicate the evidence shall testify under oath or solemn affirmation.

(3) **Testimony on promise to tell truth** — A person referred to in subsection (1) who does not understand the nature of an oath or a solemn affirmation but is able to communicate the evidence may, notwithstanding any provision of any Act requiring an oath or a solemn affirmation, testify on promising to tell the truth.

(4) **Inability to testify** — A person referred to in subsection (1) who neither understands the nature of an oath or a solemn affirmation nor is able to communicate the evidence shall not testify.

(5) **Burden as to capacity of witness** — A party who challenges the mental capacity of a proposed witness of fourteen years of age or more has the burden of satisfying the court that there is an issue as to the capacity of the proposed witness to testify under an oath or a solemn affirmation.

[R.S. 1985, c. 19 (3rd Supp.), s. 18; 1994 c. 44, s. 89]

Judicial Notice

17. Imperial Acts, etc. — Judicial notice shall be taken of all Acts of the Imperial Parliament, of all ordinances made by the Governor in Council, or the lieutenant governor in council of any province or colony that, or some portion of which, now forms or hereafter may form part of Canada, and of all the Acts of the legislature of any such province or colony, whether enacted before or after the passing of the *Constitution Act*, 1867.

18. Acts of Canada — Judicial notice shall be taken of all Acts of Parliament, public or private, without being specially pleaded.

Documentary Evidence

19. Copies by Queen's Printer — Every copy of any Act of Parliament, public or private, published by the Queen's Printer, is evidence of that Act and of its contents, and every copy purporting to be published by the Queen's Printer shall be deemed to be so published, unless the contrary is shown.

[2000, c. 5, s. 52 (in force May 1, 2000).]

20. Imperial proclamations, etc. — Imperial proclamations, orders in council, treaties, orders, warrants, licences, certificates, rules, regulations or other Imperial official records, Acts or documents may be proved

(a)   in the same manner as they may from time to time be provable in any court in England;

(b)   by the production of a copy of the *Canada Gazette*, or a volume of the Acts of Parliament purporting to contain a copy of the same or a notice thereof; or

(c)   by the production of a copy of them purporting to be published by the Queen's Printer.

[2000, c. 5, s. 53 (in force May 1, 2000).]

21. Proclamations, etc., of Governor General — Evidence of any proclamation, order, regulation or appointment, made or issued by the Governor General or by the Governor in Council, or by or under the authority of any minister or head of any department of the Government of Canada and evidence of a treaty to which Canada is a party, may be given in all or any of the following ways:

(a)   by the production of a copy of the *Canada Gazette*, or a volume of the Acts of Parliament purporting to contain a copy of the treaty, proclamation, order, regulation or appointment, or a notice thereof;

(b)   by the production of a copy of the proclamation, order, regulation or appointment, purporting to be published by the Queen's Printer;

(c)   by the production of a copy of the treaty purporting to be published by the Queen's Printer;

(d)   by the production, in the case of any proclamation, order, regulation or appointment made or issued by the Governor General or by the Governor in Council, of a copy or extract purporting to be certified to be true by the clerk or assistant or acting clerk of the Queen's Privy Council for Canada; and

(e)   by the production, in the case of any order, regulation or appointment made or issued by or under the authority of any minister or head of a department of the Government of Canada, of a copy or extract purporting to be certified to be true by the minister, by his deputy or acting deputy, or by the secretary or acting secretary of the department over which he presides.

[2000, c. 5, s. 54 (in force May 1, 2000).]

22. (1) Proclamations, etc., of lieutenant governor — Evidence of any proclamation, order, regulation or appointment made or issued by a lieutenant governor or lieutenant governor in council of any province, or by or under the authority of any member of the executive council, being the head of any department of the government of the province, may be given in all or any of the following ways:

(a)   by the production of a copy of the official gazette for the province purporting to contain a copy of the proclamation, order, regulation or appointment, or a notice thereof;

(b)   by the production of a copy of the proclamation, order, regulation or appointment purporting to be published by the government or Queen's Printer for the province; and

(c)   by the production of a copy or extract of the proclamation, order, regulation or appointment purporting to be certified to be true by the clerk or assistant or acting clerk of the executive council, by the head of any department of the government of a province, or by his deputy or acting deputy, as the case may be.

(2) **In the case of the Territories** — Evidence of any proclamation, order, regulation or appointment made by the Lieutenant Governor or Lieutenant Governor in Council of the Northwest Territories, as constituted prior to September 1, 1905, or by the Commissioner in Council of the Yukon Territory, the Commissioner in Council of the Northwest Territories or the Legislature for Nunavut, may be given by the production of a copy of the *Canada Gazette* purporting to contain a copy of the proclamation, order, regulation or appointment, or a notice thereof.

[1993, c. 28, Sch. III, s. 8 (in force April 1, 1999); 2000, c. 5, s. 55 (in force May 1, 2000).]

23. (1) **Evidence of judicial proceedings, etc.** — Evidence of any proceeding or record whatever of, in or before any court in Great Britain, the Supreme, Court, Federal Court or Tax Court of Canada, any court in any province, any court in any British colony or possession or any court of record of the United States, of any state of the United States or of any other foreign country, or before any justice of the peace or coroner in any province, may be given in any action or proceeding by an exemplification or certified copy of the proceeding or record, purporting to be under the seal of the court or under the hand or seal of the justice or coroner or court stenographer, as the case may be, without any proof of the authenticity of the seal or of the signature of the justice or coroner or court stenographer or other proof whatever.

(2) **Certificate where court has no seal** — Where any court, justice or coroner or court stenographer referred to in subsection (1) has no seal, or so certifies, the evidence may be given by a copy purporting to be certified under the signature of a judge or presiding provincial court judge or of the justice or coroner or court stenographer, without any proof of the authenticity of the signature or other proof whatever.

[R.S. 1985, c. 27 (1st Supp.), s. 203; 1993, c. 34, s. 15; 1997, c. 18, s. 117]

24. Certified copies — In every case in which the original record could be admitted in evidence,

(a)   a copy of any official or public document of Canada or of any province, purporting to be certified under the hand of the proper officer or person in whose custody the official or public document is placed, or

(b) a copy of a document, by-law, rule, regulation or proceeding, or a copy of any entry in any register or other book of any municipal or other corporation, created by charter or Act of Parliament or the legislature of any province, purporting to be certified under the seal of the corporation, and the hand of the presiding officer, clerk or secretary thereof,

is admissible in evidence without proof of the seal of the corporation, or of the signature or official character of the person or persons appearing to have signed it, and without further proof thereof.

25. Books and documents — Where a book or other document is of so public a nature as to be admissible in evidence on its mere production from the proper custody, and no other Act exists that renders its contents provable by means of a copy, a copy thereof or extract therefrom is admissible in evidence in any court of justice or before a person having, by law or by consent of parties, authority to hear, receive and examine evidence, if it is proved that it is a copy or extract purporting to be certified to be true by the officer to whose custody the original has been entrusted.

26. (1) Books kept in offices under Government of Canada — A copy of any entry in any book kept in any office or department of the Government of Canada, or in any commission, board or other branch of the public service of Canada, shall be admitted as evidence of that entry, and of the matters, transactions and accounts therein recorded, if it is proved by the oath or affidavit of an officer of the office or department, commission, board or other branch of the public service of Canada that the book was, at the time of the making of the entry, one of the ordinary books kept in the office, department, commission, board or other branch of the public service of Canada, that the entry was made in the usual and ordinary course of business of the office, department, commission, board or other branch of the public service of Canada and that the copy is a true copy thereof.

(2) Proof of non-issue of licence or document — Where by any Act of Parliament or regulation made thereunder provision is made for the issue by a department, commission, board or other branch of the public service of Canada of a licence requisite to the doing or having of any act or thing or for the issue of any other document, an affidavit of an officer of the department, commission, board or other branch of the public service, sworn before any commissioner or other person authorized to take affidavits, setting out that he has charge of the appropriate records and that after careful examination and search of those records he has been unable to find in any given case that any such licence or other document has been issued, shall be admitted in evidence as proof, in the absence of evidence to the contrary, that in that case no licence or other document has been issued.

(3) Proof of mailing departmental matter — Where by any Act of Parliament or regulation made thereunder provision is made for sending by mail any request for information, notice or demand by a department or other branch of the public service of Canada an affidavit of an officer of the department or other branch of the public service, sworn before any commissioner or other person authorized to take affidavits, setting out that he has charge of the appropriate records, that he has a knowledge of the facts in the particular case, that the request, notice or demand was sent by registered letter on a named date to the person or firm to whom it was addressed (indicating that address) and that he identifies as exhibits attached to the affidavit the post office certificate of registration of the letter and a true copy of the request, notice or demand, shall, on production and proof of the post office receipt for the delivery of the registered letter to the addressee, be admitted in evidence as proof, in the absence of evidence to the contrary, of the sending and of the request, notice or demand.

(4) **Proof of official character** — Where proof is offered by affidavit pursuant to this section, it is not necessary to prove the official character of the person making the affidavit if that information is set out in the body of the affidavit.

27. Notarial acts in Quebec — Any document purporting to be a copy of a notarial act or instrument made, filed or registered in the Province of Quebec, and to be certified by a notary or prothonotary to be a true copy of the original in his possession as such notary or prothonotary, shall be admitted in evidence in the place and stead of the original and has the same force and effect as the original would have if produced and proved, but it may be proved in rebuttal that there is no original, that the copy is not a true copy of the original in some material particular or that the original is not an instrument of such nature as may, by the law of the Province of Quebec, be taken before a notary or be filed, enrolled or registered by a notary in that Province.

28. (1) Notice of production of book or document — No copy of any book or other document shall be admitted in evidence, under the authority of section 23, 24, 25, 26 or 27, on any trial, unless the party intending to produce the copy has before the trial given to the party against whom it is intended to be produced reasonable notice of that intention.

(2) **Not less than 7 days** — The reasonableness of the notice referred to in subsection (1) shall be determined by the court, judge or other person presiding, but the notice shall not in any case be less than seven days.

29. (1) Copies of entries — Subject to this section, a copy of any entry in any book or record kept in any financial institution shall in all legal proceedings be admitted in evidence as proof, in the absence of evidence to the contrary, of the entry and of the matters, transactions and accounts therein recorded.

(2) **Admission in evidence** — A copy of an entry in the book or record described in subsection (1) shall not be admitted in evidence under this section unless it is first proved that the book or record was, at the time of the making of the entry, one of the ordinary books or records of the financial institution, that the entry was made in the usual and ordinary course of business, that the book or record is in the custody or control of the financial institution and that the copy is a true copy of it, and such proof may be given by any person employed by the financial institution who has knowledge of the book or record or the manager or accountant of the financial institution, and may be given orally or by affidavit sworn before any commissioner or other person authorized to take affidavits.

(3) **Cheques, proof of "no account"** — Where a cheque has been drawn on any financial institution or branch thereof by any person, an affidavit of the manager or accountant of the financial institution or branch, sworn before any

commissioner or other person authorized to take affidavits, setting out that he is the manager or accountant, that he has made a careful examination and search of the books and records for the purpose of ascertaining whether or not that person has an account with the financial institution or branch and that he has been unable to find such an account, shall be admitted in evidence as proof, in the absence of evidence to the contrary, that that person has no account in the financial institution or branch.

(4) **Proof of official character** — Where evidence is offered by affidavit pursuant to this section, it is not necessary to prove the signature or official character of the person making the affidavit if the official character of that person is set out in the body of the affidavit.

(5) **Compulsion of production or appearance** — A financial institution or officer of a financial institution is not in any legal proceedings to which the financial institution is not a party compellable to produce any book or record, the contents of which can be proved under this section, or to appear as a witness to prove the matters, transactions and accounts therein recorded unless by order of the court made for special cause.

(6) **Order to inspect and copy** — On the application of any party to a legal proceeding, the court may order that that party be at liberty to inspect and take copies of any entries in the books or records of a financial institution for the purposes of the legal proceeding, and the person whose account is to be inspected shall be notified of the application at least two clear days before the hearing thereof, and if it is shown to the satisfaction of the court that he cannot be notified personally, the notice may be given by addressing it to the financial institution.

(7) **Warrants to search** — Nothing in this section shall be construed as prohibiting any search of the premises of a financial institution under the authority of a warrant to search issued under any other Act of Parliament, but unless the warrant is expressly endorsed by the person under whose hand it is issued as not being limited by this section, the authority conferred by any such warrant to search the premises of a financial institution and to seize and take away anything in it shall, with respect to the books or records of the institution, be construed as limited to the searching of those premises for the purpose of inspecting and taking copies of entries in those books or records, and section 490 of the *Criminal Code* does not apply in respect of the copies of those books or records obtained under a warrant referred to in this section.

(8) **Computation of time** — Holidays shall be excluded from the computation of time under this section.

(9) **Definitions** — In this section,

"court" means the court, judge, arbitrator or person before whom a legal proceeding is held or taken;

"financial institution" means the Bank of Canada, the Business Development Bank of Canada and any institution that accepts in Canada deposits of money from its members or the public, and includes a branch, agency or office of any of those Banks or institutions;

"legal proceeding" means any civil or criminal proceeding or inquiry in which evidence is or may be given, and includes an arbitration.

[S.C. 1994, c. 44, s. 90; 1995, c. 28, s. 47(a); 1999, c. 28, s. 149]

30. (1) **Business records to be admitted in evidence** — Where oral evidence in respect of a matter would be admissible in a legal proceeding, a record made in the usual and ordinary course of business that contains information in respect of that matter is admissible in evidence under this section in the legal proceeding on production of the record.

(2) **Inference where information not in business record** — Where a record made in the usual and ordinary course of business does not contain information in respect of a matter the occurrence or existence of which might reasonably be expected to be recorded in that record, the court may on production of the record admit the record for the purpose of establishing that fact and may draw the inference that the matter did not occur or exist.

(3) **Copy of records** — Where it is not possible or reasonably practicable to produce any record described in subsection (1) or (2), a copy of the record accompanied by two documents, one that is made by a person who states why it is not possible or reasonably practicable to produce the record and one that sets out the source from which the copy was made, that attests to the copy's authenticity and that is made by the person who made the copy, is admissible in evidence under this section in the same manner as if it were the original of the record if each document is

(a) an affidavit of each of those persons sworn before a commissioner or other person authorized to take affidavits; or

(b) a certificate or other statement pertaining to the record in which the person attests that the certificate or statement is made in conformity with the laws of a foreign state, whether or not the certificate or statement is in the form of an affidavit attested to before an official of the foreign state.

(4) **Where record kept in form requiring explanation** — Where production of any record or of a copy of any record described in subsection (1) or (2) would not convey to the court the information contained in the record by reason of its having been kept in a form that requires explanation, a transcript of the explanation of the record or copy prepared by a person qualified to make the explanation is admissible in evidence under this section in the same manner as if it were the original of the record if it is accompanied by a document that sets out the person's qualifications to make the explanation, attests to the accuracy of the explanation, and is

(a) an affidavit of that person sworn before a commissioner or other person authorized to take affidavits; or

(b) a certificate or other statement pertaining to the record in which the person attests that the certificate or statement is made in conformity with the laws of a foreign state, whether or not the certificate or statement is in the form of an affidavit attested to before an official of the foreign state.

(5) **Court may order other part of record to be produced** — Where part only of a record is produced under this section by any party, the court may

examine any other part of the record and direct that, together with the part of the record previously so produced, the whole or any part of the other part thereof be produced by that party as the record produced by him.

(6) **Court may examine record and hear evidence** — For the purpose of determining whether any provision of this section applies, or for the purpose of determining the probative value, if any, to be given to information contained in any record admitted in evidence under this section, the court may, on production of any record, examine the record, admit any evidence in respect thereof given orally or by affidavit including evidence as to the circumstances in which the information contained in the record was written, recorded, stored or reproduced, and draw any reasonable inference from the form or content of the record.

(7) **Notice of intention to produce record or affidavit** — Unless the court orders otherwise, no record or affidavit shall be admitted in evidence under this section unless the party producing the record or affidavit has, at least seven days before its production, given notice of his intention to produce it to each other party to the legal proceeding and has, within five days after receiving any notice in that behalf given by any such party, produced it for inspection by that party.

(8) **Not necessary to prove signature and official character** — Where evidence is offered by affidavit under this section, it is not necessary to prove the signature or official character of the person making the affidavit if the official character of that person is set out in the body of the affidavit.

(9) **Examination on record with leave of court** — Subject to section 4, any person who has or may reasonably be expected to have knowledge of the making or contents of any record produced or received in evidence under this section may, with leave of the court, be examined or cross-examined thereon by any party to the legal proceeding.

(10) **Evidence inadmissible under this section** — Nothing in this section renders admissible in evidence in any legal proceeding
  (a)   such part of any record as is proved to be
        (i)   a record made in the course of an investigation or inquiry,
        (ii)   a record made in the course of obtaining or giving legal advice or in contemplation of a legal proceeding,
        (iii) a record in respect of the production of which any privilege exists and is claimed, or
        (iv)   a record of or alluding to a statement made by a person who is not, or if he were living and of sound mind would not be, competent and compellable to disclose in the legal proceeding a matter disclosed in the record;
  (b)   any record the production of which would be contrary to public policy; or
  (c)   any transcript or recording of evidence taken in the course of another legal proceeding.

(11) **Construction of this section** — The provisions of this section shall be deemed to be in addition to and not in derogation of

(a)   any other provision of this or any other Act of Parliament respecting the admissibility in evidence of any record or the proof of any matter; or

(b)   any existing rule of law under which any record is admissible in evidence or any matter may be proved.

(12) **Definitions** — In this section,

"business" means any business, profession, trade, calling, manufacture or undertaking of any kind carried on in Canada or elsewhere whether for profit or otherwise, including any activity or operation carried on or performed in Canada or elsewhere by any government, by any department, branch, board, commission or agency of any government, by any court or other tribunal or by any other body or authority performing a function of government;

"copy", in relation to any record, includes a print, whether enlarged or not, from a photographic film of the record, and "photographic film" includes a photographic plate, microphotographic film or photostatic negative;

"court" means the court, judge, arbitrator or person before whom a legal proceeding is held or taken;

"legal proceeding" means any civil or criminal proceeding or inquiry in which evidence is or may be given, and includes an arbitration;

"record" includes the whole or any part of any book, document, paper, card, tape or other thing on or in which information is written, recorded, stored or reproduced, and, except for the purposes of subsections (3) and (4), any copy or transcript admitted in evidence under this section pursuant to subsection (3) or (4).

[S.C. 1994, c. 44, s. 91]

31. (1) **Definitions** — In this section,

"corporation" means any bank, including the Bank of Canada and the Business Development Bank of Canada, any authorized foreign bank within the meaning of section 2 of the *Bank Act* and each of the following carrying on business in Canada, namely, every railway, express, telegraph and telephone company (except a street railway and tramway company), insurance company or society, trust company and loan company;

"government" means the government of Canada or of any province and includes any department, commission, board or branch of any such government;

"photographic film" includes any photographic plate, microphotographic film and photostatic negative.

(2) **When print admissible in evidence** — A print, whether enlarged or not, from any photographic film of

(a)   an entry in any book or record kept by any government or corporation and destroyed, lost or delivered to a customer after the film was taken,

(b)   any bill of exchange, promissory note, cheque, receipt, instrument or document held by any government or corporation and destroyed, lost or delivered to a customer after the film was taken, or

(c)   any record, document, plan, book or paper belonging to or deposited with any government or corporation, is admissible in evidence in all cases in which and for all purposes for which the object photographed would have been admitted on proof that

(d)   while the book, record, bill of exchange, promissory note, cheque, receipt, instrument or document, plan, book or paper was in the custody or control of the government or corporation, the photographic film was taken thereof in order to keep a permanent record thereof, and

(e)   the object photographed was subsequently destroyed by or in the presence of one or more of the employees of the government or corporation, or was lost or was delivered to a customer.

(3) **Evidence of compliance with conditions** — Evidence of compliance with the conditions prescribed by this section may be given by any one or more of the employees of the government or corporation, having knowledge of the taking of the photographic film, of the destruction, loss or delivery to a customer, or of the making of the print, as the case may be, either orally or by affidavit sworn in any part of Canada before any notary public or commissioner for oaths.

(4) **Proof by notarial copy** — Unless the court otherwise orders, a notarial copy of an affidavit under subsection (3) is admissible in evidence in lieu of the original affidavit.

[S.C. 1992, c. 1, s. 142(1), (Sch. V, items 9(1) and (2)); 1995, c. 28, s. 47(b); 1999, c. 28, s. 50]

31.1 Authentication of electronic documents — Any person seeking to admit an electronic document as evidence has the burden of proving its authenticity by evidence capable of supporting a finding that the electronic document is that which it is purported to be.

[added, 2000, c. 5, s. 56]

31.2 (1) Application of best evidence rule - electronic documents — The best evidence rule in respect of an electronic document is satisfied

(a)   on proof of the integrity of the electronic documents system by or in which the electronic document was recorded or stored; or

(b)   if an evidentiary presumption established under section 31.4 applies.

(2) **Printouts** — Despite subsection (1), in the absence of evidence to the contrary, an electronic document in the form of a printout satisfies the best evidence rule if the printout has been manifestly or consistently acted on, relied on or used as a record of the information recorded or stored in the printout.

[added, S.C. 2000, c. 5, s. 56]

31.3 Presumption of integrity — For the purposes of subsection 31.2(1), in the absence of evidence to the contrary, the integrity of an electronic documents system by or in which an electronic document is recorded or stored is proven

(a)   by evidence capable of supporting a finding that at all material times the computer system or other similar device used by the electronic documents system was operating properly or, if it was not, the fact of its not operating properly did not affect the integrity of the electronic document and there are no other reasonable grounds to doubt the integrity of the electronic documents system;

> (b)   if it is established that the electronic document was recorded or stored by a party who is adverse in interest to the party seeking to introduce it; or
>
> (c)   if it is established that the electronic document was recorded or stored in the usual and ordinary course of business by a person who is not a party and who did not record or store it under the control of the party seeking to introduce it.

[2000, c. 5, s. 56 (in force May 1, 2000).]

31.4 Presumptions regarding secure electronic signatures — The Governor in Council may make regulations establishing evidentiary presumptions in relation to electronic documents signed with secure electronic signatures, including regulations respecting

> (a)   the association of secure electronic signatures with persons; and
>
> (b)   the integrity of information contained in electronic documents signed with secure electronic signatures.

[added, S.C. 2000, c. 5, s. 56]

31.5 Standards may be considered — For the purpose of determining under any rule of law whether an electronic document is admissible, evidence may be presented in respect of any standard, procedure, usage or practice concerning the manner in which electronic documents are to be recorded or stored, having regard to the type of business, enterprise or endeavour that used, recorded or stored the electronic document and the nature and purpose of the electronic document.

[2000, c. 5, s. 56 (in force May 1, 2000).]

31.6 (1) Proof by affidavit — The matters referred to in subsection 31.2(2) and sections 31.3 and 31.5 and in regulations made under section 31.4 may be established by affidavit.

(2) **Cross-examination** — A party may cross-examine a deponent of an affidavit referred to in subsection (1) that has been introduced in evidence

> (a)   as of right, if the deponent is an adverse party or is under the control of an adverse party; and
>
> (b)   with leave of the court, in the case of any other deponent.

[2000, c. 5, s. 56 (in force May 1, 2000).]

31.7 Application — Sections 31.1 to 31.4 do not affect any rule of law relating to the admissibility of evidence, except the rules relating to authentication and best evidence.

[added, S.C. 2000, c. 5, s. 56]

31.8 Definitions — The definitions in this section apply in sections 31.1 to 31.6.

"computer system" means a device that, or a group of interconnected or related devices one or more of which,

> (a)   contains computer programs or other data; and
>
> (b)   pursuant to computer programs, performs logic and control, and may perform any other function.

"data" means representations of information or of concepts, in any form.

"electronic document" means data that is recorded or stored on any medium in or by a computer system or other similar device and that can be read or perceived by a person or a computer system or other similar device. It includes a display, printout or other output of that data.

"electronic documents system" includes a computer system or other similar device by or in which data is recorded or stored and any procedures related to the recording or storage of electronic documents.

"secure electronic signature" means a secure electronic signature as defined in subsection 31(1) of the **Personal Information Protection And Electronic Documents Act**.

32. (1) **Order signed by Secretary of State** — An order signed by the Secretary of State of Canada and purporting to be written by command of the Governor General shall be admitted in evidence as the order of the Governor General.

(2) **Copies published in *Canada Gazette*** — All copies of official and other notices, advertisements and documents published in the *Canada Gazette* are admissible in evidence as proof, in the absence of evidence to the contrary, of the originals and of their contents.

[S.C. 2000, c. 5, s. 57]

33. (1) **Proof of handwriting of person certifying** — No proof shall be required of the handwriting or official position of any person certifying, in pursuance of this Act, to the truth of any copy of or extract from any proclamation, order, regulation, appointment, book or other document.

(2) **Printed or written** — Any copy or extract referred to in subsection (1) may be in print or in writing, or partly in print and partly in writing.

34. (1) **Attesting witness** — It is not necessary to prove by the attesting witness any instrument to the validity of which attestation is not requisite.

(2) **Instrument, how proved** — Any instrument referred to in subsection (1) may be proved by admission or otherwise as if there had been no attesting witness thereto.

35. Impounding of forged instrument — Where any instrument that has been forged or fraudulently altered is admitted in evidence, the court or the judge or person who admits the instrument may, at the request of any person against whom it is admitted in evidence, direct that the instrument shall be impounded and be kept in the custody of an officer of the court or other proper person for such period and subject to such conditions as to the court, judge or person admitting the instrument seem meet.

36. Construction — This Part shall be deemed to be in addition to and not in derogation of any powers of proving documents given by any existing Act or existing at law.

36.1 Definition of "official" — In sections 37 to 38.16, "official" has the same meaning as in section 118 of the *Criminal Code*.

[2001, c. 41, s. 43 (in force December 24, 2001).]

Specified Public Interest

37. (1) **Objection to disclosure of information** — Subject to sections 38 to 38.16, a Minister of the Crown in right of Canada or other official may object to the disclosure of information before a court, person or body with jurisdiction to compel the production of information by certifying orally or in writing to the court, person or body that the information should not be disclosed on the grounds of a specified public interest.

(1.1) **Obligation of court, person or body** — If an objection is made under subsection (1), the court, person or body shall ensure that the information is not disclosed other than in accordance with this Act.

(2) **Objection made to superior court** — If an objection to the disclosure of information is made before a superior court, that court may determine the objection.

(3) **Objection not made to superior court** — If an objection to the disclosure of information is made before a court, person or body other than a superior court, the objection may be determined, on application, by

(a)   the Federal Court-Trial Division, in the case of a person or body vested with power to compel production by or under an Act of Parliament if the person or body is not a court established under a law of a province; or

(b)   the trial division or trial court of the superior court of the province within which the court, person or body exercises its jurisdiction, in any other case.

(4) **Limitation period** — An application under subsection (3) shall be made within 10 days after the objection is made or within any further or lesser time that the court having jurisdiction to hear the application considers appropriate in the circumstances.

(4.1) **Disclosure order** — Unless the court having jurisdiction to hear the application concludes that the disclosure of the information to which the objection was made under subsection (1) would encroach upon a specified public interest, the court may authorize by order the disclosure of the information.

(5) **Disclosure order** — If the court having jurisdiction to hear the application concludes that the disclosure of the information to which the objection was made under subsection (1) would encroach upon a specified public interest, but that the public interest in disclosure outweighs in importance the specified public interest, the court may, by order, after considering both the public interest in disclosure and the form of and conditions to disclosure that are most likely to limit any encroachment upon the specified public interest resulting from disclosure, authorize the disclosure, subject to any conditions that the court considers appropriate, of all of the information, a part or summary of the information, or a written admission of facts relating to the information.

(6) **Prohibition order** — If the court does not authorize disclosure under subsection (4.1) or (5), the court shall, by order, prohibit disclosure of the information.

(6.1) **Evidence** — The court may receive into evidence anything that, in the opinion of the court, is reliable and appropriate, even if it would not otherwise be admissible under Canadian law, and may base its decision on that evidence.

(7) **When determination takes effect** — An order of the court that authorizes disclosure does not take effect until the time provided or granted to appeal the order, or a judgment of an appeal court that confirms the order, has expired, or no further appeal from a judgment that confirms the order is available.

(8) **Introduction into evidence** — A person who wishes to introduce into evidence material the disclosure of which is authorized under subsection (5), but who may not be able to do so by reason of the rules of admissibility that apply before the court, person or body with jurisdiction to compel the production of information, may request from the court having jurisdiction under subsection (2) or (3) an order permitting the introduction into evidence of the material in a form or subject to any conditions fixed by that court, as long as that form and those conditions comply with the order made under subsection (5).

(9) **Relevant factors** — For the purpose of subsection (8), the court having jurisdiction under subsection (2) or (3) shall consider all the factors that would be relevant for a determination of admissibility before the court, person or body.

[2001, c. 41, s. 43 (in force December 24, 2001).]

37.1 (1) **Appeal to court of appeal** — An appeal lies from a determination under any of subsections 37(4.1) to (6)
  (a) to the Federal Court of Appeal from a determination of the Federal Court-Trial Division; or
  (b) to the court of appeal of a province from a determination of a trial division or trial court of a superior court of the province.

(2) **Limitation period for appeal** — An appeal under subsection (1) shall be brought within 10 days after the date of the determination appealed from or within any further time that the court having jurisdiction to hear the appeal considers appropriate in the circumstances.

[2001, c. 41, s. 43 (in force December 24, 2001).]

37.2 Limitation periods for appeals to Supreme Court of Canada — Notwithstanding any other Act of Parliament,
  (a) an application for leave to appeal to the Supreme Court of Canada from a judgment made under subsection 37.1(1) shall be made within 10 days after the date of the judgment appealed from or within any further time that the court having jurisdiction to grant leave to appeal considers appropriate in the circumstances; and
  (b) if leave to appeal is granted, the appeal shall be brought in the manner set out in subsection 60(1) of the Supreme Court Act but within the time specified by the court that grants leave.

[2001, c. 41, s. 43 (in force December 24, 2001).]

37.21 (1) **Special rules** — A hearing under subsection 37(2) or (3) or an appeal of an order made under any of subsections 37(4.1) to (6) shall be heard in private.

(2) **Representations** — The court conducting a hearing under subsection 37(2) or (3) or the court hearing an appeal of an order made under any of subsections 37(4.1) to (6) may give
(a) any person an opportunity to make representations; and
(b) any person who makes representations under paragraph (a) the opportunity to make representations ex parte.
[2001, c. 41, s. 43 (in force December 24, 2001).]

37.3 (1) **Protection of right to a fair trial** — A judge presiding at a criminal trial or other criminal proceeding may make any order that he or she considers appropriate in the circumstances to protect the right of the accused to a fair trial, as long as that order complies with the terms of any order made under any of subsections 37(4.1) to (6) in relation to that trial or proceeding or any judgment made on appeal of an order made under any of those subsections.

(2) **Potential orders** — The orders that may be made under subsection (1) include, but are not limited to, the following orders:
(a) an order dismissing specified counts of the indictment or information, or permitting the indictment or information to proceed only in respect of a lesser or included offence;
(b) an order effecting a stay of the proceedings; and
(c) an order finding against any party on any issue relating to information the disclosure of which is prohibited.
[2001, c. 41, s. 43 (in force December 24, 2001).]

International Relations and National Defence and National Security

38. Definitions — The following definitions apply in this section and in sections 38.01 to 38.15.

"judge" means the Chief Justice of the Federal Court or a judge of the Federal Court-Trial Division designated by the Chief Justice to conduct hearings under section 38.04.

"participant" means a person who, in connection with a proceeding, is required to disclose, or expects to disclose or cause the disclosure of, information.

"potentially injurious information" means information of a type that, if it were disclosed to the public, could injure international relations or national defence or national security.

"proceeding" means a proceeding before a court, person or body with jurisdiction to compel the production of information.

"prosecutor" means an agent of the Attorney General of Canada or of the Attorney General of a province, the Director of Military Prosecutions under the National Defence Act or an individual who acts as a prosecutor in a proceeding.

"sensitive information" means information relating to international relations or national defence or national security that is in the possession of the Government of Canada, whether originating from inside or outside Canada, and is of a type that the Government of Canada is taking measures to safeguard.

[2001, c. 41, s. 43 (in force December 24, 2001).]

38.01 (1) **Notice to Attorney General of Canada** — Every participant who, in connection with a proceeding, is required to disclose, or expects to disclose or cause the disclosure of, information that the participant believes is sensitive information or potentially injurious information shall, as soon as possible, notify the Attorney General of Canada in writing of the possibility of the disclosure, and of the nature, date and place of the proceeding.

(2) **During a proceeding** — Every participant who believes that sensitive information or potentially injurious information is about to be disclosed, whether by the participant or another person, in the course of a proceeding shall raise the matter with the person presiding at the proceeding and notify the Attorney General of Canada in writing of the matter as soon as possible, whether or not notice has been given under subsection (1). In such circumstances, the person presiding at the proceeding shall ensure that the information is not disclosed other than in accordance with this Act.

(3) **Notice of disclosure from official** — An official, other than a participant, who believes that sensitive information or potentially injurious information may be disclosed in connection with a proceeding may notify the Attorney General of Canada in writing of the possibility of the disclosure, and of the nature, date and place of the proceeding.

(4) **During a proceeding** — An official, other than a participant, who believes that sensitive information or potentially injurious information is about to be disclosed in the course of a proceeding may raise the matter with the person presiding at the proceeding. If the official raises the matter, he or she shall notify the Attorney General of Canada in writing of the matter as soon as possible, whether or not notice has been given under subsection (3), and the person presiding at the proceeding shall ensure that the information is not disclosed other than in accordance with this Act.

(5) **Military proceedings** — In the case of a proceeding under Part III of the *National Defence Act*, notice under any of subsections (1) to (4) shall be given to both the Attorney General of Canada and the Minister of National Defence.

(6) **Exception** — This section does not apply when
(a)   the information is disclosed by a person to their solicitor in connection with a proceeding, if the information is relevant to that proceeding;
(b)   the information is disclosed to enable the Attorney General of Canada, the Minister of National Defence, a judge or a court hearing an appeal from, or a review of, an order of the judge to discharge their responsibilities under section 38, this section and sections 38.02 to 38.13, 38.15 and 38.16;
(c)   disclosure of the information is authorized by the government institution in which or for which the information was produced or, if the information was not produced in or for a government institution, the government institution in which it was first received; or
(d)   the information is disclosed to an entity and, where applicable, for a purpose listed in the schedule.

(7) **Exception** — Subsections (1) and (2) do not apply to a participant if a government institution referred to in paragraph (6)(c) advises the participant that it is not necessary, in order to prevent disclosure of the information referred to in that paragraph, to give notice to the Attorney General of Canada under subsection (1) or to raise the matter with the person presiding under subsection (2).

(8) **Schedule** — The Governor in Council may, by order, add to or delete from the schedule a reference to any entity or purpose, or amend such a reference.

[2001, c. 41, s. 43 (in force December 24, 2001).]

38.02 (1) **Disclosure prohibited** — Subject to subsection 38.01(6), no person shall disclose in connection with a proceeding

   (a) information about which notice is given under any of subsections 38.01(1) to (4);

   (b) the fact that notice is given to the Attorney General of Canada under any of subsections 38.01(1) to (4), or to the Attorney General of Canada and the Minister of National Defence under subsection 38.01(5);

   (c) the fact that an application is made to the Federal Court-Trial Division under section 38.04 or that an appeal or review of an order made under any of subsections 38.06(1) to (3) in connection with the application is instituted; or

   (d) the fact that an agreement is entered into under section 38.031 or subsection 38.04(6).

(1.1) **Entities** — When an entity listed in the schedule, for any purpose listed there in relation to that entity, makes a decision or order that would result in the disclosure of sensitive information or potentially injurious information, the entity shall not disclose the information or cause it to be disclosed until notice of intention to disclose the information has been given to the Attorney General of Canada and a period of 10 days has elapsed after notice was given.

(2) **Exceptions** — Disclosure of the information or the facts referred to in subsection (1) is not prohibited if

   (a) the Attorney General of Canada authorizes the disclosure in writing under section 38.03 or by agreement under section 38.031 or subsection 38.04(6); or

   (b) a judge authorizes the disclosure under subsection 38.06(1) or (2) or a court hearing an appeal from, or a review of, the order of the judge authorizes the disclosure, and either the time provided to appeal the order or judgment has expired or no further appeal is available.

[2001, c. 41, s. 43 (in force December 24, 2001).]

38.03 (1) **Authorization by Attorney General of Canada** — The Attorney General of Canada may, at any time and subject to any conditions that he or she considers appropriate, authorize the disclosure of all or part of the information and facts the disclosure of which is prohibited under subsection 38.02(1).

(2) **Military proceedings** — In the case of a proceeding under Part III of the *National Defence Act*, the Attorney General of Canada may authorize disclosure only with the agreement of the Minister of National Defence.

(3) **Notice** — The Attorney General of Canada shall, within 10 days after the day on which he or she first receives a notice about information under any of subsections 38.01(1) to (4), notify in writing every person who provided notice under section 38.01 about that information of his or her decision with respect to disclosure of the information.

[2001, c. 41, s. 43 (in force December 24, 2001).]

38.031 (1) **Disclosure agreement** — The Attorney General of Canada and a person who has given notice under subsection 38.01(1) or (2) and is not required to disclose information but wishes, in connection with a proceeding, to disclose any facts referred to in paragraphs 38.02(1)(b) to (d) or information about which he or she gave the notice, or to cause that disclosure, may, before the person applies to the Federal Court-Trial Division under paragraph 38.04(2)(c), enter into an agreement that permits the disclosure of part of the facts or information or disclosure of the facts or information subject to conditions.

(2) **No application to Federal Court** — If an agreement is entered into under subsection (1), the person may not apply to the Federal Court-Trial Division under paragraph 38.04(2)(c) with respect to the information about which he or she gave notice to the Attorney General of Canada under subsection 38.01(1) or (2).

[2001, c. 41, s. 43 (in force December 24, 2001).]

38.04 (1) **Application to Federal Court — Attorney General of Canada** — The Attorney General of Canada may, at any time and in any circumstances, apply to the Federal Court-Trial Division for an order with respect to the disclosure of information about which notice was given under any of subsections 38.01(1) to (4).

(2) **Application to Federal Court — general** — If, with respect to information about which notice was given under any of subsections 38.01(1) to (4), the Attorney General of Canada does not provide notice of a decision in accordance with subsection 38.03(3) or, other than by an agreement under section 38.031, authorizes the disclosure of only part of the information or disclosure subject to any conditions,

  (a) the Attorney General of Canada shall apply to the Federal Court-Trial Division for an order with respect to disclosure of the information if a person who gave notice under subsection 38.01(1) or (2) is a witness;

  (b) a person, other than a witness, who is required to disclose information in connection with a proceeding shall apply to the Federal Court-Trial Division for an order with respect to disclosure of the information; and

  (c) a person who is not required to disclose information in connection with a proceeding but who wishes to disclose it or to cause its disclosure may apply to the Federal Court-Trial Division for an order with respect to disclosure of the information.

(3) **Notice to Attorney General of Canada** — A person who applies to the Federal Court-Trial Division under paragraph (2)(b) or (c) shall provide notice of the application to the Attorney General of Canada.

(4) **Court records** — An application under this section is confidential. Subject to section 38.12, the Administrator of the Federal Court may take any measure that he or she considers appropriate to protect the confidentiality of the application and the information to which it relates.

(5) **Procedure** — As soon as the Federal Court-Trial Division is seized of an application under this section, the judge

(a) shall hear the representations of the Attorney General of Canada and, in the case of a proceeding under Part III of the *National Defence Act*, the Minister of National Defence, concerning the identity of all parties or witnesses whose interests may be affected by either the prohibition of disclosure or the conditions to which disclosure is subject, and concerning the persons who should be given notice of any hearing of the matter;

(b) shall decide whether it is necessary to hold any hearing of the matter;

(c) if he or she decides that a hearing should be held, shall
   (i) determine who should be given notice of the hearing,
   (ii) order the Attorney General of Canada to notify those persons, and
   (iii) determine the content and form of the notice; and

(d) if he or she considers it appropriate in the circumstances, may give any person the opportunity to make representations.

(6) **Disclosure agreement** — After the Federal Court-Trial Division is seized of an application made under paragraph (2)(c) or, in the case of an appeal from, or a review of, an order of the judge made under any of subsections 38.06(1) to (3) in connection with that application, before the appeal or review is disposed of,

(a) the Attorney General of Canada and the person who made the application may enter into an agreement that permits the disclosure of part of the facts referred to in paragraphs 38.02(1)(b) to (d) or part of the information, or disclosure of the facts or information subject to conditions; and

(b) if an agreement is entered into, the Court's consideration of the application or any hearing, review or appeal shall be terminated.

(7) **Termination of Court consideration, hearing, review or appeal** — Subject to subsection (6), after the Federal Court-Trial Division is seized of an application made under this section or, in the case of an appeal from, or a review of, an order of the judge made under any of subsections 38.06(1) to (3) before the appeal or review is disposed of, if the Attorney General of Canada authorizes the disclosure of all or part of the information or withdraws conditions to which the disclosure is subject, the Court's consideration of the application or any hearing, appeal or review shall be terminated in relation to that information, to the extent of the authorization or the withdrawal.

[2001, c. 41, s. 43 (in force December 24, 2001).]

38.05 Report relating to proceedings — If he or she receives notice of a hearing under paragraph 38.04(5)(c), a person presiding or designated to preside at the proceeding to which the information relates or, if no person is designated, the person who has the authority to designate a person to preside may, within 10 days after the day on which he or she receives the notice, provide the judge with a report concerning any matter relating to the proceeding that the person considers may be of assistance to the judge.

[2001, c. 41, s. 43 (in force December 24, 2001).]

38.06 (1) **Disclosure order** — Unless the judge concludes that the disclosure of the information would be injurious to international relations or national defence or national security, the judge may, by order, authorize the disclosure of the information.

(2) **Disclosure order** — If the judge concludes that the disclosure of the information would be injurious to international relations or national defence or national security but that the public interest in disclosure outweighs in importance the public interest in non-disclosure, the judge may by order, after considering both the public interest in disclosure and the form of and conditions to disclosure that are most likely to limit any injury to international relations or national defence or national security resulting from disclosure, authorize the disclosure, subject to any conditions that the judge considers appropriate, of all of the information, a part or summary of the information, or a written admission of facts relating to the information.

(3) **Order confirming prohibition** — If the judge does not authorize disclosure under subsection (1) or (2), the judge shall, by order, confirm the prohibition of disclosure.

(3.1) **Evidence** — The judge may receive into evidence anything that, in the opinion of the judge, is reliable and appropriate, even if it would not otherwise be admissible under Canadian law, and may base his or her decision on that evidence.

(4) **Introduction into evidence** — A person who wishes to introduce into evidence material the disclosure of which is authorized under subsection (2) but who may not be able to do so in a proceeding by reason of the rules of admissibility that apply in the proceeding may request from a judge an order permitting the introduction into evidence of the material in a form or subject to any conditions fixed by that judge, as long as that form and those conditions comply with the order made under subsection (2).

(5) **Relevant factors** — For the purpose of subsection (4), the judge shall consider all the factors that would be relevant for a determination of admissibility in the proceeding.

[2001, c. 41, s. 43 (in force December 24, 2001).]

38.07 Notice of order — The judge may order the Attorney General of Canada to give notice of an order made under any of subsections 38.06(1) to (3) to any person who, in the opinion of the judge, should be notified.

[2001, c. 41, s. 43 (in force December 24, 2001).]

38.08 Automatic review — If the judge determines that a party to the proceeding whose interests are adversely affected by an order made under any of subsections 38.06(1) to (3) was not given the opportunity to make representations under paragraph 38.04(5)(d), the judge shall refer the order to the Federal Court of Appeal for review.

[2001, c. 41, s. 43 (in force December 24, 2001).]

38.09 (1) **Appeal to Federal Court of Appeal** — An order made under any of subsections 38.06(1) to (3) may be appealed to the Federal Court of Appeal.

(2) **Limitation period for appeal** — An appeal shall be brought within 10 days after the day on which the order is made or within any further time that the Court considers appropriate in the circumstances.

[2001, c. 41, s. 43 (in force December 24, 2001).]

38.1 Limitation periods for appeals to Supreme Court of Canada — Notwithstanding any other Act of Parliament,

(a)   an application for leave to appeal to the Supreme Court of Canada from a judgment made on appeal shall be made within 10 days after the day on which the judgment appealed from is made or within any further time that the Supreme Court of Canada considers appropriate in the circumstances; and

(b)   if leave to appeal is granted, the appeal shall be brought in the manner set out in subsection 60(1) of the *Supreme Court Act* but within the time specified by the Supreme Court of Canada.

[2001, c. 41, s. 43 (in force December 24, 2001).]

38.11 (1) **Special rules** — A hearing under subsection 38.04(5) or an appeal or review of an order made under any of subsections 38.06(1) to (3) shall be heard in private and, at the request of either the Attorney General of Canada or, in the case of a proceeding under Part III of the *National Defence Act*, the Minister of National Defence, shall be heard in the National Capital Region, as described in the schedule to the *National Capital Act*.

(2) **Ex parte representations** — The judge conducting a hearing under subsection 38.04(5) or the court hearing an appeal or review of an order made under any of subsections 38.06(1) to (3) may give any person who makes representations under paragraph 38.04(5)(d), and shall give the Attorney General of Canada and, in the case of a proceeding under Part III of the *National Defence Act*, the Minister of National Defence, the opportunity to make representations ex parte.

[2001, c. 41, s. 43 (in force December 24, 2001).]

38.12 (1) **Protective order** — The judge conducting a hearing under subsection 38.04(5) or the court hearing an appeal or review of an order made under any of subsections 38.06(1) to (3) may make any order that the judge or the court considers appropriate in the circumstances to protect the confidentiality of the information to which the hearing, appeal or review relates.

(2) **Court records** — The court records relating to the hearing, appeal or review are confidential. The judge or the court may order that the records be sealed and kept in a location to which the public has no access.

[2001, c. 41, s. 43 (in force December 24, 2001).]

38.13 (1) **Certificate of Attorney General of Canada** — The Attorney General of Canada may personally issue a certificate that prohibits the disclosure of information in connection with a proceeding for the purpose of protecting information obtained in confidence from, or in relation to, a foreign entity as defined in subsection 2(1) of the *Security of Information Act* or for the purpose of protecting national defence or national security. The certificate may only be issued after an order or decision that would result in the disclosure of the information to be subject to the certificate has been made under this or any other Act of Parliament.

(2) **Military proceedings** — In the case of a proceeding under Part III of the *National Defence Act*, the Attorney General of Canada may issue the certificate only with the agreement, given personally, of the Minister of National Defence.

(3) **Service of certificate** — The Attorney General of Canada shall cause a copy of the certificate to be served on

   (a)   the person presiding or designated to preside at the proceeding to which the information relates or, if no person is designated, the person who has the authority to designate a person to preside;

   (b)   every party to the proceeding;

   (c)   every person who gives notice under section 38.01 in connection with the proceeding;

   (d)   every person who, in connection with the proceeding, may disclose, is required to disclose or may cause the disclosure of the information about which the Attorney General of Canada has received notice under section 38.01;

   (e)   every party to a hearing under subsection 38.04(5) or to an appeal of an order made under any of subsections 38.06(1) to (3) in relation to the information;

   (f)   the judge who conducts a hearing under subsection 38.04(5) and any court that hears an appeal from, or review of, an order made under any of subsections 38.06(1) to (3) in relation to the information; and

   (g)   any other person who, in the opinion of the Attorney General of Canada, should be served.

(4) **Filing of certificate** — The Attorney General of Canada shall cause a copy of the certificate to be filed

   (a)   with the person responsible for the records of the proceeding to which the information relates; and

   (b)   in the Registry of the Federal Court and the registry of any court that hears an appeal from, or review of, an order made under any of subsections 38.06(1) to (3).

(5) **Effect of certificate** — If the Attorney General of Canada issues a certificate, then, notwithstanding any other provision of this Act, disclosure of the information shall be prohibited in accordance with the terms of the certificate.

(6) **Statutory Instruments Act does not apply** — *The Statutory Instruments Act* does not apply to a certificate issued under subsection (1).

(7) **Publication** — The Attorney General of Canada shall, without delay after a certificate is issued, cause the certificate to be published in the *Canada Gazette*.

(8) **Restriction** — The certificate and any matters arising out of it are not subject to review or to be restrained, prohibited, removed, set aside or otherwise dealt with, except in accordance with section 38.131.

(9) **Expiration** — The certificate expires 15 years after the day on which it is issued and may be reissued.

[2001, c. 41, s. 43 (in force December 24, 2001).]

38.131 (1) **Application for review of certificate** — A party to the proceeding referred to in section 38.13 may apply to the Federal Court of Appeal for an order varying or cancelling a certificate issued under that section on the grounds referred to in subsection (8) or (9), as the case may be.

(2) **Notice to Attorney General of Canada** — The applicant shall give notice of the application to the Attorney General of Canada.

(3) **Military proceedings** — In the case of proceedings under Part III of the *National Defence Act*, notice under subsection (2) shall be given to both the Attorney General of Canada and the Minister of National Defence.

(4) **Single judge** — Notwithstanding section 16 of the *Federal Court Act*, for the purposes of the application, the Federal Court of Appeal consists of a single judge of that Court.

(5) **Admissible information** — In considering the application, the judge may receive into evidence anything that, in the opinion of the judge, is reliable and appropriate, even if it would not otherwise be admissible under Canadian law, and may base a determination made under any of subsections (8) to (10) on that evidence.

(6) **Special rules and protective order** — Sections 38.11 and 38.12 apply, with any necessary modifications, to an application made under subsection (1).

(7) **Expedited consideration** — The judge shall consider the application as soon as reasonably possible, but not later than 10 days after the application is made under subsection (1).

(8) **Varying the certificate** — If the judge determines that some of the information subject to the certificate does not relate either to information obtained in confidence from, or in relation to, a foreign entity as defined in subsection 2(1) of the *Security of Information Act*, or to national defence or security, the judge shall make an order varying the certificate accordingly.

(9) **Cancelling the certificate** — If the judge determines that none of the information subject to the certificate relates to information obtained in confidence from, or in relation to, a foreign entity as defined in subsection 2(1) of the *Security of Information Act*, or to national defence or security, the judge shall make an order cancelling the certificate.

(10) **Confirming the certificate** — If the judge determines that all of the information subject to the certificate relates to information obtained in confidence from, or in relation to, a foreign entity as defined in subsection 2(1) of the *Security*

of Information Act, or to national defence or security, the judge shall make an order confirming the certificate.

(11) **Determination is final** — Notwithstanding any other Act of Parliament, a determination of a judge under any of subsections (8) to (10) is final and is not subject to review or appeal by any court.

(12) **Publication** — If a certificate is varied or cancelled under this section, the Attorney General of Canada shall, as soon as possible after the decision of the judge and in a manner that mentions the original publication of the certificate, cause to be published in the *Canada Gazette*

(a) the certificate as varied under subsection (8); or

(b) a notice of the cancellation of the certificate under subsection (9).

[2001, c. 41, s. 43 (in force December 24, 2001).]

38.14 (1) **Protection of right to a fair trial** — The person presiding at a criminal proceeding may make any order that he or she considers appropriate in the circumstances to protect the right of the accused to a fair trial, as long as that order complies with the terms of any order made under any of subsections 38.06(1) to (3) in relation to that proceeding, any judgment made on appeal from, or review of, the order, or any certificate issued under section 38.13.

(2) **Potential orders** — The orders that may be made under subsection (1) include, but are not limited to, the following orders:

(a) an order dismissing specified counts of the indictment or information, or permitting the indictment or information to proceed only in respect of a lesser or included offence;

(b) an order effecting a stay of the proceedings; and

(c) an order finding against any party on any issue relating to information the disclosure of which is prohibited.

[2001, c. 41, s. 43 (in force December 24, 2001).]

38.15 (1) **Fiat** — If sensitive information or potentially injurious information may be disclosed in connection with a prosecution that is not instituted by the Attorney General of Canada or on his or her behalf, the Attorney General of Canada may issue a fiat and serve the fiat on the prosecutor.

(2) **Effect of fiat** — When a fiat is served on a prosecutor, the fiat establishes the exclusive authority of the Attorney General of Canada with respect to the conduct of the prosecution described in the fiat or any related process.

(3) **Fiat filed in court** — If a prosecution described in the fiat or any related process is conducted by or on behalf of the Attorney General of Canada, the fiat or a copy of the fiat shall be filed with the court in which the prosecution or process is conducted.

(4) **Fiat constitutes conclusive proof** — The fiat or a copy of the fiat

(a) is conclusive proof that the prosecution described in the fiat or any related process may be conducted by or on behalf of the Attorney General of Canada; and

(b) is admissible in evidence without proof of the signature or official character of the Attorney General of Canada.

(5) **Military proceedings** — This section does not apply to a proceeding under Part III of the *National Defence Act*.

[2001, c. 41, s. 43 (in force December 24, 2001).]

38.16 Regulations — The Governor in Council may make any regulations that the Governor in Council considers necessary to carry into effect the purposes and provisions of sections 38 to 38.15, including regulations respecting the notices, certificates and the fiat.

[2001, c. 41, s. 43 (in force December 24, 2001).]

39. (1) **Objection relating to a confidence of the Queen's Privy Council** — Where a minister of the Crown or the Clerk of the Privy Council objects to the disclosure of information before a court, person or body with jurisdiction to compel the production of information by certifying in writing that the information constitutes a confidence of the Queen's Privy Council for Canada, disclosure of the information shall be refused without examination or hearing of the information by the court, person or body.

(2) **Definition** — For the purpose of subsection (1), "a confidence of the Queen's Privy Council for Canada" includes, without restricting the generality thereof, information contained in

(a)   a memorandum the purpose of which is to present proposals or recommendations to Council;

(b)   a discussion paper the purpose of which is to present background explanations, analyses of problems or policy options to Council for consideration by Council in making decisions;

(c)   an agendum of Council or a record recording deliberations or decisions of Council;

(d)   a record used for or reflecting communications or discussions between ministers of the Crown on matters relating to the making of government decisions or the formulation of government policy;

(e)   a record the purpose of which is to brief Ministers of the Crown in relation to matters that are brought before, or are proposed to be brought before, Council or that are the subject of communications or discussions referred to in paragraph (d); and

(f)   draft legislation.

(3) **Definition of "Council"** — For the purposes of subsection (2), "Council" means the Queen's Privy Council for Canada, committees of the Queen's Privy Council for Canada, Cabinet and committees of Cabinet.

(4) **Exception** — Subsection (1) does not apply in respect of

(a)   a confidence of the Queen's Privy Council for Canada that has been in existence for more than twenty years; or

(b)   a discussion paper described in paragraph (2)(b)

(i)   if the decisions to which the discussion paper relates have been made public, or

(ii) where the decisions have not been made public, if four years have passed since the decisions were made.

[S.C. 1992, c. 1, s. 144 (Sch. VII, item 5)(F)]

Provincial Laws of Evidence

40. How applicable — In all proceedings over which Parliament has legislative authority, the laws of evidence in force in the province in which those proceedings are taken, including the laws of proof of service of any warrant, summons, subpoena or other document, subject to this Act and other Acts of Parliament, apply to those proceedings.

Statutory Declarations

41. Solemn declaration — Any judge, notary public, justice of the peace, provincial court judge, recorder, mayor or commissioner authorized to take affidavits to be used either in the provincial or federal courts, or any other functionary authorized by law to administer an oath in any matter, may receive the solemn declaration of any person voluntarily making the declaration before him, in the following form, in attestation of the execution of any writing, deed or instrument, or of the truth of any fact, or of any account rendered in writing:

> I,................, solemnly declare that (*state the fact or facts declared to*), and I make this solemn declaration conscientiously believing it to be true, and knowing that it is of the same force and effect as if made under oath.
>
> Declared before me.................... at.................... this.................... day of....................
> 19.............

[R.S. 1985, c. 27 (1st Supp.), s. 203]

Insurance Proofs

42. Affidavits, etc. — Any affidavit, solemn affirmation or declaration required by any insurance company authorized by law to do business in Canada, in regard to any loss of or injury to person, property or life insured or assured therein, may be taken before any commissioner or other person authorized to take affidavits, before any justice of the peace or before any notary public for any province, and the commissioner, person, justice of the peace or notary public is required to take the affidavit, solemn affirmation or declaration.

Application

43. Foreign courts — This Part applies to the taking of evidence relating to proceedings in courts out of Canada.

Interpretation

44. Definitions — In this Part,

"cause" includes a proceeding against a criminal;

"court" means any superior court in any province;

"judge" means any judge of any superior court in any province;

"oath" includes a solemn affirmation in cases in which, by the law of Canada, or of a province, as the case may be, a solemn affirmation is allowed instead of an oath.

45. Construction — This Part shall not be so construed as to interfere with the right of legislation of the legislature of any province requisite or desirable for the carrying out of the objects hereof.

Procedure

46. Order for examination of witness in Canada — If, on an application for that purpose, it is made to appear to any court or judge that any court or tribunal outside Canada, before which any civil, commercial or criminal matter is pending, is desirous of obtaining the testimony in relation to that matter of a party or witness within the jurisdiction of the first mentioned court, of the court to which the judge belongs or of the judge, the court or judge may, in its or their discretion, order the examination on oath on interrogatories, or otherwise, before any person or persons named in the order, of that party or witness accordingly, and by the same or any subsequent order may command the attendance of that party or witness for the purpose of being examined, and for the production of any writings or other documents mentioned in the order and of any other writings or documents relating to the matter in question that are in the possession or power of that party or witness.

(2) **Video links, etc.** — For greater certainty, testimony for the purposes of subsection (1) may be given by means of technology that permits the virtual presence of the party or witness before the court or tribunal outside Canada or that permits that court or tribunal, and the parties, to hear and examine the party or witness.

[S.C. 1999, c. 18, s. 89]

47. Enforcement of the order — On the service on the party or witness of an order referred to in section 46, and of an appointment of a time and place for the examination of the party or witness signed by the person named in the order for taking the examination, or, if more than one person is named, by one of the persons named, and on payment or tender of the like conduct money as is properly payable on attendance at a trial, the order may be enforced in like manner as an order made by the court or judge in a cause pending in that court or before that judge.

48. Expenses and conduct money — Every person whose attendance is required in the manner described in section 47 is entitled to the like conduct money and payment for expenses and loss of time as on attendance at a trial.

49. Administering oath — On any examination of parties or witnesses, under the authority of any order made in pursuance of this Part, the oath shall be administered by the person authorized to take the examination, or, if more than one person is authorized, by one of those persons.

50. (1) **Right of refusal to answer or produce document** — Any person examined under any order made under this Part has the like right to refuse to answer questions tending to criminate himself, or other questions, as a party or witness, as the case may be, would have in any cause pending in the court by which, or by a judge whereof, the order is made.

(1.1) **Laws about witnesses to apply - video links etc.** — Despite subsection (1), when a party or witness gives evidence under subsection 46(2), the evidence shall be given as though they were physically before the court or tribunal outside Canada, for the purposes of the laws relating to evidence and procedure but only to the extent that giving the evidence would not disclose information otherwise protected by the Canadian law of non-disclosure of information or privilege.

(1.2) **Contempt of court in Canada** — When a party or witness gives evidence under subsection 46(2), the Canadian law relating to contempt of court applies with respect to a refusal by the party or witness to answer a question or to produce a writing or document referred to in subsection 46(1), as ordered under that subsection by the court or judge.

(2) **Nature of right** — No person shall be compelled to produce, under any order referred to in subsection (1), any writing or other document that he could not be compelled to produce at a trial of such a cause.

[S.C. 1999, c. 18, s. 90]

51. (1) **Rules of court** — The court may frame rules and orders in relation to procedure and to the evidence to be produced in support of the application for an order for examination of parties and witnesses under this Part, and generally for carrying this Part into effect.

(2) **Letters rogatory** — In the absence of any order in relation to the evidence to be produced in support of the application referred to in subsection (1), letters rogatory from a court or tribunal outside Canada in which the civil, commercial or criminal matter is pending, are deemed and taken to be sufficient evidence in support of the application.

[1999, c. 18, s. 91 (in force June 17, 1999).]

Part III

Application

52. Application of this Part — This Part extends to the following classes of persons:

(a) officers of any of Her Majesty's diplomatic or consular services while performing their functions in any foreign country, including ambassadors, envoys, ministers, charges d'affaires, counsellors, secretaries, attaches, consuls general, consuls, vice-consuls, pro-consuls, consular agents, acting consuls general, acting consuls, acting vice-consuls and acting consular agents;

(b) officers of the Canadian diplomatic, consular and representative services while performing their functions in any foreign country or in any part of the Commonwealth and Dependent Territories other than Canada, including, in addition to the diplomatic and consular officers mentioned in paragraph (a), high commissioners, permanent delegates, acting high commissioners, acting permanent delegates, counsellors and secretaries;

(c) Canadian Government Trade Commissioners and Assistant Canadian Government Trade Commissioners while performing their functions in any foreign country or in any part of the Commonwealth and Dependent Territories other than Canada;

(d) honorary consular officers of Canada while performing their functions in any foreign country or in any part of the Commonwealth and Dependent Territories other than Canada;

(e) judicial officials in a foreign country in respect of oaths, affidavits, solemn affirmations, declarations or similar documents that the official is authorized to administer, take or receive; and

(f) persons locally engaged and designated by the Deputy Minister of Foreign Affairs or any other person authorized by that Deputy Minister while performing their functions in any foreign country or in any part of the Commonwealth and Dependent Territories other than Canada.

[S.C. 1994, c. 44, s. 92; 1997, c. 18, s. 118]

Oaths and Solemn Affirmations

53. Oaths taken abroad — Oaths, affidavits, solemn affirmations or declarations administered, taken or received outside Canada by any person mentioned in section 52 are as valid and effectual and are of the like force and effect to all intents and purposes as if they had been administered, taken or received in Canada by a person authorized to administer, take or receive oaths, affidavits, solemn affirmations or declarations therein that are valid and effectual under this Act.

Documentary Evidence

54. (1) **Documents to be admitted in evidence** — Any document that purports to have affixed, impressed or subscribed on it or to it the signature of any person authorized by any of paragraphs 52(a) to (d) to administer, take or receive oaths, affidavits, solemn affirmations or declarations, together with their seal or with the seal or stamp of their office, or the office to which the person is attached, in testimony of any oath, affidavit, solemn affirmation or declaration being administered, taken or received by the person, shall be admitted in evidence, without proof of the seal or stamp or of the person's signature or official character.

(2) **Status of statements** — An affidavit, solemn affirmation, declaration or other similar statement taken or received in a foreign country by an official referred to in paragraph 52(e) shall be admitted in evidence without proof of the signature or official character of the official appearing to have signed the affidavit, solemn affirmation, declaration or other statement.

[S.C. 1994, c. 44, s. 93]

RELATED PROVISIONS

From An Act to amend the Criminal Code and the *Canada Evidence Act*

R.S.C., 1985, c. 19 (3rd Supp.), s. 19:

"**19**. (1) **Review after four years** — On the expiration of four years after the coming into force of this Act, the provisions contained herein shall be referred to such committee of the House of Commons, of the Senate, or of both Houses of Parliament as may be designated or established by Parliament for that purpose.

(2) **Report** — The committee designated or established by Parliament for the purpose of subsection (1) shall, as soon as practicable, undertake a comprehensive review of the provisions and operation of this Act and shall, within one year after the review is undertaken or within such further time as the House of Commons may authorize, submit a report to Parliament thereon including such recommendations pertaining to the continuation of those sections and changes required therein as the committee may wish to make."

Appendix C

EVIDENCE ACT

R.S.O. 1990, c. E.23

1. Definitions — In this Act,

"action" includes an issue, matter, arbitration, reference, investigation, inquiry, a prosecution for an offence committed against a statute of Ontario or against a by-law or regulation made under any such statute and any other proceeding authorized or permitted to be tried, heard, had or taken by or before a court under the law of Ontario;

"court" includes a judge, arbitrator, umpire, commissioner, justice of the peace or other officer or person having by law or by consent of parties authority to hear, receive and examine evidence.

2. Application of Act — This Act applies to all actions and other matters whatsoever respecting which the Legislature has jurisdiction.

3. (1) **Administration of oaths and affirmations** — Where by any Act of the Legislature or order of the Assembly an oath or affirmation is authorized or directed to be administered, the oath or affirmation may be administered by any person authorized to take affidavits in Ontario.

(2) **By courts** — Every court has power to administer or cause to be administered an oath or affirmation to every witness who is called to give evidence before the court.

4. Certification — Where an oath, affirmation or declaration is directed to be made before a person, he or she has power and authority to administer it and to certify to its having been made.

5. (1) **Recording of evidence, etc.** — Despite any Act, regulation or the rules of court, a stenographic reporter, shorthand writer, stenographer or other person who is authorized to record evidence and proceedings in an action in a court or in a proceeding authorized by or under any Act may record the evidence and the proceedings by any form of shorthand or by any device for recording sound of a type approved by the Attorney General.

(2) **Admissibility of transcripts** — Despite any Act or regulation or the rules of court, a transcript of the whole or a part of any evidence that has or proceedings that have been recorded in accordance with subsection (1) and that has or have been certified in accordance with the Act, regulation or rule of court, if any, applicable thereto and that is otherwise admissible by law is admissible in evidence whether or not the witness or any of the parties to the action or proceeding has approved the method used to record the evidence and the proceedings and whether or not he or she has read or signed the transcript.

(3) **Regulations** — The Lieutenant Governor in Council may make regulations,

(a) requiring the certification of recordings of evidence and proceedings under subsection (1), and respecting the certification of those recordings;

(b) requiring the certification of transcripts under subsection (2), and respecting the certification of those transcripts; and

(c) prescribing the format, wording or content of certificates to be used in connection with certification under clauses (a) and (b).

[2001, c. 9, Sch. B, s. 8 (in force June 29, 2001).]

6. Witnesses, not incapacitated by crime, etc. — No person offered as a witness in an action shall be excluded from giving evidence by reason of any alleged incapacity from crime or interest.

7. Admissibility notwithstanding interest or crime — Every person offered as a witness shall be admitted to give evidence although he or she has an interest in the matter in question or in the event of the action and although he or she has been previously convicted of a crime or offence.

8. (1) **Evidence of parties** — The parties to an action and the persons on whose behalf it is brought, instituted, opposed or defended are, except as hereinafter otherwise provided, competent and compellable to give evidence on behalf of themselves or of any of the parties, and the husbands and wives of such parties and persons are, except as hereinafter otherwise provided, competent and compellable to give evidence on behalf of any of the parties.

(2) **Evidence of husband and wife** — Without limiting the generality of subsection (1), a husband or a wife may in an action give evidence that he or she did or did not have sexual intercourse with the other party to the marriage at any time or within any period of time before or during the marriage.

9. (1) **Witness not excused from answering questions tending to criminate** — A witness shall not be excused from answering any question upon the ground that the answer may tend to criminate the witness or may tend to establish his or her liability to a civil proceeding at the instance of the Crown or of any person or to a prosecution under any Act of the Legislature.

(2) **Answer not to be used in evidence against witness** — If, with respect to a question, a witness objects to answer upon any of the grounds mentioned in subsection (1) and if, but for this section or any Act of the Parliament of Canada, he or she would therefore be excused from answering such question, then, although the witness is by reason of this section or by reason of any Act of the Parliament of Canada compelled to answer, the answer so given shall not be used or receivable in evidence against him or her in any civil proceeding or in any proceeding under any Act of the Legislature.

10. Evidence in proceedings in consequence of adultery — The parties to a proceeding instituted in consequence of adultery and the husbands and wives of such parties are competent to give evidence in such proceedings, but no witness in any such proceeding, whether a party to the suit or not, is liable to be asked or bound to answer any question tending to show that he or she is guilty of adultery, unless such witness has already given evidence in the same proceeding in disproof of his or her alleged adultery.

11. Communications made during marriage — A husband is not compellable to disclose any communication made to him by his wife during the marriage, nor is a wife compellable to disclose any communication made to her by her husband during the marriage.

12. Expert evidence — Where it is intended by a party to examine as witnesses persons entitled, according to the law or practice, to give opinion evidence, not more than three of such witnesses may be called upon either side without the leave of the judge or other person presiding.

13. Actions by or against heirs, etc. — In an action by or against the heirs, next of kin, executors, administrators or assigns of a deceased person, an opposite or interested party shall not obtain a verdict, judgment or decision on his or her own evidence in respect of any matter occurring before the death of the deceased person, unless such evidence is corroborated by some other material evidence.

14. Actions by or against persons under disability — In an action by or against a mentally incompetent person so found, or a patient in a psychiatric facility, or a person who from unsoundness of mind is incapable of giving evidence, an opposite or interested party shall not obtain a verdict, judgment or decision on his or her own evidence, unless such evidence is corroborated by some other material evidence.

15. Use of examination for discovery of officer or employee of corporation at trial — An examination for discovery, or any party thereof, of an officer or employee of a corporation made under the rules of court may be used as evidence at the trial by any party adverse in interest to the corporation, subject to such protection to the corporation as the rules of court provide.

16. Mode of administering oath — Where an oath may be lawfully taken, it may be administered to a person while such person holds in his or her hand a copy of the Old or New Testament without requiring him or her to kiss the same, or, when the person objects to being sworn in this manner or declares that the oath so administered is not binding upon the person's conscience, then in such manner and form and with such ceremonies as he or she declares to be binding.

17. (1) **Affirmation in lieu of oath** — Where a person objects to being sworn from conscientious scruples, or on the ground of his or her religious belief, or on the ground that the taking of an oath would have no binding effect on the person's conscience, he or she may, in lieu of taking an oath, make an affirmation or declaration that is of the same force and effect as if the person had taken an oath in the usual form.

(2) **Certifying affirmation** — Where the evidence is in the form of an affidavit or written deposition, the person before whom it is taken shall certify that the deponent satisfied him or her that the deponent was a person entitled to affirm.

18. (1) **Presumption of competency** — A person of any age is presumed to be competent to give evidence.

(2) **Challenge, examination** — When a person's competence is challenged, the judge, justice or other presiding officer shall examine the person.

(3) **Exception** — However, if the judge, justice or other presiding officer is of the opinion that the person's ability to give evidence might be adversely affected if he or she examined the person, the person may be examined by counsel instead.

[1995, c. 6, s. 6]

18.1 (1) **Evidence of witness under 14** — When the competence of a proposed witness who is a person under the age of 14 is challenged, the court may admit the person's evidence if the person is able to communicate the evidence, understands the nature of an oath or solemn affirmation and testifies under oath or solemn affirmation.

(2) **Same** — The court may admit the person's evidence, if the person is able to communicate the evidence, even though the person does not understand the nature of an oath or solemn affirmation, if the person understands what it means to tell the truth and promises to tell the truth.

(3) **Further discretion** — If the court is of the opinion that the person's evidence is sufficiently reliable, the court has discretion to admit it, if the person is able to communicate the evidence, even if the person understands neither the nature of an oath or solemn affirmation nor what it means to tell the truth.

[1995, c. 6, s. 6]

18.2 (1) **Corroboration not required, witness under 14** — Evidence given by a person under the age of 14 need not be corroborated.

(2) **No mandatory warning** — It is not necessary to instruct the trier of fact that it is unsafe to rely on the uncorroborated evidence of a person under the age of 14.

[1995, c. 6, s. 6]

18.3 (1) **Videotaped testimony, witness under 18** — A videotape of the testimony of a witness under the age of 18 that satisfies the conditions set out in subsection (2) may be admitted in evidence, if the court is of the opinion that this is likely to help the witness give complete and accurate testimony or that it is in the best interests of the witness.

(2) **Conditions** — The judge or other person who is to preside at the trial and the lawyers of the parties to the proceeding shall be present when the testimony is given, and the lawyers shall be given an opportunity to examine the witness in the same way as if he or she were testifying in the courtroom.

(3) **Screen, support person** — Subsection 18.4 (1) and section 18.5 apply with necessary modifications when testimony is being videotaped.

(4) **Effect of admitting videotape** — If a videotape is admitted under subsection (1), the witness need not attend or testify and shall not be summoned to testify.

(5) **Exception** — However, in exceptional circumstances, the court may require the witness to attend and testify even though a videotape of his or her testimony has been admitted in evidence.

(6) **Videotaped interview** — With the leave of the court, a videotape of an interview with a person under the age of 18 may be admitted in evidence if the person, while testifying, adopts the contents of the videotape.

(7) **Hearsay exceptions preserved** — Subsection (6) is in addition to any rule of law under which a videotape may be admitted in evidence.

[1995, c. 6, s. 6]

18.4 (1) **Screen, witness under 18** — A witness under the age of 18 may testify behind a screen or similar device that allows the witness not to see an adverse party, if the court is of the opinion that this is likely to help the witness give complete and accurate testimony or that it is in the best interests of the witness, and if the condition set out in subsection (4) is satisfied.

(2) **Closed-circuit television** — The court may order that closed-circuit television be used instead of a screen or similar device if the court is of the opinion that,

    (a)   a screen or similar device is insufficient to allow the witness to give complete and accurate testimony; or

    (b)   the best interests of the witness require the use of closed-circuit television.

(3) **Same** — If the court makes an order under subsection (2), the witness shall testify outside the courtroom and his or her testimony shall be shown in the courtroom by means of closed circuit television.

(4) **Condition** — When a screen or similar device or closed-circuit television is used, the judge and jury and the parties to the proceeding and their lawyers shall be able to see and hear the witness testify.

[1995, c. 6, s. 6]

    18.5 (1) **Support person, witness under 18** — During the testimony of a witness under the age of 18, a support person chosen by the witness may accompany him or her.

(2) **Court's discretion** — If the court determines that the support person chosen by the witness is not appropriate for any reason, the witness is entitled to choose another support person.

(3) **Examples** — The following are examples of reasons on the basis of which the court may determine that the support person chosen by a witness is not appropriate:

    1.   The court is of the opinion that the support person may attempt to influence the testimony of the witness.

    2.   The support person behaves in a disruptive manner.

    3.   The support person is also a witness in the proceeding.

[1995, c. 6, s. 6]

    18.6 (1) **Personal cross-examination by adverse party** — The court may prohibit personal cross-examination of a witness under the age of 18 by an adverse party if the court is of the opinion that such a cross-examination,

    (a)   would be likely to affect adversely the ability of the witness to give evidence; or

    (b)   would not be in the best interests of the witness.

(2) **Alternatives** — If the court prohibits personal cross-examination by the adverse party, the cross-examination may be conducted in some other appropriate way (for example, by means of questions written by the adverse party and read to the witness by the court).

[1995, c. 6, s. 6]

    19. Attendance of witnesses — A witness served in due time with a summons issued out of a court in Ontario, and paid proper witness fees and conduct money, who makes default in obeying such summons, without any lawful and reasonable impediment, in addition to any penalty he or she may incur as for a contempt of court, is liable to an action on the part of the person by whom, or on whose behalf, he or she has been summonsed for any damage that such person may sustain or be put to by reason of such default.

[The following provisions were enacted by the Province of Canada as part of Chapter 9 of 1854. They were carried into the Consolidated Statutes of Canada, 1859 as sections 4-11 and 13 of Chapter 79. They have appeared in their present form in successive revisions since Confederation. They are revised in the Revised Statutes of Ontario to provide for gender-neutrality and to include a French version. See Rideout v. Rideout (1956), O.W.N. 644].

4. **Courts may issue subpoenas to any part of Canada** — If in any action or suit depending in any of Her Majesty's Superior Courts of Law or Equity in Canada, it appears to the Court, or when not sitting, it appears to any Judge of the Court that it is proper to compel the personal attendance at any trial or enquête or examination of witnesses, of any person who may not be within the jurisdiction of the Court in which the action or suit is pending, the Court or Judge, in their or his or her discretion, may order that a writ called a writ of subpoena ad testificandum or of subpoena duces tecum shall issue in special form, commanding such person to attend as a witness at such trial or enquête or examination of witnesses wherever he or she may be in Canada.

5. **Service thereof in any part of Canada to be good** — The service of any such writ or process in any part of Canada, shall be valid and effectual to all intents and purposes, as if the same had been served within the jurisdiction of the Court from which it has issued, according to the practice of such Court.

6. **When not to be issued** — No such writ shall be issued in any case in which an action is pending for the same cause of action, in that section of the Province, whether Upper or Lower Canada respectively, within which such witness or witnesses may reside.

7. **Writs to be specially noted** — Every such writ shall have at the foot, or in the margin thereof, a statement or notice that the same is issued by the special order of the Court or Judge making such order, and no such writ shall issue without such special order.

8. **Consequences of disobedience** — In case any person so served does not appear according to the exigency of such writ or process, the Court out of which the same issued, may, upon proof made of the service thereof, and of such default to the satisfaction of such Court, transmit a certificate of such default, under the seal of the same Court, to any of Her Majesty's Superior Courts of Law or Equity in that part of Canada in which the person so served may reside, being out of the jurisdiction of the Court transmitting such certificate, and the Court to which such certificate is sent, shall thereupon proceed against and punish such person so having made default, in like manner as they might have done if such person had neglected or refused to appear to a writ of subpoena or other similar process issued out of such last mentioned Court.

9. **If expenses paid or tendered** — No such certificate of default shall be transmitted by any Court, nor shall any person be punished for neglect or refusal to attend any trial or enquête or examination of witnesses, in obedience to any such subpoena or other similar process, unless it be made to appear to the Court transmitting and also to the Court receiving such certificate, that a reasonable and sufficient sum of money, according to the rate per diem and per mile allowed to witnesses by the law and practice of the Superior Court of Law within the jurisdiction of which such person was found, to defray the expenses of coming and attending to give evidence and of returning from giving evidence, had been

tendered to such person at the time when the writ of subpoena, or other similar process was served upon him or her.

10. **How service proved** — The service of such writs of subpoena or other similar process, in Lower Canada, shall be proved by the certificate of a Bailiff within the jurisdiction where the service has been made, under his or her oath of office, and such service in Upper Canada by the affidavit of service endorsed on or annexed to such writ by the person who served the same.

11. **Costs of attendance provided for** — The costs of the attendance of any such witness shall not be taxed against the adverse party to such suit, beyond the amount that would have been allowed on a commission rogatoire, or to examine witnesses unless the Court or Judge before whom such trial or enquête or examination of witnesses is had, so orders.

. . . . .

13. **Power to issue commissions to examine witnesses preserved** — Nothing herein contained shall affect the power of any Court to issue a commission for the examination of witnesses out of its jurisdiction, nor affect the admissibility of any evidence at any trial or proceeding, where such evidence is now by law receivable, on the ground of any witness being beyond the jurisdiction of the Court.

20. Examination of witnesses, proof of contradictory written statements — A witness may be cross-examined as to previous statements made by him or her in writing, or reduced into writing, relative to the matter in question, without the writing being shown to the witness, but, if it is intended to contradict the witness by the writing, his or her attention shall, before such contradictory proof is given, be called to those parts of the writing that are to be used for the purpose of so contradicting the witness, and the judge or other person presiding at any time during the trial or proceeding may require the production of the writing for his or her inspection, and may thereupon make such use of it for the purposes of the trial or proceeding as he or she thinks fit.

21. Proof of contradictory oral statements — If a witness upon cross-examination as to a former statement made by him or her relative to the matter in question and inconsistent with his or her present testimony does not distinctly admit that he or she did make such statement, proof may be given that the witness did in fact make it, but before such proof is given the circumstances of the supposed statement sufficient to designate the particular occasion shall be mentioned to the witness, and the witness shall be asked whether or not he or she did make such statement.

22. (1) **Proof of previous conviction of a witness** — A witness may be asked whether he or she has been convicted of any crime, and upon being so asked, if the witness either denies the fact or refuses to answer, the conviction may be proved, and a certificate containing the substance and effect only, omitting the formal part, of the charge and of the conviction, purporting to be signed by the officer having the custody of the records of the court at which the offender was convicted, or by the deputy of the officer, is, upon proof of the identity of the witness as such convict, sufficient evidence of the conviction, without proof of the signature or of the official character of the person appearing to have signed the certificate.

(2) [Repealed, 1995, c. 6, s. 6]

[1995, c. 6, s. 6]

22.1 (1) **Proof of conviction or discharge** — Proof that a person has been convicted or discharged anywhere in Canada of a crime is proof, in the absence of evidence to the contrary, that the crime was committed by the person, if,

(a)   no appeal of the conviction or discharge was taken and the time for an appeal has expired; or

(b)   an appeal of the conviction or discharge was taken but was dismissed or abandoned and no further appeal is available.

(2) **Same** — Subsection (1) applies whether or not the convicted or discharged person is a party to the proceeding.

(3) **Same** — For the purposes of subsection (1), a certificate containing the substance and effect only, omitting the formal part, of the charge and of the conviction or discharge, purporting to be signed by the officer having the custody of the records of the court at which the offender was convicted or discharged, or by the deputy of the officer, is, on proof of the identity of the person named as convicted or discharged person in the certificate, sufficient evidence of the conviction or discharge of that person, without proof of the signature or of the official character of the person appearing to have signed the certificate.

[1995, c. 6, s. 6]

23. How far a party may discredit his or her own witness — A party producing a witness shall not be allowed to impeach his or her credit by general evidence of bad character, but the party may contradict the witness by other evidence, or, if the witness in the opinion of the judge or other person presiding proves adverse, such party may, by leave of the judge or other person presiding, prove that the witness made at some other time a statement inconsistent with his or her present testimony, but before such last-mentioned proof is given the circumstances of the proposed statement sufficient to designate the particular occasion shall be mentioned to the witness and the witness shall be asked whether or not he or she did make such statement.

24. Letters patent — Letters patent under the Great Seal of the United Kingdom, or of any other of Her Majesty's dominions, may be proved by the production of an exemplification thereof, or of the enrolment thereof, under the Great Seal under which such letters patent were issued, and such exemplification has the like force and effect for all purposes as the letters patent thereby exemplified or enrolled, as well against Her Majesty as against all other persons whomsoever.

24.1 (1) **Office consolidations of statutes or regulations** — A document that purports to be printed by the Queen's Printer for Ontario as an office consolidation of a statute or regulation shall be received in evidence, in the absence of evidence to the contrary, as an accurate consolidation of the statute or regulation as it read on the date indicated on the document.

(2) **Electronic consolidations** — A CD-ROM disk or other electronic information storage device prescribed by the regulations that purports to be published by the Queen's Printer for Ontario as a consolidation of statutes or regulations shall be received in evidence, in the absence of evidence to the contrary, as an accurate consolidation of the statutes or regulations as they read on the date indicated by the disk or other device.

(3) **Same** — Subsections (1) and (2) do not apply to a document, CD-ROM disk or device that has a disclaimer to the effect that is prepared for the purposes of convenience only and is not intended as authoritative text.

(4) **Regulations** — The Lieutenant Governor in Council may make regulations prescribing electronic information storage devices for the purposes of this section.

[1998, c. 18, Sched. B, s. 7(1) (in force December 18, 1998)]

25. Copies of statutes, etc. — Copies of statutes, official gazettes, ordinances, regulations, proclamations, journals, orders, appointments to office, notices thereof and other public documents purporting to be printed by or under the authority of the Parliament of the United Kingdom, or of the Imperial Government or by or under the authority of the government or of any legislative body of any dominion, commonwealth, state, province, colony, territory or possession within the Queen's dominions, shall be admitted in evidence to prove the contents thereof.

26. Proclamations, orders, etc. — Proof in the absence of evidence to the contrary of a proclamation, order, regulation or appointment to office made or issued,

(a)　by the Governor General or the Governor General in Council, or other chief executive officer or administrator of the Government of Canada; or

(b)　by or under the authority of a minister or head of a department of the Government of Canada or of a provincial or territorial government in Canada; or

(c)　by a Lieutenant Governor or Lieutenant Governor in Council or other chief executive officer or administrator of Ontario or of any other province or territory in Canada,

may be given by the production of,

(d)　a copy of the *Canada Gazette* or of the official gazette for a province or territory purporting to contain a notice of such proclamation, order, regulation or appointment; or

(e)　a copy of such proclamation, order, regulation or appointment purporting to be printed by the Queen's Printer or by the government printer for the province or territory; or

(f)　a copy of or extract from such proclamation, order, regulation or appointment purporting to be certified to be a true copy by such minister or head of a department or by the clerk, or assistant or acting clerk of the Executive Council or by the head of a department of the Government of Canada or of a provincial or territorial government or by his or her deputy or acting deputy.

[1993, c. 27, Sch.]

27. Orders signed by Secretary of State or member of Executive Council — An order in writing purporting to be signed by the Secretary of State of Canada and to be written by command of the Governor General shall be received in evidence as the order of the Governor General and an order in writing purporting to be signed by a member of the Executive Council and to be written by command of the Lieutenant Governor shall be received in evidence as the order of the Lieutenant Governor.

28. Notices in *Gazette* — Copies of proclamations and of official and other documents, notices and advertisements printed in the *Canada Gazette*, or in The *Ontario Gazette*, or in the official gazette of any province or territory in Canada are proof, in the absence of evidence to the contrary, of the originals and of the contents thereof.

29. Public or official documents — Where the original record could be received in evidence, a copy of an official or public document in Ontario, purporting to be certified under the hand of the proper officer, or the person in whose custody such official or public document is placed, or of a document, by-law, rule, regulation or proceeding, or of an entry in a register or other book of a corporation, created by charter or statute in Ontario, purporting to be certified under the seal of the corporation and the hand of the presiding officer or secretary thereof, is receivable in evidence without proof of the seal of the corporation, or of the signature or of the official character of the person or persons appearing to have signed the same, and without further proof thereof.

30. Privilege in case of official documents — Where a document is in the official possession, custody or power of a member of the Executive Council, or of the head of a ministry of the public service of Ontario, if the deputy head or other officer of the ministry has the document in his or her personal possession, and is called as a witness, he or she is entitled, acting herein by the direction and on behalf of such member of the Executive Council or head of the ministry, to object to producing the document on the ground that it is privileged, and such objection may be taken by him or her in the same manner, and has the same effect, as if such member of the Executive Council or head of the ministry were personally present and made the objection.

31. (1) **Definition** — In this section, "municipality" means a regional, metropolitan or district municipality, the County of Oxford, a county, city, town, village, township or improvement district.

(2) **Entries in books** — A copy of an entry in a book of account kept by a municipality or in a department of the Government of Canada or of Ontario shall be received as proof in the absence of evidence to the contrary of such entry and of the matters, transactions and accounts recorded therein, if it is proved by the oath, affirmation or affidavit of an officer of the municipality or of the department,

    (a)   that the book was, at the time of the making of the entry, one of the ordinary books kept by the municipality or in the department;

    (b)   that the entry was apparently, and as the deponent believes, made in the usual and ordinary course of business of the municipality or department; and

    (c)   that such copy is a true copy thereof.

[1993, c. 27, Sch.]

32. (1) **Copies of public books or documents** — Where a book or other document is of so public a nature as to be admissible in evidence on its mere production from the proper custody, a copy thereof or extract therefrom is admissible in evidence if it is proved that it is an examined copy or extract, or that it purports to be signed and certified as a true copy or extract by the officer to whose custody the original was entrusted.

(2) **Copies to be delivered if required** — Such officer shall furnish the certified copy or extract to any person applying for it at a reasonable time, upon the person paying therefor a sum not exceeding 10 cents for every folio of 100 words.

33. (1) **Definition** — In this section, "bank" means a bank to which the *Bank Act* (Canada) applies or the Province of Ontario Savings Office, and includes a branch, agency or office of any of them.

(2) **Copies of entries in books as evidence** — Subject to this section, a copy of an entry in a book or record kept in a bank is in any action to which the bank is not a party proof in the absence of evidence to the contrary of such entry and of the matters, transactions and accounts therein recorded.

[S.O. 1993, c. 27, Sch.]

(3) **Proof required as to entry in ordinary course of business** — A copy of an entry in such book or record shall not be received in evidence under this section unless it is first proved that the book or record was at the time of making the entry one of the ordinary books or records of the bank, that the entry was made in the usual and ordinary course of business, that the book or record is in the custody or control of the bank, or its successor, and that such copy is a true copy thereof, and such proof may be given by the manager or accountant, or a former manager of the bank or its successor, and may be given orally or by affidavit.

(4) **Production of books to be required only under order** — A bank or officer of a bank is not, in an action to which the bank is not a party, compellable to produce any book or record the contents of which can be proved under this section, or to appear as a witness to prove the matters, transactions and accounts therein recorded, unless by order of the court or a judge made for special cause.

(5) **Inspection of account** — On the application of a party to an action, the court or judge may order that such party be at liberty to inspect and take copies of any entries in the books or records of a bank for the purposes of such proceeding, but a person whose account is to be inspected shall be served with notice of the application at least two clear days before the hearing thereof, and, if it is shown to the satisfaction of the court or judge that such person cannot be notified personally, such notice may be given by addressing it to the bank.

(6) **Costs** — The costs of an application to a court or judge under or for the purposes of this section, and the costs of any thing done or to be done under an order of a court or judge made under or for the purposes of this section, are in the discretion of the court or judge who may order such costs or any part thereof to be paid to a party by the bank, where such costs have been occasioned by a default or delay on the part of the bank, and any such order against a bank may be enforced as if the bank were a party to the proceeding.

34. (1) **Definitions** — In this section,
"person" includes,

    (a)   the Government of Canada and of a province of Canada, and a department, commission, board or branch of any such government,

    (b)   a corporation, its successors and assigns, and

    (c)   the heirs, executors, administrators or other legal representatives of a person;

"photographic film" includes any photographic plate, microphotographic film and photostatic negative, and "photograph" has a corresponding meaning.

(2) **Admissible in evidence** — Where a bill of exchange, promissory note, cheque, receipt, instrument, agreement, document, plan or a record or book or entry therein kept or held by a person,

(a)   is photographed in the course of an established practice of such person of photographing objects of the same or a similar class in order to keep a permanent record thereof; and

(b)   is destroyed by or in the presence of such person or of one or more of the person's employees or delivered to another person in the ordinary course of business or lost,

a print from the photographic film is admissible in evidence in all cases and for all purposes for which the object photographed would have been admissible.

(3) [Repealed, 1999, c. 12, Sch. B. s. 7 (in force June 30, 2000)]

(4) [Repealed, 1999, c. 12, Sch. B. s. 7 (in force June 30, 2000)]

(5) **Proof of compliance with conditions** — Proof of compliance with the conditions prescribed by this section may be given by any person having knowledge of the facts either orally or by affidavit sworn or affirmed before a notary public, and, unless the court otherwise orders, a notarial copy of any such affidavit is admissible in evidence in lieu of the original affidavit.

[1999, c. 12, Sch. B, s. 7 (in force June 30, 2000).]

34.1 (1) **Definitions** — In this section,

"data" means representations, in any form, of information or concepts;

"electronic record" means data that is recorded or stored on any medium in or by a computer system or other similar device, that can be read or perceived by a person or a computer system or other similar device, and includes a display, printout or other output of that data, other than a printout referred to in subsection (6);

"electronic records system" includes the computer system or other similar device by or in which data is recorded or stored, and any procedures related to the recording and storage of electronic records.

(2) **Application** — This section does not modify any common law or statutory rule relating to the admissibility of records, except the rules relating to authentication and best evidence.

(3) **Power of court** — A court may have regard to evidence adduced under this section in applying any common law or statutory rule relating to the admissibility of records.

(4) **Authentication** — The person seeking to introduce an electronic record has the burden of proving its authenticity by evidence capable of supporting a finding that the electronic record is what the person claims it to be.

(5) **Application of best evidence rule** — Subject to subsection (6), where the best evidence rule is applicable in respect of an electronic record, it is satisfied on proof of the integrity of the electronic records system by or in which the data was recorded or stored.

(5.1) **Same** — The integrity of an electronic record may be proved by evidence of the integrity of the electronic records system by or in which the data was recorded or stored, or by evidence that reliable encryption techniques were used to support the integrity of the electronic record.

(6) **What constitutes record** — An electronic record in the form of a printout that has been manifestly or consistently acted on, relied upon, or used as the record of the information recorded or stored on the printout, is the record for the purposes of the best evidence rule.

(7) **Presumption of integrity** — In the absence of evidence to the contrary, the integrity of the electronic records system by or in which an electronic record is recorded or stored is proved for the purposes of subsection (5),

(a) by evidence that supports a finding that at all material times the computer system or other similar device was operating properly or, if it was not, the fact of its not operating properly did not affect the integrity of the electronic record, and there are no other reasonable grounds to doubt the integrity of the electronic records system;

(b) if it is established that the electronic record was recorded or stored by a party to the proceeding who is adverse in interest to the party seeking to introduce it; or

(c) if it is established that the electronic record was recorded or stored in the usual and ordinary course of business by a person who is not a party to the proceeding and who did not record or store it under the control of the party seeking to introduce the record.

(8) **Standards** — For the purpose of determining under any rule of law whether an electronic record is admissible, evidence may be presented in respect of any standard, procedure, usage or practice on how electronic records are to be recorded or stored, having regard to the type of business or endeavour that used, recorded or stored the electronic record and the nature and purpose of the electronic record.

(9) **Proof by affidavit** — The matters referred to in subsections (6), (7) and (8) may be established by an affidavit given to the best of the deponent's knowledge and belief.

(10) **Cross-examination** — A deponent of an affidavit referred to in subsection (9) that has been introduced in evidence may be cross-examined as of right by a party to the proceeding who is adverse in interest to the party who has introduced the affidavit or has caused the affidavit to be introduced.

(11) **Same** — Any party to the proceeding may, with leave of the court, cross-examine a person referred to in clause (7) (c).

[1999, c. 12, Sch. B, s. 7 (in force June 30, 2000); 2000, c. 26, Sch. A s. 7(1) (in force April 15, 2001).]

35. (1) **Definitions** — In this section,

"business" includes every kind of business, profession, occupation, calling, operation or activity, whether carried on for profit or otherwise;

"record" includes any information that is recorded or stored by means of any device.

(2) **Where business records admissible** — Any writing or record made of any act, transaction, occurrence or event is admissible as evidence of such act, transaction, occurrence or event if made in the usual and ordinary course of any business and if it was in the usual and ordinary course of such business to make such writing or record at the time of such act, transaction, occurrence or event or within a reasonable time thereafter.

(3) **Notice and production** — Subsection (2) does not apply unless the party tendering the writing or record has given at least seven days notice of the party's intention to all other parties in the action, and any party to the action is entitled to obtain from the person who has possession thereof production for inspection of the writing or record within five days after giving notice to produce the same.

(4) **Surrounding circumstances** — The circumstances of the making of such a writing or record, including lack of personal knowledge by the maker, may be shown to affect its weight, but such circumstances do not affect its admissibility.

(5) **Previous rules as to admissibility and privileged documents not affected** — Nothing in this section affects the admissibility of any evidence that would be admissible apart from this section or makes admissible any writing or record that is privileged.

36. (1) **Judicial notice to be taken of signatures of judges, etc.** — All courts, judges, justices, masters, case management masters, clerks of courts, commissioners and other officers acting judicially, shall take judicial notice of the signature of any judge of any court in Canada, in Ontario and in every other province and territory in Canada, where the judge's signature is appended or attached to a decree, order, certificate, affidavit, or judicial or official document.

(2) **Interpretation** — The members of the Canadian Transport Commission and of the Ontario Municipal Board, the Mining and Lands Commissioner appointed under the *Ministry of Natural Resources Act* and a referee appointed under the *Drainage Act* shall be deemed judges for the purposes of this section.

[1996, c. 25, s. 5 (in force October 31, 1996)]

37. Proof of handwriting, when not required — No proof is required of the handwriting or official position of a person certifying to the truth of a copy of or extract from any proclamation, order, regulation or appointment, or to any matter or thing as to which he or she is by law authorized or required to certify.

38. Foreign judgments, etc., how proved — A judgment, decree or other judicial proceeding recovered, made, had or taken in the Supreme Court of Judicature or in any court of record in England or Ireland or in any of the superior courts of law, equity or bankruptcy in Scotland, or in any court of record in Canada, or in any of the provinces or territories in Canada, or in any British colony or possession, or in any court of record of the United States of America, or of any state of the United States of America, may be proved by an exemplification of the same under the seal of the court without any proof of the authenticity of such seal or other proof whatever, in the same manner as a judgment, decree or other judicial proceeding of the Superior Court of Justice may be proved by an exemplification thereof.

[2000, c. 26, Sch. A, s. 7 (in force December 6, 2000).]

39. (1) **Copies of notarial acts in Quebec admissible** — A copy of a notarial act or instrument in writing made in Quebec before a notary and filed, enrolled or enregistered by such notary, certified by a notary or prothonotary to be a true copy of the original thereby certified to be in his or her possession as such notary or prothonotary, is receivable in evidence in the place and stead of the original, and has the same force and effect as the original would have if produced and proved.

(2) **How impeached** — The proof of such certified copy may be rebutted or set aside by proof that there is no such original, or that the copy is not a true copy of the original in some material particular, or that the original is not an instrument of such nature as may, by the law of Quebec, be taken before a notary, or be filed, enrolled or enregistered by a notary.

40. Protests of bills and notes — A protest of a bill of exchange or promissory note purporting to be under the hand of a notary public wherever made is proof, in the absence of evidence to the contrary, of the allegations and facts therein stated.

41. Effect of certain certificates of notaries — Any note, memorandum or certificate purporting to be made by a notary public in Canada, in his or her own handwriting or to be signed by him or her at the foot of or embodied in any protest, or in a regular register of official acts purporting to be kept by him or her is proof, in the absence of evidence to the contrary, of the fact of notice of non-acceptance or non-payment of a bill of exchange or promissory note having been sent or delivered at the time and in the manner stated in such note, certificate or memorandum.

42. Proving titles under Small Claims Court executions — In proving a title under a sheriff's conveyance based upon an execution issued from the Small Claims Court, it is sufficient to prove the judgment recovered in the Small Claims Court without proof of any prior proceedings.

43. Solemn declaration — Any person authorized to take declarations in Ontario may receive the solemn declaration of any person in attestation of the truth of any fact or of any account rendered in writing and the declaration and any declaration authorized or required by any Act of the Legislature shall be in the following form:

I, ..., solemnly declare that (*state* the fact or facts declared to), and I make this solemn declaration conscientiously believing it to be true and knowing that it is of the same force and effect as if made under oath.

Declared before me at the of this day of , 20

A Commissioner, etc.

44. (1) **Oaths, etc., administered by commissioned officers** — An oath, affidavit, affirmation or statutory declaration administered, sworn, affirmed or made in or outside Ontario before a person who holds a commission as an officer in the Canadian Forces and is on full-time service is as valid and effectual to all intents and purposes as if it had been duly administered, sworn, affirmed or made in Ontario before a commissioner for taking affidavits in Ontario.

(2) **Admissibility** — A document that purports to be signed by a person mentioned in subsection (1) in testimony of an oath, affidavit, affirmation or statutory declaration having been administered, sworn, affirmed or made before him or her and on which the officer's rank and unit are shown below his or her signature is admissible in evidence without proof of the signature or rank or unit or that he or she is on full-time service.

45. (1) **Oaths, etc., administered outside Ontario** — An oath, affidavit, affirmation or statutory declaration administered, sworn, affirmed or made outside Ontario before,

(a) a judge;

(b) a magistrate;

(c) an officer of a court of justice;

(d) a commissioner for taking affidavits or other competent authority of the like nature;

(e) a notary public;

(f) the head of a city, town, village, township or other municipality;

(g) an officer of any of Her Majesty's diplomatic or consular services, including an ambassador, envoy, minister, charge d'affairs, counsellor, secretary, attache, consul-general, consul, vice-consul, pro-consul, consular agent, acting consul-general, acting consul, acting vice-consul and acting consular agent;

(h) an officer of the Canadian diplomatic, consular or representative services, including, in addition to the diplomatic and consular officers mentioned in clause (g), a high commissioner, permanent delegate, acting high commissioner, acting permanent delegate, counsellor and secretary; or

(i) a Canadian Government trade commissioner or assistant trade commissioner,

exercising his or her functions or having jurisdiction or authority as such in the place in which it is administered, sworn, affirmed or made, is as valid and effectual to all intents and purposes as if it had been duly administered, sworn, affirmed or made in Ontario before a commissioner for taking affidavits in Ontario.

(2) **Idem** — An oath, affidavit, affirmation or statutory declaration administered, sworn, affirmed or made outside Ontario before a notary public for Ontario or before a commissioner for taking affidavits in Ontario is as valid and effectual to all intents and purposes as if it had been duly administered, sworn, affirmed or made in Ontario before a commissioner for taking affidavits in Ontario.

(3) **Admissibility** — A document that purports to be signed by a person mentioned in subsection (1) or (2) in testimony of an oath, affidavit, affirmation or statutory declaration having been administered, sworn, affirmed or made before him or her, and on which the person's office is shown below his or her signature, and

(a)   in the case of a notary public, that purports to have impressed thereon or attached thereto his or her official seal;

(b)   in the case of a person mentioned in clause (1) (f), that purports to have impressed thereon or attached thereto the seal of the municipality;

(c)   in the case of a person mentioned in clause (1) (g), (h) or (i), that purports to have impressed thereon or attached thereto his or her seal or the seal or stamp of his or her office or of the office to which he or she is attached, is admissible in evidence without proof of his or her signature or of his or her office or official character or of the seal or stamp and without proof that he or she was exercising his or her functions or had jurisdiction or authority in the place in which the oath, affidavit, affirmation or statutory declaration was administered, sworn, affirmed or made.

46. Formal defects, when not to vitiate — No informality in the heading or other formal requisites to any affidavit, declaration or affirmation made or taken before a commissioner or other person authorized to take affidavits under the Commissioners for taking Affidavits Act, or under this Act, is any objection to its reception in evidence if the court or judge before whom it is tendered thinks proper to receive it.

47. Affidavit sworn by solicitor for a party — An affidavit or declaration is not inadmissible or unusable in evidence in an action for the reason only that it is made before the solicitor of a party to the action or before the partner, associate, clerk or agent of such solicitor.

48. (1) **Admissibility of copies of depositions** — Where an examination or deposition of a party or witness has been taken before a judge or other officer or person appointed to take it, copies of it, certified under the hand of the judge, officer or other person taking it, shall, without proof of the signature, be received and read in evidence, saving all just exceptions.

(2) **Presumption** — An examination or deposition received or read in evidence under subsection (1) shall be presumed to represent accurately the evidence of the party or witness, unless there is good reason to doubt its accuracy.

49. Effect of probate, etc., as evidence of will, etc. — In order to establish a devise or other testamentary disposition of or affecting real estate, probate of the will or letters of administration with the will annexed containing such devise or disposition, or a copy thereof, under the seal of the court that granted it or under the seal of the Superior Court of Justice, are proof, in the absence of evidence to the contrary, of the will and of its validity and contents.

[2000, c. 26, Sch. A, s. 7 (in force December 6, 2000).]

50. (1) **Proof in the case of will of real estate filed in courts outside Ontario** — Where a person dies in any of Her Majesty's possessions outside Ontario having made a will sufficient to pass real estate in Ontario, purporting to devise, charge or affect real estate in Ontario, the party desiring to establish any such disposition, after giving one month's notice to the opposite party to the proceeding of the party's intentions so to do, may produce and file the probate of the will or letters of administration with the will annexed or a certified copy thereof under the seal of the court that granted the same with a certificate of the judge, registrar or clerk of such court that the original will is filed and remains in the court and purports to have been executed before two witnesses, and such probate or letters of administration or certified copy with such certificate is, unless the court otherwise orders, proof in the absence of evidence to the contrary of the will and of its validity and contents.

(2) **Effect of certificate** — The production of the certificate mentioned in subsection (1) is proof in the absence of evidence to the contrary of the facts therein stated and of the authority of the judge, registrar or clerk, without proof of his or her appointment, authority or signature.

[1993, c. 27, Sch.]

51. Military records — The production of a certificate, purporting to be signed by an authority authorized in that behalf by the *National Defence Act* (Canada) or by regulations made thereunder, stating that the person named in the certificate died, or was deemed to have died, on a date set forth therein, is proof, in the absence of evidence to the contrary, for any purpose to which the authority of the Legislature extends that the person so named died on that date, and also of the office, authority and signature of the person signing the certificate, without any proof of his or her appointment, authority or signature.

52. (1) **Definition** — In this section,
"practitioner" means,

(a) a member of a College as defined in subsection 1(1) of the *Regulated Health Professions Act*, 1991,

(b) a drugless practitioner registered under the *Drugless Practitioners Act*,

(c) a person licensed or registered to practise in another part of Canada under an Act that is similar to an Act referred to in clause (a) or (b).

(d) [Repealed, 1998, c. 18, Sched. G, s. 50 (in force February 1, 1999)]

(e) [Repealed, 1998, c. 18, Sched. G, s. 50 (in force February 1, 1999)]

(f) [Repealed, 1998, c. 18, Sched. G, s. 50 (in force February 1, 1999)]

(2) **Medical reports** — A report obtained by or prepared for a party to an action and signed by a practitioner and any other report of the practitioner that relates to the action are, with leave of the court and after at least ten days notice has been given to all other parties, admissible in evidence in the action.

(3) **Entitlement** — Unless otherwise ordered by the court, a party to an action is entitled, at the time that notice is given under subsection (2), to a copy of the report together with any other report of the practitioner that relates to the action.

(4) **Report required** — Except by leave of the judge presiding at the trial, a practitioner who signs a report with respect to a party shall not give evidence at the trial unless the report is given to all other parties in accordance with subsection (2).

(5) **If practitioner called unnecessarily** — If a practitioner is required to give evidence in person in an action and the court is of the opinion that the evidence could have been produced as effectively by way of a report, the court may order the party that required the attendance of the practitioner to pay as costs therefor such sum as the court considers appropriate.

[1998, c. 18, Sched. G, s. 50 (in force February 1, 1999)]

53. (1) **Definition** — In this section, "instrument" has the meaning assigned to it in section 1 of the *Registry Act*.

(2) **Registered instrument as evidence** — A copy of an instrument or memorial, certified to be a true copy by the land registrar in whose office the instrument or memorial is deposited, filed, kept or registered, is proof of the original, in the absence of evidence to the contrary, except in the cases provided for in subsection (3).

(3) **Where certified copies of registered instruments may be used** — Where it would be necessary to produce and prove an instrument or memorial that has been so deposited, filed, kept or registered in order to establish such instrument or memorial and the contents thereof, the party intending to prove it may give notice to the opposite party, at least ten days before the trial or other proceeding in which the proof is intended to be adduced, that the party intends at the trial or other proceeding to give in evidence, as proof of the instrument or memorial, a copy thereof certified by the land registrar and in every such case the copy so certified is sufficient evidence of the instrument or memorial and of its validity and contents unless the party receiving the notice, within four days after such receipt, gives notice that the party disputes its validity, in which case the costs of producing and proving it may be ordered to be paid by any or either of the parties as is considered just.

[1993, c. 27, Sch.; 1998, c. 18, Sched. B, s. 7 (in force December 18, 1998)]

54. (1) **Filing copies of official documents** — Where a public officer produces upon a summons an original document, it shall not be deposited in court unless otherwise ordered, but, if the document or a copy is needed for subsequent reference or use, a copy thereof or of so much thereof as is considered necessary, certified under the hand of the officer producing the document or otherwise proved, shall be filed as an exhibit in the place of the original, and the officer is entitled to receive in addition to his or her ordinary fees the fees for any certified copy, to be paid to the officer before it is delivered or filed.

(2) **When original to be retained** — Where an order is made that the original be retained, the order shall be delivered to the public officer and the exhibit shall be retained in court and filed.

55. (1) **Proof of certain written instruments** — A party intending to prove the original of a telegram, letter, shipping bill, bill of lading, delivery order, receipt, account or other written instrument used in business or other transactions, may give notice to the opposite party, ten days at least before the trial or other proceeding in which the proof is intended to be adduced, that the party intends to give in evidence as proof of the contents a writing purporting to be a copy of the documents, and in the notice shall name some convenient time and place for the inspection thereof.

(2) **Inspection** — Such copy may then be inspected by the opposite party, and is without further proof sufficient evidence of the contents of the original document, and shall be accepted and taken in lieu of the original, unless the party receiving the notice within four days after the time mentioned for such inspection gives notice that the party intends to dispute the correctness or genuineness of the copy at the trial or proceeding, and to require proof of the original, and the costs

attending any production or proof of the original document are in the discretion of the court.

56. Where no attestation required — It is not necessary to prove, by the attesting witness, an instrument to the validity of which attestation is not requisite.

57. Comparison of disputed writing with genuine — Comparison of a disputed writing with a writing proved to the satisfaction of the court to be genuine shall be permitted to be made by a witness, and such writings and the evidence of witnesses respecting them may be submitted to the court or jury as evidence of the genuineness or otherwise of the writing in dispute.

58. Where instruments offered in evidence may be impounded — Where a document is received in evidence, the court admitting it may direct that it be impounded and kept in such custody for such period and subject to such conditions as seem proper, or until the further order of the court or of the Superior Court of Justice or of a judge thereof, as the case may be.

[2000, c. 26, Sch. A, s. 7 (in force December 6, 2000).]

59. Evidence dispensed with under *Vendors and Purchasers Act* — It is not necessary in an action to produce any evidence that, by section 1 of the *Vendors and Purchasers Act*, is dispensed with as between vendor and purchaser, and the evidence declared to be sufficient in the absence of evidence to the contrary as between vendor and purchaser is sufficient for the purposes of the action.

[1993, c. 27, Sch.]

60. (1) **Evidence for foreign tribunals** — Where it is made to appear to the Superior Court of Justice or a judge thereof, that a court or tribunal of competent jurisdiction in a foreign country has duly authorized, by commission, order or other process, for a purpose for which a letter of request could be issued under the rules of court, the obtaining of the testimony in or in relation to an action, suit or proceeding pending in or before such foreign court or tribunal, of a witness out of the jurisdiction thereof and within the jurisdiction of the court or judge so applied to, such court or judge may order the examination of such witness before the person appointed, and in the manner and form directed by the commission, order or other process, and may, by the same or by a subsequent order, command the attendance of a person named therein for the purpose of being examined, or the production of a writing or other document or thing mentioned in the order, and may give all such directions as to the time and place of the examination, and all other matters connected therewith as seem proper, and the order may be enforced, and any disobedience thereto punished, in like manner as in the case of an order made by the court or judge in an action pending in the court or before a judge of the court.

(2) **Payment of expenses of witness** — A person whose attendance is so ordered is entitled to the like conduct money and payment for expenses and loss of time as upon attendance at a trial in the Superior Court of Justice.

(3) **Right of refusal to answer questions and to produce documents** — A person examined under such commission, order or process has the like right to object to answer questions tending to criminate himself or herself, and to refuse to answer any questions that, in an action pending in the court by which or by a judge whereof or before the judge by whom the order for examination was made,

the witness would be entitled to object or to refuse to answer, and no person shall be compelled to produce at the examination any writing, document or thing that the person could not be compelled to produce at the trial of such an action.

(4) **Administration of oath** — Where the commission, order or other process, or the instructions of the court accompanying the same, direct that the person to be examined shall be sworn or shall affirm, the person so appointed has authority to administer the oath to the person or take his or her affirmation.

[2000, c. 26, Sch. A, s. 7 (in force December 6, 2000).]

Appendix D

COURTS OF JUSTICE ACT
RULES OF CIVIL PROCEDURE

R.R.O. 1990, Reg. 194

Trials
Rule 53 Evidence At Trial

Evidence By Witnesses

53.01 (1) **Oral Evidence as General Rule** — Unless these rules provide otherwise, witnesses at the trial of an action shall be examined orally in court and the examination may consist of direct examination, cross-examination and re-examination.

(2) **Trial Judge to Exercise Control** — The trial judge shall exercise reasonable control over the mode of interrogation of a witness so as to protect the witness from undue harassment or embarrassment and may disallow a question put to a witness that is vexatious or irrelevant to any matter that may properly be inquired into at the trial.

(3) The trial judge may at any time direct that a witness be recalled for further examination.

(4) **Leading Questions on Direct Examination** — Where a witness appears unwilling or unable to give responsive answers, the trial judge may permit the party calling the witness to examine him or her by means of leading questions.

(5) **Interpreter** — Where a witness does not understand the language or languages in which the examination is to be conducted or is deaf or mute, a competent and independent interpreter shall, before the witness is called, take an oath or make an affirmation to interpret accurately the administration of the oath or affirmation to the witness, the questions put to the witness and his or her answers.

(6) Where an interpreter is required under subrule (5), the party calling the witness shall provide the interpreter, unless the interpretation is to be from English to French or from French to English and an interpreter is provided by the Ministry of the Attorney General.

Evidence By Affidavit

53.02 (1) **With Leave of Court** — Before or at the trial of an action, the court may make an order allowing the evidence of a witness or proof of a particular fact or document to be given by affidavit, unless an adverse party reasonably requires the attendance of the deponent at trial for cross-examination.

(2) Where an order is made under subrule (1) before the trial, it may be set aside or varied by the trial judge where it appears necessary to do so in the interest of justice.

Expert Witnesses

53.03 (1) **Experts' Reports** — A party who intends to call an expert witness at trial shall, not less than 90 days before the commencement of the trial, serve on every other party to the action a report, signed by the expert, setting out his or her name, address and qualifications and the substance of his or her proposed testimony.

(2) A party who intends to call an expert witness at trial to respond to the expert witness of another party shall, not less than 60 days before the commencement of the trial, serve on every other party to the action a report, signed by the expert setting out his or her name, address and qualifications and the substance of his or her proposed testimony.

(3) **Sanction for Failure to Address Issue in Report or Supplementary Report** — An expert witness may not testify with respect to an issue, except with leave of the trial judge, unless the substance of his or her testimony with respect to that issue is set out in,

(a)   a report served under this rule; or

(b)   a supplementary report served on every other party to the action not less than 30 days before the commencement of the trial.

(4) **Extension or Abridgment of Time** — The time provided for service of a report or supplementary report under this rule may be extended or abridged,

(a)   by the judge or case management master at the pre-trial conference or at any conference under Rule 77; or

(b)   by the court, on motion.

[O. Reg. 348/97, s. 3 (in force October 20, 1997); O. Reg. 570/98, s. 3 (in force January 4, 1999).]

[Note: O. Reg. 348/97, s. 8 (in force October 20, 1997) provides as follows:
8. Despite section 7, rule 53.03 of the Regulation, as it read on October 19, 1997, continues to apply with respect to actions in which the trial commences before February 16, 1998.
Section 7 provides as follows:
This Regulation comes into force on October 20, 1997.]

Compelling Attendance At Trial

53.04 (1) **By Summons to Witness** — A party who requires the attendance of a person in Ontario as a witness at a trial may serve the person with a summons to witness (Form 53A) requiring him or her to attend the trial at the time and place stated in the summons, and the summons may also require the person to produce at the trial the documents or other things in his or her possession, control or power relating to the matters in question in the action that are specified in the summons.

(2) **Summons may be Issued in Blank** — On the request of a party or a solicitor and on payment of the prescribed fee, a registrar shall sign, seal and issue a blank summons to witness and the party or solicitor may complete the summons and insert the names of any number of witnesses.

(3) **Where Document may be Proved by Certified Copy** — No summons to witness for the production of an original record or document that may be proved by a certified copy shall be served without leave of the court.

(4) **Summons to be Served Personally** — A summons to witness shall be served on the witness personally and not by an alternative to personal service and, at the same time, attendance money calculated in accordance with Tariff A shall be paid or tendered to the witness.

(5) Service of a summons to witness and the payment or tender of attendance money may be proved by affidavit.

(6) **Summons in Effect until Attendance No Longer Required** — A summons to witness continues to have effect until the attendance of the witness is no longer required.

(7) **Sanctions for Failure to Obey Summons** — Where a witness whose evidence is material to an action is served with a summons to witness and the proper attendance money is paid or tendered to him or her, and the witness fails to attend at the trial or to remain in attendance in accordance with the requirements of the summons, the presiding judge may by a warrant for arrest (Form 53B) cause the witness to be apprehended anywhere within Ontario and forthwith brought before the court.

(8) On being apprehended, the witness may be detained in custody until his or her presence is no longer required, or released on such terms as are just, and the witness may be ordered to pay the costs arising out of the failure to attend or remain in attendance.

Interprovincial Subpoena

53.05 A summons to a witness outside Ontario to compel his or her attendance under the *Interprovincial Summonses Act* shall be in (Form 53C).

Compelling Attendance Of Witness In Custody

53.06 The court may make an order (Form 53D) for attendance of a witness in custody whose evidence is material to an action, directing the officer having custody of a prisoner to produce him or her, on payment of the fee prescribed under the *Administration of Justice Act*, for an examination authorized by these rules or as a witness at a hearing.

Calling Adverse Party As Witness

53.07 Persons to Whom Rule Applies — (1) Subrules (2) to (7) apply in respect of the following persons:

1. An adverse party.
2. An officer, director, employee or sole proprietor of an adverse party.
3. A partner of a partnership that is an adverse party.

(2) **Securing Attendance** — A party may secure the attendance of a person referred to in subrule (1) as a witness at a trial,

(a) by serving the person with a summons to witness, or by serving on the adverse party or the solicitor for the adverse party, at least 10 days before the commencement of the trial, a notice of intention to call the person as a witness; and

(b) by paying or tendering attendance money calculated in accordance with Tariff A at the same time.

(3) If a person referred to in subrule (1) is in attendance at the trial, it is unnecessary to serve the person with a summons or to pay attendance money to call the person as a witness.

(4) **When Adverse Party may be Called** — A party may call a person referred to in subrule (1) as a witness unless,

(a) the person has already testified; or

(b) the adverse party or the adverse's party counsel undertakes to call the person as a witness.

(5) **Cross-examination** — A person referred to in subrule (1) may be cross-examined by the party who called him or her as a witness and by any other party who is adverse in interest to that person.

(6) **Re-examination** — After a cross-examination under subrule (5), the person may be re-examined by any party who is not entitled to cross-examine under that subrule.

(7) **Failure to testify** — The court may grant judgment in favour of the party calling the witness, adjourn the trial or make such other order as is just where a person required to testify under this rule,

(a) refuses or neglects to attend at the trial or to remain in attendance at the trial;

(b) refuses to be sworn; or

(c) refuses to answer any proper question put to him or her or to produce any document or other thing that he or she is required to produce.

[O. Reg. 536/96, s. 4 (in force December 12, 1996).]

Evidence Admissible Only With Leave

53.08 (1) If evidence is admissible only with leave of the trial judge under a provision listed in subrule (2), leave shall be granted on such terms as are just and with an adjournment if necessary, unless to do so will cause prejudice to the opposite party or will cause undue delay in the conduct of the trial.

(2) Subrule (1) applies with respect to the following provisions:
1. Subrule 30.08(1) (failure to disclose document).
2. Rule 30.09 (failure to abandon claim of privilege).
3. Rule 31.07 (refusal to disclose information on discovery).
4. Subrule 31.09(3) (failure to correct answers on discovery).
5. Subrule 53.03(3) (failure to serve expert's report).
6. Subrule 76.03(3) (failure to disclose witness).

[O. Reg. 533/95, s. 5 (in force March 11, 1996); O. Reg. 348/97, s. 4 (in force October 20, 1997); O. Reg. 284/01, s. 13 (in force January 1, 2002).]

Calculation Of Awards For Future Pecuniary Damages

53.09 (1) **Discount Rate** — The discount rate to be used in determining the amount of an award in respect of future pecuniary damages, to the extent that it reflects the difference between estimated investment and price inflation rates, is,

(a) for the 15-year period that follows the start of the trial, the average of the value for the last Wednesday in each month of the real rate of interest on long-term Government of Canada real return bonds (Series B113911), as published in the Bank of Canada Weekly Financial Statistics for the 12 months ending on August 31 in the year before the year in which the trial begins, less 1 per cent and rounded to the nearest 1/4 per cent; and

(b) for any later period covered by the award, 2.5 per cent per year.

(2) **Gross Up** — In calculating the amount to be included in the award to offset any liability for income tax on income from investment of the award, the court shall,

(a) assume that the entire award will be invested in fixed income securities; and

(b) determine the rate to be assumed for future inflation in accordance with the following formula:

g rounded to the nearest 1/4 per cent where,

$$g = \frac{1+i}{1+d} - 1$$

"i" is the average of the value for the last Wednesday in each month of the nominal rate of interest on long-term Government of Canada bonds (Series B113867), as published in the Bank of Canada Weekly Financial Statistics, for the 12 months ending on August 31 in the year before the year in which the trial begins;

"d" is

(a) for the 15-year period that follows the start of the trial, the average of the value for the last Wednesday in each month of the real rate of interest on long-term Government of Canada real return bonds (Series B113911), as published in the Bank of Canada Weekly Financial Statistics for the 12 months ending on August 31 in the year before the year in which the trial begins, less 1 per cent, and

(b) for any later period covered by the award, 2.5 percent per year.

[O. Reg. 465/93, s. 5 (in force October 4, 1993); O. Reg. 288/99, s. 16 (in force January 1, 2000); O. Reg. 488/99, s. 2 (in force January 1, 2000).]

[NOTE: Despite O. Reg. 288/99, subsection 31(3), and O. Reg 488/99, subsection 3(2), rule 53.09 of the Regulation, as it read on December 31, 1999, continues to apply with respect to actions in which the trial commences before January 1, 2000.]

Prejudgment Interest Rate For Non-Pecuniary Damages

53.10 The prejudgment interest rate on damages for non-pecuniary loss in an action for personal injury is 5 per cent per year.

Index